TELEVISION STYLE

Style matters. Television relies on style—setting, lighting, videography, editing, and so on—to set moods, hail viewers, construct meanings, build narratives, sell products, and shape information. Yet, to date, style has been the most understudied aspect of the medium. In this book, Jeremy G. Butler examines the meanings behind television's stylistic conventions.

Television Style dissects how style signifies and what significance it has had in specific television contexts. Using hundreds of frame captures from television programs, *Television Style* dares to look closely at television. *Miami Vice*, *ER*, soap operas, sitcoms, and commercials, among other prototypical television texts, are deconstructed in an attempt to understand how style functions in television. *Television Style* also assays the state of style during an era of media convergence and the ostensible demise of network television.

This book is a much needed introduction to television style, and essential reading at a moment when the medium is undergoing radical transformation, perhaps even a stylistic renaissance.

Discover additional examples and resources on the companion website: **www.tvstylebook.com**

Jeremy G. Butler is Professor of Telecommunication and Film at the University of Alabama. He is author of *Television: Critical Methods and Applications* (3rd edition, 2006).

TELEVISION STYLE

Jeremy G. Butler

Routledge
Taylor & Francis Group

NEW YORK AND LONDON

10 06629823

First published 2010
by Routledge
270 Madison Ave, New York, NY 10016

Simultaneously published in the UK
by Routledge
2 Park Square, Milton Park, Abingdon, Oxon OX14 4RN

Routledge is an imprint of the Taylor & Francis Group, an informa business

Typeset in Minion Pro by Wearset Ltd, Boldon, Tyne and Wear
Printed and bound in the United States of America on acid-free paper
by Edwards Brothers, Inc.

Library of Congress Cataloging in Publication Data
Butler, Jeremy G., 1954-
Television style / Jeremy G. Butler.
p. cm.
Includes bibliographical references and index.
1. Television–Aesthetics. I. Title.
PN1992.55.B88 2009
791.45–dc22

2009020055

ISBN10: 0-415-96511-X (hbk)
ISBN10: 0-415-96512-8 (pbk)
ISBN10: 0-203-87957-0 (ebk)

ISBN13: 978-0-415-96511-8 (hbk)
ISBN13: 978-0-415-96512-5 (pbk)
ISBN13: 978-0-203-87957-3 (ebk)

For my father and mother, both of whom are lovers of words on a printed page.

Contents

Preface

When it comes to illustrations, a book on style in television is inevitably constricted by the limitation of the printed form. We have struggled against this limitation by including hundreds of frame captures from television programs, but that does little to illuminate the movements of motion images and nothing to illustrate the sound accompanying these images. And, of course, these frame captures are presented here in black-and-white and in reduced size. To ameliorate the situation somewhat we have created a companion website that displays enlarged, color versions of all the illustrations. Also, when not bound by copyright issues, we have included short video clips. You will find this website at:

www.TVStyleBook.com

Some of its material is password protected and may be accessed with the following:

Account name: tvstyle
Password: telestylistics

Please use all lowercase letters when entering the account name and password. Further, TVStyleBook.com contains many of the links to which I refer in the text, which are augmented with other television-style online resources.

With very few exceptions, the illustrations presented here were digitally captured from DVDs and video files. Any number of software packages can create such stills, but I have come to rely on the VLC media player, open-source software that runs on Windows, Mac, and Linux operating systems. Not only is VLC free, but it is also quite full featured and creates image files that may be used by the Shot Logger statistical style project (www.ShotLogger. org). Tutorials on frame capture and Shot Logger are provided on TVStyle-Book.com.

Acknowledgments

These chapters, often in embarrassingly rough form, have benefitted from review by Marysia Galbraith, Patrick Leary, Greg M. Smith, and Frederick Whiting. Although David Bordwell and Kristin Thompson were not directly involved in the creation of *Television Style*, I would be remiss if I did not acknowledge how instrumental their work has been to my own thinking on style in television and film, beginning with the first edition of *Film Art* in 1979. I also wish to thank several television practitioners who were generous with their time and allowed me to pepper them with (probably naive) questions about standard craft practices: Thomas Azzari, Tom Cherones, Dean Holland, Michael Laibson, Greg Stroud, and Ken Kwapis. Peter Bradberry transcribed several interviews for me and I was ably assisted in the preparation of illustrations by Laura Lineberry and Jung Kim. I am grateful to my editor at Routledge, Matthew Byrnie, for his belief in this project and for his encouragement in bringing it to fruition.

Marysia Galbraith is well experienced in the running of marathons (and 5Ks and 10Ks) and she provided expert advice, affection, and support during the marathon that is the writing of a book. I thank Ian Butler for giving me an excuse to watch *The Wonder Pets*, whose motto—"What's going to work? Teamwork!"—is applicable to so many things in life.

Chapters 1–4 are updated, revised, and enlarged versions of essays that have previously appeared in print over the past 25 years. I am grateful for permission to reprint the following: "Notes on the Soap Opera Apparatus: Televisual Style and *As the World Turns*," *Cinema Journal* 25, no. 3 (spring 1986): 53–70; "*Miami Vice*: The Legacy of Film Noir," *Journal of Popular Film and Television* 13, no. 3 (fall 1985): 126–38; "The Television Commercial," in *Television: Critical Methods and Applications*, 3rd edn (Mahweh: Lawrence Erlbaum Associates, 2007), 363–415; "VR in the ER: *ER*'s Use of E-Media," *Screen* 42, no. 4 (winter 2001): 313–31.

Jeremy G. Butler
Tuscaloosa, Alabama
jbutler@ua.edu
April 2009
www.TVStyleBook.com

Introduction

Dare We Look Closely at Television?

> Television is a relative of motorcar and airplane: it is a means of cultural transportation. To be sure, it is a mere instrument of transmission, which does not offer new means for the artistic interpretation of reality—as radio and film did.[1]
>
> (Rudolf Arnheim, 1935)

Many factors have militated against the study of style in television. Rudolf Arnheim dismissed the artistic potential of television a good ten years before it existed as a viable mass medium. Implicit within his dismissal is a denial of television style. For Arnheim and others of the first wave of film theorists—notably, Lev Kuleshov and Sergei Eisenstein—it was through a patterned implementation of a medium's techniques that true artists interpreted reality. Film-as-art was thus established in terms of how film artists *transformed* reality through style, how film images *differed* from reality. Style was paramount; it made film into art. These theorists felt this transformation was essential to elevate a mechanical recording device to what Alexandre Astruc later called "*la caméra stylo*," the camera as stylus, a device capable of rendering reality into aesthetic form. The film camera was not an artistic implement until it was elevated beyond its base recording function. Similarly, the television camera could never be an artistic implement because, to Arnheim, it was impossible for it to get beyond its transmission function. An entire book devoted to television style would be unfathomable to him.

We might today scoff at Arnheim's short-sighted presumption that television could never become the artistic equal of film (or radio!), but his characterization of television-as-transmission persists in contemporary television studies and has contributed to the dearth of television stylistic analyses. When authors discuss the essential "liveness" or immediacy of television and its lack of Roland Barthes' "photo effect," they rely on the same presumption as Arnheim, that television is defined fundamentally by its ability to transmit events that occur simultaneous to the time of viewing.[2] This same presumption feeds into early journalistic criticism of television in the 1950s, where the pinnacle of television art is seen to be the live transmission of well-respected plays. The "art" of these productions is not in the television medium itself, but, rather, in the play that is being transmitted. The only notice paid to television style is negative—attributes of the small, high-contrast, black-and-white image and the primitive, monaural sound. In classical film theory, the differences between human perception of reality and reality's representation on screen are interpreted as artistic opportunities. For instance, black-and-white cinematography is said to allow the film artist to emphasize compositional elements by eliminating color tonality. Similar claims were not made for television's limitations in the 1950s.

The television-as-transmission concept has had other impacts on the study of style. In fact, it shapes many empirical approaches to the medium. Cultural-studies ethnographers prefer to examine the recipient of the transmission and not the transmission itself. I am over-simplifying here, but the empirical emphasis on the recipient and not the text means that the text's stylistic aspects are of less interest than the recipient's use of the text's signifieds. Cultural-studies scholars, for example, have examined viewers' responses to television soap opera by talking to the genre's fans and by examining materials they (the viewers) have written about the programs. What interests the scholars most is how viewers understand the characters and relate them to their own lives and not how the viewers feel about stylistic attributes like shot-counter shot editing or a zoom-in to conclude a scene.

However, not all impediments to stylistic analysis can be blamed on television's roots in sound-image transmission. Auteurism, shot through with romantic notions of the artist, views style as a manifestation of the individual's unique "vision." When François Truffaut and his colleagues at *Cahiers du Cinéma* launched the auteur theory in the mid-1950s, they never thought to unearth auteurs within the television industry, because the medium was seen to be aesthetically stunted and an industrial product—even more so than the Hollywood film studio system's products. In 1953, the year before Truffaut issued auteurism's manifesto, André Bazin predicted, "the television picture will always retain its mediocre legibility."[3] How could it possibly aspire to the art of the cinema? Moreover, Truffaut *et al.* were aspiring directors themselves and so they looked for the auteur's signature in a cinematic aspect that directors control: principally, elements of visual style. In television, then as now, a single director seldom controls the visual style of a program. Over the course of a program's season, ten or 20 directors might be called upon. The auteur of a television program is most likely to be the producer and the producer is more likely to be a screenwriter than a director. Thus, auteurists have been frustrated in their limited attempts to find auteurs in television and, in their view, there can be no style without an auteur.

Taken together, these factors explain why there has been no comprehensive television stylistics or poetics on a par with David Bordwell's *Poetics of Cinema* and no historical poetics of the same scope as Bordwell, Kristin Thompson, and Janet Staiger's *The Classical Hollywood Cinema: Film Style and Mode of Production to 1960*.[4] These factors also suggest why the recent crop of television studies anthologies and introductory texts give style short shrift.[5] The present volume contributes to a poetics of television, although on a much more modest level than Bordwell's work. It brings together chapters that contribute to a critical tendency within television studies that has been largely overlooked. I do not, however, intend to overstate their uniqueness. Despite the longstanding bias against television style, despite some quarters which deny that it exists or believe that its analysis is frivolous, there have been some substantive analyses of television style upon which this book heavily relies. Some of the most useful have also been influenced by pertinent work in film studies, such as Bordwell's. To begin a consideration of television stylistics, therefore, we must first survey some prominent antecedent efforts.

Style and Media Studies

> Film style matters because what people call content comes to us in and through the patterned use of the medium's techniques.... Style is the tangible texture of a film, the perceptual surface we encounter as we watch and listen, and that surface is our point of departure in moving to plot, theme, feeling—everything else that matters to us.[6]
>
> (David Bordwell)

Certain elements are common to all stylistic work in media studies. All media-studies stylisticians must develop a method for describing, in Bordwell's terms, the "perceptual surface" of a television program or film. They must also make a case for why the phenomenon they have described is significant, which results in some form of analysis, interpretation and/or evaluation of that which they have described. A final step may be to describe how style has changed over time and also to suggest causes for that change, although some stylisticians favor a synchronic approach over such a diachronic one. In my review of work in this area—limiting myself predominantly to studies of television and film—I have found that media stylistics can be divided into four strains:

1. Descriptive stylistics
2. Analytic stylistics (interpretation)
3. Evaluative stylistics (aesthetics)
4. Historical stylistics

Most commonly, analytic and evaluative stylistics build upon descriptive stylistics and historical stylistics may engage the other three strains, but I have found it methodologically illuminating to separate these four aspects in order to examine their fundamental assumptions about television style and its functioning. I also believe strongly in grounding all theory in its practical application to specific texts and to that end I have selected a fairly random shot from *CSI: Crime Scene Investigation*—a program known for its sound-image flair—and will discuss how descriptive, analytic, and evaluative stylistic methods would approach it. Since a historical stylistic analysis would extend well beyond the province of this individual program, I have left that for another occasion.

Descriptive Stylistics

To discuss style, one must first be able to describe it. This would seem to be an obvious first step, but it is one that has caused much analytical and theoretical stumbling. Describing style requires the analyst to hew to a well-defined understanding of what style is and how it functions in television. Semiotics offers the most comprehensive set of tools for accomplishing the detailed description of television style. The initial formal implementation of semiotics in media studies, in the 1960s, was concerned with the larger questions of narrative form rather than the enunciation of that form in sound and image— as can be seen in Christian Metz's categorization of film scenes, or syntagms, into "*la grande syntagmatique*" and his syntagm-by-syntagm analysis of the film, *Adieu Philippine*.[7] However, film semioticians soon zeroed in on the organization of individual shots within syntagms.[8] These close readings were often accomplished by putting a film print on an editor to facilitate frame-by-frame analysis and they commonly included frame enlargements when they were published in journals such as *Screen*. Raymond Bellour and Stephen Heath further illustrated their descriptions of style with tables and diagrams of camera angles and shot scales. Thus, the close semiotic analysis of film in the 1970s incorporated verbal descriptions of individual series of shots, tables that arrayed the shots into columns and rows, diagrams of camera positions and blocking, and visual "descriptions" of the shots' composition (i.e., still frames representing the moving image).

The semiotic description of television found early application in John Fiske and John Hartley's slim volume, *Reading Television*, in 1978.[9] They engage in a brief "analysis of a TV syntagm"—a five-shot segment of the documentary, *Cathy Come Home* (1966).[10] Without diagrams or still-image illustrations, they rely on a verbal shot list. Clearly influenced by Metz, they articulate the syntagmatic and paradigmatic structure of the program's sign system, and attempt to account for its "aesthetic codes"—that is, its set of conventionalized stylistic elements.[11] Fiske continued this work nine years later in *Television Culture*.[12] His detailed analyses of television texts such as Madonna's music videos and *Miami Vice* (1984–9) do not include frame captures, but they do describe framing, camera movement, editing, and so on, in detail. As before, Fiske promotes the studying of these techniques within specific codes, which he defines as "a rule-governed system of signs, whose rules and conventions are shared amongst members of a culture, and which is used to generate and circulate meanings in and for that culture."[13] Stylistic description, thus, is not just a description of techniques in individual shots. Rather, it is always a matter of placing those techniques in broader contexts. To do so, Fiske divides television's stylistic codes into "technical codes" governing television's image and sound techniques and "social codes," sets of conventions of dress, hair style and the like that belong to the host culture.[14] Fiske does not want to be associated with an empty formalism that ignores cultural values and when he describes stylistic codes he is always alert to their cultural significance. He contends,

A textual study of television, then, involves three foci: the formal qualities of television programs [that is, their style] and their flow; the intertextual relations of television within itself, with other media, and with conversation; and the study of socially situated readers and the process of reading.[15]

Fiske's last focus clearly bears the influence of cultural studies, but the first two are more comfortable within the province of semiotics.

Originally published in 1987, the same year as *Television Culture*, the *Channels of Discourse: Television and Contemporary Criticism* anthology was an important milestone in television studies' development as a discipline of critical studies—sharply distinguishing itself from quantitative, "mass-communication," empirical approaches to the medium.[16] Each chapter summarizes a critical method or theory and explicates its approach to television. In Ellen Seiter's contribution to that volume, she articulates how semiotics might benefit television studies and she does so through a close analysis of a cartoon program's title sequence and television coverage of the space shuttle *Challenger* disaster, among other examples.[17] Her analyses begin with a shot-by-shot description and then seek to describe the television text's syntagmatic and paradigmatic structures, and the codes that govern them. Seiter relies upon Fiske and Hartley's method and she draws heavily on another study that was also inspired by Fisk and Hartley: Robert Hodge and David Tripp's *Children and Television: A Semiotic Approach*, published the year before the first edition of *Channels of Discourse*.[18] Hodge and Tripp "solve" the description problem with numerous shot lists and transcriptions of dialogue from *Fangface*, the children's program they analyze in depth. They include just two, low-quality frame captures in the book, but one senses they would have had many more had the video technology and copyright law of mid-1980s publishing supported it. In Seiter's discussion of *Children and Television*, she comments on Hodge and Tripp's analysis of *Fangface*'s first nine shots,

> it is the typical founding gesture of the semiotician to gather a small, manageable, and synchronic (contemporaneous) text or set of texts for analysis and, using the text as a basis, try to establish the conventions governing the larger system (in this case the series *Fangface* and the larger system of children's animated television).[19]

Semiotics aspires to an objective system of description (and interpretation) of sign systems, although it seldom entirely achieves that goal. The desire for precision, if not necessarily objectivity, has led some media stylisticians to employ quantitative methods. Antecedents to this approach include stylometry in quantitative linguistics and literary criticism. In those fields, according to Katie Wales, "Stylometry uses statistical analyses to investigate *stylistic* patterns in order to determine authorship of texts ... Linguistic features commonly examined in stylometry include word length; sentence length, connectives; collocations" (emphasis added).[20] Stylometry may be traced to logician Augustus D. Morgan's work in 1851, but as a method of television and film analysis it has only recently become viable.[21] Barry Salt pioneered a statistical method and has been a (sometimes contentious) advocate for it under the banner of "practical film theory."[22] The work he has done attempts to measure cinematic stylistic elements by counting them and then analyzing them through statistical tests.[23] This process builds upon "descriptive statistics," where the measuring of a phenomenon is said to describe that phenomenon. Salt, for example, has noted the following parameters in hundreds of films and a few dozen television programs: average shot length (ASL), reverse angles, point-of-view shots, inserts, shot scale, and camera movement.[24] And he has done so through the painstakingly slow process of watching the films and programs on editing machines and recording these parameters. More recent work in stylometry relies upon computer software to generate these descriptive statistics.[25] In screen studies this effort has been facilitated by Cine-Metrics and Shot Logger. In the former, Yuri Tsivian and Gunars Civjans have built a data-entry and data-display system containing shot-length and shot-scale data on hundreds of films and a few television programs.[26] For Shot Logger, I have constructed data-entry software that uses video time code embedded in frame captures to automatically measure shot length and then perform some rudimentary statistical analyses (average shot length, minimum/maximum shot length, range between minimum and maximum shot lengths, and standard deviation).[27] Both CineMetrics and Shot Logger are online efforts that enlist the help of volunteer stylisticians to amass a large body of data.

The following chapters frequently engage television texts in the manner of a semiotician—seeking to find the essence of style in television's sound-image details. It is, of course, possible to get lost in television's minutiae in this manner, but I agree with authors such as Bordwell, Thompson, and Salt who contend that one must "reverse engineer" media texts in order to fully understand their style.[28] Thus the same attention to detail that scriptwriters, directors, cinematographers, editors, and so on, put into the *construction* of a television text must be employed in the *deconstruction* of that text. This is a lesson of film and television analysis that I learned long ago when, as an undergraduate, I was forced to perform shot-by-shot scene *découpages* in a French cinema class. Initially, I hated the assignment, but those weekly encounters with the cinema's building blocks soon taught me a new way of seeing film, an understanding of how it functions as a sign system, and an appreciation of the skills of Jean Renoir, René Clair, François Truffaut, and many others. I regularly "inflict" (as I thought of it then) that assignment on my own television-studies students now. And it seldom fails to provide them with moments of insight when they suddenly realize that television is a constructed medium, right down to the smallest minutiae of its *mise-en-scène*.

Pedagogical exercises often demand precise descriptions of television and in television and film textbooks one finds useful attention to the details of sound-image style. Bordwell and Thompson led the way with the 1979 publication of the first edition of *Film Art: An Introduction*, which has had enormous impact on media-studies curricula and is currently in its eighth edition. A virtual manifesto for the study of style in visual media, it inspired my own more modest introduction to television studies, *Television: Critical Methods and Applications*, which was first published in 1994.[29] From the perspective of television stylistics, it is disappointing that the number of well-illustrated television textbooks released since the mid-1990s remains relatively small, especially when contrasted with the numerous film studies textbooks. However, it is not clear whether this is due to inherent difficulties in television stylistic pedagogy, or the simple fact that the market for television-studies books is much smaller than that for film studies. One exception to the general paucity of visually sophisticated television textbooks is Herbert Zettl's *Sight Sound Motion: Applied Media Aesthetics*, which has been published since 1973.[30] Zettl has been taken to task for his sometimes idiosyncratic terminology, but there is no denying the precision with which he describes sound-image style and the pedagogical efficacy of the hundreds of illustrations in *Sight Sound Motion*.

Descriptive stylistics, in one form or another, is often the first step in an analysis of *CSI: Crime Scene Investigation*. In fact, several of the essays in *Reading* CSI: *Crime TV Under the Microscope* do just that.[31] The program is commonly presumed to be highly "stylized," to eschew classical film's transparent style in favor of an aggressive articulation of sound and image that confronts the viewer. But how would my own brand of semiotics-inflected stylistics describe a shot selected virtually at random from the Nathan Hope-directed *CSI* episode, "Kill Me If You Can" (February 26, 2009)? The first step is to "describe" the television text with a series of silent, still images (Figures 0.1–0.8). It may be tempting to claim that since video is made of 30 *still* frames per second (in the U.S. broadcast system), that a single one of those frames accurately describes the shot, but the obvious truth is that we experience television as images *in motion*, over time, and a still image, a television *fragment*, is always going to be an approximation of that. In metonymic fashion, we are describing a phenomenon with an element of that phenomenon itself, but the fragment (a frame) and the whole (a moving-image shot, with sound) offer two very different experiences. For television scholars of the 1970s, before the advent of video on personal computers and even before the existence of consumer-grade VCRs, this visual description was arduously difficult to obtain. As Penelope Houston, a film critic from a previous generation, admitted, "The unattractive truth, of course, is … that the film, because it cannot be taken home and studied like a novel or a play, invites reactions and impressions rather than sustained analysis."[32] Up until the 1990s, television stylisticians had to rely on photographs of the video image to create still frames—resulting in visual distortions, evident scan lines, and low-resolution images that did not reproduce well in print publications.[33] The introduction of DVD drives into personal computers—and the release of hundreds of television programs in that format—has facilitated "sustained analysis" of television and has made the acquisition of television frames quite trivial, the result of just a few key strokes. The captured image is still rather low resolution by the standards of print publications, but high-definition video is improving on that. Figures 0.1–0.8 were captured at 1280 × 720 pixels from an HD video of a *CSI* episode, purchased through iTunes, viewed on my computer, and captured by pressing the "PrtScn" ("print screen") key.

Figure 0.1 CSI: a shot begins on the detail of a pottery book and then the camera moves on to...

Figure 0.2 ...a reconstructed pot, which contains clues to a murder. The focus shifts from the book to the pot, and then it pulls to...

Figure 0.3 ...lab technician Wendy working on reassembling the pot and musing about a missing piece.

Figure 0.4 As the shot continues, Dr Raymond Langston pokes into the frame with the missing piece in a jar. The camera pulls focus to it...

Figure 0.5 ...and then back to Wendy.

Figure 0.6 She moves around him, bringing the focus with her and...

Figure 0.7 ...then she situates the missing piece in its place. The camera and focus follow her hand.

Figure 0.8 The shot ends with Wendy in focus and Dr. Langston out of focus.

The logistics of image capture were not the only impediment to the publication of frame captures in the 1970s and 1980s. In the United States and other countries with restrictive intellectual property laws, the publication of frame captures was in a legal grey area. Was this copyright infringement or was it "fair use"? Once again, it was Thompson who took a leadership role that went beyond *Film Art*'s bold use of film frame enlargements. In 1993, she chaired a committee of the Society for Cinema Studies (since renamed the Society for Cinema and Media Studies) that studied the "Fair Usage Publication of Film Stills" and published a report in *Cinema Journal* that advocated for authors to claim fair use of stills in books, and, moreover, to not even request permission from copyright holders.[34] Her report emboldened many authors and publishers to rely on fair use in their publication of stylistic analyses of television and film. Any author who has published television stylistic analyses before the 1990s has his or her own copyright horror story and there are still occasional problems that arise, but fair use and its advocates have largely eliminated them, thus paving the way for visual stylistic descriptions.[35] Obviously, *Television Style* benefits from the frequent use of frame captures.

If I were doing a stylistic analysis of *CSI*, my description of this shot would depend upon the context of my analysis and the interpretation I was pursuing. I could describe the shot's short depth of field and the five rack focuses. Or I might emphasize Hope's use of a mobile frame and off/on-screen space in Figure 0.4, which conceals the entrance of Dr Raymond Langston (Laurence Fishburne), just as his entrance is initially unnoticed by lab technician Wendy Glenn (Darcy Farrell). In regards to *mise-en-scène*, I could remark on the crime lab's relatively low-key lighting, which seems unusual for a setting in which small pieces of evidence are being visually examined. Shot length is also an aspect of style, of the program's visual rhythm, and I could rely on statistical data to contextualize the shot's 24-second length. Table 0.1 arrays data on the average shot length of nine *CSI* episodes. The main, post-credits segment of "Kill Me If You Can" clocks in at a 3.3 ASL. The other eight episodes in Table 0.1 are from the first season of the show and none of them contain ASLs under 3.5. The longest shot in this episode is 39 seconds and the longest of all the episodes is 44 seconds. The length of shots may be graphed through CineMetrics' system, which in the case of this *CSI* episode results in the graph found in Figure 0.9. In the graph, each shot is represented by a vertical line. The *x*-axis legend displays the time at which the shot begins and the *y*-axis indicates the length of each shot, with zero at the top and 20 seconds at the bottom (allowing some longer shots to extend beyond this limit). The shot analyzed here occurs between 5:19 and 7:24 on the *x*-axis. It stands out because it is the only shot longer than 20 seconds in the first 28 minutes of the episode. A trend line is automatically drawn horizontally across the graph, bumping downward toward the end of the episode as the shots get longer. The graph thus visually describes the episode's editing rhythms, allowing the researcher to note editing patterns. Of course, descriptive stylistics must not limit itself to the visual components. It must also account for sound design. In this shot (and most of this scene), the sound is relatively barren—only sync

Table 0.1 CSI statistical data

Title	Date	Length	# of Shots	ASL	Min SL	Max SL	Range
Burked	09/27/2001	2,619	669	3.9	1	36	35
Chaos Theory	10/04/2001	2,602	634	4.1	1	41	40
Scuba Doobie-Doo	10/25/2001	2,518	585	4.3	1	23	22
Alter Boys	11/01/2001	2,641	739	3.5	1	33	32
And Then There Were None	11/22/2001	2,418	672	3.5	1	28	27
Identity Crisis	01/17/2002	2,621	575	4.5	1	44	43
Stalker	04/04/2002	2,637	549	4.8	1	44	43
Anatomy of a Lye	05/02/2002	2,653	531	4.9	1	37	36
Kill Me If You Can (pre-credits)	02/26/2009	154	42	3.6	1	12	11
Kill Me If You Can (post-credits)	02/26/2009	2,407	713	3.3	1	39	38
Kill Me If You Can (combined)	02/26/2009	2,561	755	3.4	1	39	38

Figure 0.9 A CineMetrics graph in which the length of each shot is represented by one line. The height of the graph ranges from 0 to 20 seconds.

dialogue and no music, diegetic or non-diegetic. Such quiet scenes contrast with the distinctive sound effect that signals *CSI*'s ratiocinative flashbacks.

My description of this shot's style engages terms borrowed from television production practices. Depth of field, rack focus, and low-key lighting were not invented by semioticians to describe stylistic features—as the term "syntagm," for instance, was coined to refer to the smallest narrative unit. Rather, they are terms that depend upon knowledge of how those shots were created. It is here that the reverse engineering aspect of stylistic analysis becomes obvious. The stylistician must tap into the production culture of a particular time in order to understand stylistic conventions and thus it is reasonable that we, as stylisticians, employ terms rooted in that culture. However, we should not allow production culture to dictate our vocabulary either. Just because most television producers do not use the term "*mise-en-scène*," does not mean that it is an unproductive analytical concept. Stylistic description incorporates a hybrid terminology, part industry jargon and part scholarly neologisms.

As should be obvious from my attempt to limit myself to descriptive stylistics, I cannot truly do so without straying into interpretation. Formal features become salient based on the end goal of an analysis. Description initiates interpretation. If not, then descriptions would have to account for every pixel of every frame—clearly an impossible task and one which would generate unreadable exegeses. A description of a television show should not replicate that show. It should, obviously enough, only serve to further the analysis.

Analytic Stylistics

Analyses of style in television depend upon explicit or implicit assumptions about style's purpose and function in the text. The stylistician's job then becomes deconstructing how style fulfills that function. To do so, the stylistician examines the workings of style within the textual system—seeking patterns of stylistic elements and, on a higher level, the relationships among those patterns themselves. The overall form of a television program depends on how shots relate to one another, on how the lighting style of shot A relates to that of shot B, on the juxtaposition of a musical theme with a particular image, on short shots being contrasted with long shots, and on and on. In my emphasis on function, am echoing Noël Carroll's "functional theory of style" in the cinema. Using "style" and "form" interchangeably, he contends,

> According to the functional account of film form, *the form* [or style] *of an individual film is the ensemble of choices intended to realize the point or the purpose of the film.* This approach to film form is different from the descriptive account. The descriptive account says that the form of the film is the sum total of *all* the relations between the elements of the film. The functional account says that film form comprises *only* the elements and relations intended to serve as the means to the end of the film.[36]

Carroll here helpfully distinguishes his approach from descriptive stylistics and identifies a useful way for thinking about television stylistics. Most analytical stylistics of television presume style serves one or more functions ("means") to the end of a television program. Certainly, all of the chapters in this volume do. Thus, to best understand analytic stylistics we must define style's functions in television.

In *Figures Traced in Light: On Cinematic Staging,* Bordwell outlines film style's "four broad functions."[37] I will begin with his four functions, but television style has additional functions unique to the medium that must be addressed. Television stylisticians have contended that style can:

1. Denote
2. Express
3. Symbolize
4. Decorate
5. Persuade
6. Hail or interpellate
7. Differentiate
8. Signify liveness

Each chapter in *Television Style* investigates aspects of style's function in more detail, but a few summary comments are in order here.

First, Bordwell suggests that the denotative function of film style controls "the description of settings and characters, the account given of their motives, the presentation of dialogue and movement."[38] This is style at its most fundamental, the level at which semiotic analysis begins. If I discuss how my sample *CSI* shot uses rack focuses to reveal and conceal narratively significant objects, then I am breaking down a stylistic element's denotative function. Textbooks such as *Sight Sound Motion* often stress this basic function of style.

Bordwell's second style function, its expressive quality, refers to the emotions that a film's style displays and those that it elicits in the viewer: "We can distinguish between style *presenting* feelingful qualities ('The shot exudes sadness') and *causing* feelings in the perceiver ('The shot makes me sad')."[39] The former, to which he limits himself in most of his work, "can be carried by light, color, performances, music, and certain camera movements."[40] Television stylisticians might occasionally discuss "feelingful qualities," but the more systematic interpretation of this sense of expression is to be found in *quantitative* empirical research into the feelings caused by television's "formal features," as style is commonly referred to in this context. Numerous empirical studies of style view it principally as a stimulus, as a factor that provokes emotions or actions, heightens/decreases attention, has an impact on cognition or otherwise affects its "subjects."[41] One empirical study, for example, examines the effect that voiceover narration has on viewer comprehension of television news.[42] A group of subjects was shown a news story with narration that redundantly explained the images. Another group was shown a story where the sound was kept the same, but the shots were re-ordered—thus eliminating redundancy of sound and image and altering the style or formal features of the video. Then both groups were given some tests to gauge their recall of audio information and other factors and the results were then quantified. This study's hypotheses revolve around the effect of this stylistic change on the subjects' cognitive processing. Other research in this same vein finds psychophysiological methods for quantifying the emotional impact of formal features—tracking heart rate, skin conductance, facial electromyography (EMG), and so on.[43]

The third function of style Bordwell explicates is its ability to "yield more abstract, conceptual meanings."[44] The set design of our *CSI* shot is typical of the program: the technician works in a room surrounded by glass, revealing other offices surrounding her. In Karen Lury's *CSI* study, she makes a case for specific themes associated with this *mise-en-scène*: "This sense of both depth and transparency at a visual level neatly echoes the push towards 'transparency' and truth in the crime-solving narrative."[45] Visual transparency in the style thus becomes a metaphor for ratiocinative clarity.

Bordwell's final style function, decoration, deserves a bit more extensive exploration than the first three, because, in television stylistics, some grand claims have been made for decorative style. "Decoration," Bordwell writes, "Asks us to apprehend the sheer pattern-making possibilities of the medium."[46] In other words, this is style for style's sake. It does not denote, express, or symbolize anything other than style itself. The decorative function of style has gone by many names: parametric narration, mannerism, the picture effect, excessive style, and so on. Television stylisticians have often asserted the radical or postmodern effect of television style such as this that does not labor on behalf of the narrative or theme. In the picture effect, John Caldwell finds the essential basis of "televisuality" in 1980s television. He declares, in enthusiastic italics, *"The new television does not depend upon the reality effect or the fiction effect, but upon the picture effect."*[47] In similarly fervent prose, Fiske proclaims,

> Images are neither the bearers of ideology, nor the representations of the real, but what [Jean] Baudrillard calls "the hyperreal": the television image, the advertisement, the pop song becomes more "real" than "reality," their sensuous imperative is so strong that they *are* our experience, they are our pleasure.[48]

He makes this claim in a chapter on *Miami Vice* and has even stronger words for style in Madonna's music videos:

> Style is a recycling of images that wrenches them out of the original context that enabled them to make sense and reduces them to free-floating signifiers whose only signification is that they are free, outside the control of the normal sense and sense-making, and thus able to enter the world of pleasure where their materiality can work directly on the sensual eye, running the boundary between culture and nature, between ideology and its absence.[49]

Fiske's approach to style draws upon Mikhail Bakhtin's notion of carnival: "In the postmodern world, style performs many of the functions of carnival. It is essentially liberating, acting as an empowering language for the subordinate."[50] Viewing *Miami Vice* and Madonna's 1980s video work today, it may be difficult to see their liberating, empowering, free-floating signifiers. Those television texts have been rendered virtually quaint in contrast to the stylistic exhibitionism of programs such as *CSI* whose "sensuous imperative" is far more extreme. Still, Caldwell's and Fiske's efforts were some of the very few to address television style at a time (the 1980s) when the medium was presumed to have none. They cleared the way for studies of programs with very distinctive styles. Indeed, it's quite easy to get lost in the visual and sound "ornamentation" that *CSI* offers and which is evident even in Figures 0.1–0.8.

Bordwell's four functions of style are well suited to much of television analysis, but his focus on narrative cinema means that he is less interested in documentary or propaganda film. Television, however, is laced with propaganda, with persuasive material in the form of editorials, sports commentaries, and, of course, commercials. Style is an essential part of commercials' persuasive efforts and commercials have, due to their short length, more carefully crafted sound-image style than any 30- or 60-minute program. Surprisingly little has been invested in the analysis of the persuasive function of style in television commercials—if you discount the massive amount of proprietary marketing research (focus groups and the like) done by advertisers regarding their own products. Chapter 3, on style and the television commercial, attempts to redress this neglect with a consideration of how television style persuades. In this effort, I draw upon an account of visual style in print advertising by Paul Messaris who identifies many of the stylistic methods that an image may use to convince us to buy a product.[51]

Also discussed in Chapter 3 is television style's hailing function, but this function underpins virtually all of the chapters. The larger concept of hailing finds its genesis in Louis Althusser's theory of ideology and the subject: "All ideology hails or interpellates concrete individuals as concrete subjects."[52] Hailing is the process by which a society's ideology calls out, "Hey, you!" and encourages you to become one of its subjects. Television during the network era was clearly an hegemonic instrument of dominant ideology, interpellating television's subjects—although cracks and fissures were always possible in that edifice.[53] Style participated in this interpellation as the device through which the hailing was accomplished, but it also hailed viewers in a narrower sense—calling to them to watch the television flow (stopping other household activities) and entreating them not to interrupt the flow by changing to one of the three or four other channels. This specific hailing function is moot in the cinema, where spectators have purchased a ticket and already decided to devote their attention to the illuminated screen displayed in the darkened theater. Further, even though television is no longer dominated by three networks, it still relies heavily on hailing, particularly since viewers' attention is being pulled in so many more directions. The age of convergence is also one of divergence and distraction. Distinctive style is a significant weapon used by television practitioners to combat the distraction factor of the modern mediascape.

Sound style, in particular, is an invaluable stimulus for pulling viewers to the television flow.[54] *CSI*, for instance, uses a distinctive sound cue to signal a flashback when the investigators theorize about how a crime happened. The shot I selected above is relatively quiet (dialogue only, no non-diegetic music), as is typical of much of the program. The visual style of this shot—with its complicated camera movement and rack focuses—serves a subtle hailing function, too. It demands a sustained gaze at the image. The narrative information of that shot (a missing pottery piece) is conveyed through this articulation of the visuals. To get that information, you *must* be paying attention—not looking at e-mail or playing *World of Warcraft* while you are watching *CSI*. The program rewards the sustained gaze, as do visually sophisticated programs such as *Miami Vice*, *ER*, and single-camera sitcoms—the subjects of Chapters 2, 4, and 5, respectively.

Once a viewer has been hailed, been enticed to view a particular program, style is then used to help differentiate brand identities. As discussed in Chapter 4, when *ER* debuted, it needed a way to distinguish itself from other hospital dramas, particularly *Chicago Hope*, which debuted in the same season and was programmed in the same time-slot. *ER*'s solution for brand differentiation was part narrative form and actor performance, of course, but it also depended upon an aggressive use of the Steadicam (one of the first television programs to do so) and four-walled sets to achieve a swirling, dizzying style of camera movement that effectively echoed the hectic life in the emergency room. Thus, the same premise necessary to differentiate Coke from Pepsi also obtains in television programs. *CSI* clearly illustrates the power of branding as its producer, Jerry Bruckheimer, has been able to use the program's style to stand out from other contemporary crime dramas and to develop a profitable *CSI* franchise: three television programs (*CSI: Crime Scene Investigation* [2000–], *CSI: Miami* [2002–], and *CSI: NY* [2004–]), graphic novels, and several video games, among other merchandise.

The final function of style, to signify liveness, returns us to the beginning of this introduction. If we accept Stephen Heath, Gillian Skirrow, and others' contention that viewers perceive television as live, then we must look to television style for the signifiers of that liveness. Aside from the occasional declaration of liveness ("Live, from New York! It's Saturday Night!"), it is stylistic elements such as haphazard framing and "bad" audio recording that convey a strong sense of liveness. This can be observed most clearly in genres that were once live and could be again, such as the case study of the soap opera in Chapter 1. As I note at this chapter's beginning, some critics interpret this "clumsy" articulation of sound-image techniques as emblematic of a *lack* of "style," or as zero-degree style. I prefer to think of it as a set or code of conventionalized techniques that have come to represent liveness, but could be used in broadcasts that are not actually live. Soap operas are recorded "live-on-tape" and come by this code "naturally," but mockumentaries such as *The Office* can be coded as "spontaneous" without actually employing modes of production that are "live" or "live-on-tape." The stylistic signifiers of spontaneity and liveness have become so familiar to viewers that they read the text as live even when it is not. This code of liveness is as significant a style as Nathan Hope's rendering of a *CSI* script. Throughout *Television Style*, I advocate for an understanding of style as *any* patterning of sound-image technique that serves a function within the television text. I thereby reject the definition of style as the mark of the individual genius on a text (although certainly geniuses create elements of television) or as a flourish somehow layered on top of the narrative (although some style is decorative). A program does not need geniuses or flourishes in order to possess style. Axiomatic to every chapter in this book is that *all television texts contain style*. Style is their texture, their surface, the web that holds together their signifiers and through which their signifieds are communicated.

Evaluative Stylistics

As may be gleaned from my passion for zero-degree style, I am more eager to describe and analyze style than I am to evaluate it. And television studies, in general, has not developed a coherent method for evaluating television as a medium or style as a portion of it. What efforts there have been in this area have engaged with an evaluative aesthetics, with aesthetic *judgment*. Of course, "aesthetics" has a very long and complicated history within various philosophical and art historical traditions. One must consequently be very clear about its meaning. Within television studies the term can be used in a non-judgmental manner, as we have already seen with Fiske and Hartley's investigation of "aesthetic codes." In this sense, "aesthetic" means elements of image-sound style and "codes" refers to sets of image-sound conventions. Fiske and Hartley are not evaluating or judging those codes. They are only describing and analyzing them. More recently, however, a strain of television studies has evolved that does propose aesthetic evaluation of the medium. Christine Geraghty is one television scholar who advocates for the aesthetic judgment of television, but she acknowledges that this will be an uphill battle. She neatly summarizes several reasons for the neglect of aesthetic judgment within television studies:

> the impact of semiotics on the genesis of media studies with its pseudo-scientific claims about objectivity; the impact of postmodernism with its emphasis on diversity, decentering and play; the need to establish popular culture and television, in particular, as worthy of study that involved refusing the traditional modes of judgment; the impact of feminist work, with its demand that certain kinds of denigrated fictions should be treated seriously; the notion, coming rather differently from [Michel] Foucault and [Pierre] Bourdieu, that to make aesthetic judgments was to impose the cultural norms of the powerful.[55]

To these reasons, we might add Jason Jacobs' observation regarding an unwarranted prejudice against television style:

> The continued sense that the television text is mostly inferior to the film text and cannot withstand concentrated critical pressure because it lacks "symbolic density", rich *mise-en-scène*, and the promotion of identification as a means of securing audience proximity, has to be revised in the light of contemporary television.[56]

Jacobs clarifies that television might indeed have been "textually anaemic" in the decades before the 1980s, but that stylistically lavish, even excessive, programs have been developing since then.[57] He contends such programs reward close textual analysis. I would certainly agree and argue in Chapter 2 that *Miami Vice* led the charge toward lavish style that was followed across several genres and networks by programs such as *Homicide: Life on the Street* (1993–9), *Ally McBeal* (1997–2002), *The Sopranos* (1999–2007), *Arrested Development* (2003–6), *Deadwood* (2004–6), and, of course, the test case for this introduction, *CSI* (2000–). Another voice within television studies that has called for aesthetic evaluation is Greg Smith. In *Beautiful TV: The Art and*

Argument of Ally McBeal he ponders why "it is acceptable to do a book-length aesthetic analysis of a film, but to analyze a television series on primarily aesthetic and narrative terms is a radical notion."[58]

These authors make persuasive cases for the aesthetic judgment of television, but they are less persuasive about how such judgment would proceed. Smith states the aesthetic principle underpinning his analysis: "The concept of beauty that emerges from this book is a fairly old-fashioned one: a cohesive system in which elegant, innovative formal technique serves to convey a unified, complex argument suitable for moral and ethical insight."[59] And *Beautiful TV* does engage intelligently with *Ally McBeal's* complex narrative system and its moral/ethical thematic structure, describing how ground-breaking stylistic techniques convey them.[60] However, the bulk of his book's exegesis is *descriptive* and *analytical*, not *evaluative* or *judgmental*. Further, Smith recognizes that his intentionally provocative, "old-fashioned" aesthetic can be a worrisome one:

> By calling this show "beautiful," I am not saying that elegance and complexity are the only qualities that can constitute beauty, world without end, amen. I am saying that at a moment when television is widely frowned upon as a denigrated object, using these old-fashioned words can help us to see television more clearly.... In arguing for the art and argument of a quite silly (and often annoying) television series, I want to reclaim our ability to talk openly, unashamedly, unironically, and rigorously about television as a beautiful object.[61]

In sum, Smith is using aesthetic judgment as a justification for his chosen object of study, but aside from using some descriptive words with evaluative connotations—such as "elegant," "complex," and "innovative"—he does not focus on the beauty of *Ally McBeal* in the main part of his analysis.[62] Similarly, Geraghty's and Jacobs' analyses fall predominantly into the descriptive and analytic stylistics categories I have discussed above. Geraghty summarizes her approach thus:

> I am not suggesting that aesthetic or quality norms should be imposed without discussion of their provenance but that textual work provides the possibility of engagement with such issues through an approach that emphasizes *analytic description* and evaluative discussion across a range of programmes (emphasis added).[63]

To date, television aestheticians have not systematically defined the medium's aesthetic norms of evaluation. Rather, those norms have been composed of problematic, ideologically loaded terms such a "elegance," "complexity," "organic unity," "expressiveness," "uniqueness," "artistic vision," and so on. If television studies is to develop a method of aesthetic judgment, then it will need to be one quite distinct from antecedent norms found in art history, literature, music, and even the cinema.

The search for beauty in television has led some scholars to import the debunked auteur theory into television studies from film studies. *CSI* receives this treatment in Sue Turnbull's essay on "The Hook and the Look: *CSI* and the Aesthetics of the Television Crime Series."[64] For her, what makes *CSI* a good program is its auteurist lineage from director Danny Cannon to Michael Mann. *CSI* creator/producer Bruckheimer had worked with Mann on the feature films, *Thief* (1981) and *Manhunter* (1986), during the time of *Miami Vice* (1984–90). Bruckheimer hired Cannon and instructed him to get that "cinematic look," in general, and to emulate Mann's style, in particular.[65] Turnbull thus relies on the unexamined evaluative criteria that, first, cinematic style is superior to television style and, second, that style is good when it is the expression of the auteur's vision. Chapter 2 of this volume devotes much of its discussion of *Miami Vice* to identifying cinematic style and examining its crossover into television. However, I do not share Turnbull's aesthetic hierarchy or her emphasis on the auteur. Auteurs do exist in television—Paul Henning and Joss Whedon come to mind— but their "vision" is not necessary to make a program good. Much like a medieval cathedral, beautiful television may be the product of dozens of workers' efforts. A Byronic auteur need not be at the helm. One final reason to avoid auteurist aesthetics is that auteurism has an amorphous sense of the beautiful. Individual authors more often describe or point to a beautiful moment instead of explaining why it is beautiful. The result is mysticism.[66] Andrew Sarris, in the 1962 essay largely responsible for importing the auteur theory to U.S. film criticism, argues that the marks of true auteurs are in their aesthetic implementations of style—"close to what Astruc defines as *mise-en-scène*, but not quite."[67] Sarris avers that Jean Renoir qualifies as an auteur and, as proof, refers the reader to a tiny moment from *Rules of the Game*:

> Renoir gallops up the stairs, turns to his right with a lurching movement, stops in hop-like uncertainty when his name is called by a coquettish maid [Figure 0.10], and, then, with marvelous postreflex continuity, resumes his bearishly shambling journey to the heroine's boudoir. If I could describe the musical grace note of that momentary suspension, *and I can't*, I might be able to provide a more precise definition of the auteur theory. As it is, all I can do is point at *the specific beauties* of interior meaning on the screen and, later, *catalogue the moments of recognition* (emphasis added).[68]

Much auteurist writing on film and television presumes this "you recognize it or you don't" attitude toward beauty and style. It is less aesthetic analysis than it is elitism.

Aesthetic evaluation of *CSI* could point to the elaborate camera movement that Nathan Hope staged in our test-case shot and demand the reader accept the labeling of it as television beauty and Hope as an auteur even though he has mostly worked as a cinematographer, with very few directing credits aside from *CSI*. The aesthetician could also argue for this shot's elegance and complexity, as Smith does for style in *Ally McBeal*. But, to some, camera movement is overused in "beautiful" programs such as *CSI*, *ER*, and *The West Wing*. For such a critic, this moment is anything but beautiful.

Until television studies develops an aesthetic system that goes beyond taste and dominant culture norms, we must admit that semiotics, postmodernism, cultural studies, feminism, Foucault, and Bourdieu (remembering Geraghty's list) are correct to caution us about the hazards of television evaluation, especially if it portends a return to auteurism. "Can we have a television aesthetic, and do we want one?" asks Charlotte Brunsdon pointedly.[69] Her answer is mostly negative:

Figure 0.10 Rules of the Game: One of the "specific beauties" of interior meaning, according to Andrew Sarris.

> An aesthetic of television would thus, in some ways, have to be an anti-aesthetic to be adequate to its object and the practices constituting it. Engaging with the popular, the domestic, and the functional, it [television] undercuts the very constitution of classical aesthetic judgment.[70]

Historical Stylistics

Several chapters in this book place individual programs into larger contexts of television-style history. Most notably, Chapter 4 unpacks the layers of media texts that converged on *ER* in the mid-1990s and Chapter 5 discusses the resurrection, through stylistic innovation, of the sitcom in the 2000s. My fundamental approach to television-style history is that style exists at the intersection of economics, technology, industry standards, and semiotic/aesthetic codes; and each of these elements has their own, semi-independent history. To pick an illustrative example: the technology for the zoom shot was introduced to the cinema in the 1930s. Early television cameras, however, had turret lenses, not zooms, although zoom lenses became standard in television studios in the 1960s. Consequently, studio-based programs of the 1940s and 1950s have few zoom shots. The television industry of the late 1960s and 1970s, however, came to rely on zoom lenses for efficient, inexpensive shooting of soap operas, game shows, talk shows, sports programs, and the like—an economic decision. But the choice of ending a soap-opera scene with a zoom-in on a character has no economic, technological, or industrial imperative. It draws purely on semiotic codes of narrative signification.

In media studies, the most methodical historical stylistician is undoubtedly David Bordwell. *Poetics of Cinema* (2008) is the result of his most recent labor in the cinepoetics vineyards, but 20 years earlier, in *Ozu and the Poetics of Cinema* (1988), Bordwell establishes that "'Poetics' refers to the study of how films are put together and how, in determinate contexts, they elicit particular effects."[71] He later clarifies that poetics extends beyond stylistics to include "thematics" and "large-scale form" and that stylistics, in particular, "deals with the materials and patterning of the medium as components of the constructive process."[72] Poetics is thus no "mere" formalism. Rather, it approaches style as the physical manifestation of theme and narrative, in the case of fiction film. And these elements are always culturally situated. In Bordwell's words, "A narrative film exhibits a total form consisting of materials—subject matter, themes—shaped and transformed by overall composition (e.g., narrative structure, narrational logic) and stylistic patterning."[73] Also, Bordwell brings to the analytical table a knowledge of cognitive psychology, which undergirds his understanding of style's effects on viewers.

To comprehend how Bordwell's poetics approaches the history of style, it is worth quoting *Figures Traced in Light* at some length:

> I propose that we can fruitfully analyze and explain the historical dynamic of film style by inferring, *on the basis of the films and what we know about their making*, some pertinent craft traditions. The *traditions preserve favored practices*, practices that are the result of choices among alternatives. In choosing, filmmakers exercise their skill and judgment, thereby replicating, revising, or rejecting options supplied by their predecessors and peers (emphasis added).[74]

Bordwell conceptualizes craft practices as standardized routines that guide practitioners as they make films. He gathers these routines together into sets or schemas, a concept he appropriates from the work of art historian E.H. Gombrich.[75] Bordwell explains, "Schemas are bare-bone, routinized devices that solve perennial problems."[76] Individual practitioners can follow, modify or reject these routines, but these routines remain "favored" or, shall we say, generally dominant within specific film cultures at specific times, or within specific genres or movements or modes of production. The schemas comprise the flexible rules of film-making, the ever-changing grammar of image-sound signification. On his understanding of the function of schemas—as providing solutions to problems—Bordwell builds his theory of the history of film style, which he refers to as the "problem/solution model."[77] Film practitioners are faced with common problems—for example, how to position actors on a stage to best communicate narrative information.[78] During certain time periods, in certain countries, using certain modes of production, this problem *tends to be* solved in specific ways by certain practitioners—e.g., having the actors stand in a line perpendicular to the camera, as was often done in the early 1900s. But that solution to the problem is no longer the norm and so the cinepoetician must ask, "How have the norms altered or maintained across history? What factors have promoted stability as well as change?"[79] Colin Burnett accurately sums Bordwell's model:

> Problem-solving is cast *as a motor of short- and long-term historical development*—a logic that describes the nature of practical filmic creativity, links the problems faced by filmmakers working in different contexts, and ultimately drives the history of the art.[80]

I have gone into Bordwell's historical cinepoetics in significant detail because the overarching project of *Television Style* is to begin the process of building a television poetics, a telepoetics, if you will. The reader will note traces of Bordwell's approach throughout the following chapters. Particularly fruitful to the study of television style is the notion of schemas, which enable the researcher to characterize accurately the stylistic traits of certain modes of production (e.g., in-studio multiple-camera production of situation comedies) and discuss their functions and significance. Bordwell's problem/solution model of stylistic history also underpins certain *Television Style* analyses—such as my consideration of how single-camera situation comedies found different solutions to the problems of narrative and humor presentation than those of the multiple-camera norm. Moreover, I am not alone in my incorporation of Bordwell's methods in the analysis of television. Jason Mittell decries the fact that "the formal attributes of television texts have been given little scholarly attention."[81] He advocates Bordwell's approach and contends, "By looking at *Dragnet* via a historical poetic analysis to examine how cultural meanings and assumptions were encoded in the program, we can see how these textual elements fit into larger cultural and generic categories."[82]

Articles of Faith

> Style is not simply window-dressing draped over a script; it is the very flesh of the work.[83]
>
> (David Bordwell)

The chapters that follow are built on two axioms, two virtual articles of faith:

1. Television style exists.
2. Television style is significant.

I begin *Television Style* by making the case for style's existence in a television genre often presumed to have none, the lowly soap opera. In Chapter 1, the schema governing the soap opera is articulated and its signification of liveness, among other meanings, is explicated. Chapter 2 continues the consideration of stylistic genre schemas in television by examining the impact of an aggressively stylized film genre, the film noir, upon a television program, *Miami Vice*. It is here that we will first encounter Caldwell's notion of the "televisual," of the medium's "visual exhibitionism," which also twines through Chapter 3.[84] The televisual is a significant stylistic device used by advertisers to convince us to consume conspicuously, but it is not the only one. This chapter documents seven other stylistic techniques in their arsenal, all of which serve the stylistic function of interpellation.

To my axiom, "television style exists," I should add a short corollary: *television exists*. As I write this introduction in spring 2009, there are signs too numerous to discuss that the network-television era is coming to a close. For some, this signals an end to television itself, but the reality of the matter is complex. Television will continue to exist in some form or another for the foreseeable future. Chapter 4 tries to make some sense of the collision of old media and new media—both with their own stylistic schemas—by examining an example of failed convergence. The online efforts of *ER* in the 1990s illustrate how *not* to leverage an old-media property into the new media, but they also provide an illuminating example of how television style must adapt to new-media exigencies. *Television Style*'s final chapter is yet another genre study, the mirror image of the first chapter on the soap opera. However, where the soap opera has been denigrated as being bereft of style, the single-camera sitcom of the early 2000s was often chided for having "too much" style, for using style as a gimmick or unnecessary visual flourish. It seems fitting, therefore, to close on a genre on the opposite end of the stylistic hierarchy.

From the style-less to the style-full, from attenuated style to the televisual, these chapters weave together the core issues in television stylistics. They incorporate a method that blends close semiotic description with articulations of stylistic schemas that are the result of problem-solving by television practitioners whose craft practices are governed by technological, economic, and aesthetic/cultural systems. My project in each chapter is to understand how style functions in a specific television text—a genre, a program, an online version of a show, a commercial, a particular practitioner's work, and so on. My larger goal is to begin the work of a television poetics and to advocate for greater attention to style in future television studies. We can no longer use Penelope Houston's excuse that our texts cannot be examined as closely as a novel or a play because we cannot take them home to study. Not only can we study, in extremely detailed fashion, the television text from the comfort of our computer screens, but we can visually "describe" that text with frames easily captured from the flow of images. The digital age has provided all the necessary tools for a renaissance in image-sound analysis. We need only dare to look closely at television.

Notes

1. Rudolf Arnheim, "A Forecast of Television," in *Film as Art* (Berkeley: University of California Press, 1957), 194.
2. One early television-studies essay that emphasizes television's immediacy is Stephen Heath and Gillian Skirrow, "Television, a World in Action," *Screen* 18, no. 2 (summer 1977): 7–59.
3. André Bazin, "Will CinemaScope Save the Film Industry?," in *Bazin at Work: Major Essays and Reviews from the Forties and Fifties*, trans. Alain Piette and Bert Cardullo, ed. Bert Cardullo (New York: Routledge, 1997), 80.
4. David Bordwell, *Poetics of Cinema* (New York: Routledge, 2008); David Bordwell, Kristin Thompson, and Janet Staiger, *The Classical Hollywood Cinema: Film Style and Mode of Production to 1960* (New York: Columbia University Press, 1985).
5. Robert C. Allen and Annette Hill, eds., *The Television Studies Reader* (New York: Routledge, 2004) runs 629 pages, but does not include a single essay on style or a single image to illustrate stylistic analysis.
6. David Bordwell, *Figures Traced in Light: On Cinematic Staging* (Berkeley: University of California Press, 2005), 32.
7. Christian Metz, *Film Language: A Semiotics of the Cinema*, trans. Michael Taylor (Chicago: University of Chicago Press, 1991). Among the essays in this collection is "The Cinema: Language or Language System," originally published as "*Le*

cinéma: langue ou langage?" in *Communications* 4 (1964) and commonly regarded as the first major article about film semiotics.

8. Several of Bellour's essays have been compiled in *The Analysis of Film*, ed. Constance Penley (Bloomington: Indiana University Press, 2000). One of Heath's earliest close readings was published as "Film and System: Terms of Analysis, Part I," *Screen* 16, no. 1 (spring 1975): 7–77; and "Film and System: Terms of Analysis, Part II," *Screen* 16, no. 2 (summer 1975): 91–113.

9. John Fiske and John Hartley, *Reading Television* (New York: Methuen, 1978). The authors provide an annotated bibliography of "semiotic/textual analyses of television," 205–8.

10. Ibid., 55–8.

11. Ibid., 61–3.

12. John Fiske, *Television Culture* (New York: Methuen, 1987).

13. Ibid., 4.

14. Ibid., 5.

15. Ibid., 16.

16. Robert C. Allen, ed., *Channels of Discourse: Television and Contemporary Criticism* (New York: Routledge, 1987). A second edition, *Channels of Discourse, Reassembled*, was released five years later, but there have been no further editions. Consequently, its claim to "contemporary" criticism is becoming increasingly dated.

17. Ellen Seiter, "Semiotics, Structuralism, and Television," in *Channels of Discourse, Reassembled*, ed. Robert C. Allen (Chapel Hill: University of North Carolina Press, 1992), 31–66.

18. Robert Hodge and David Tripp, *Children and Television: A Semiotic Approach* (Cambridge: Polity Press, 1986).

19. Seiter, "Semiotics," 50–1.

20. Katie Wales, *A Dictionary of Stylistics* (New York: Longman, 1989), 439.

21. David I. Holmes, "The Evolution of Stylometry in Humanities Scholarship," *Literary and Linguistic Computing* 13, no. 3 (1998): 112.

22. Barry Salt, "Practical Film Theory and its Application to TV Series Dramas," *Journal of Media Practice* 2, no. 2 (2001): 98–114.

23. Thomas Elsaesser and Warren Buckland gloss the statistical style analysis of the cinema in *Studying Contemporary American Film: A Guide to Movie Analysis* (London: Arnold, 2002), 102–16.

24. A sample of these data is displayed on the CineMetrics website. "Barry Salt's Database," CineMetrics, www.cinemetrics.lv/saltdb.php (accessed March 31, 2009).

25. According to Holmes, "The growing power of the computer and the ready availability of machine-readable texts are now transforming modern stylometry" in humanities scholarship. Holmes, "The Evolution," 111.

26. "CineMetrics Database," CineMetrics, www.cinemetrics.lv/database.php (accessed March 8, 2009).

27. Jeremy Butler, "Shot Logger," www.shotlogger.org (accessed March 12, 2008).

28. The phrase is used in Bordwell, *Figures Traced in Light*, 250; but the general concept underpins other stylisticians' approaches. There may be concerns that reverse engineering risks returning to the intentional fallacy. Bordwell responds, "This framework does not claim access to intentions as mental episodes, only to intentions as posited sources of patterns of action. Again, we reverse-engineer" (257).

29. Jeremy G. Butler, *Television: Critical Methods and Applications*, 3rd edn (Mahweh: Lawrence Erlbaum, 2007).

30. Herbert Zettl, *Sight Sound Motion: Applied Media Aesthetics* (Belmont: Wadsworth, 1973). Now in its fifth edition.

31. Michael Allen, ed., *Reading* CSI: *Crime TV Under the Microscope* (New York: I.B. Tauris, 2007).

32. Penelope Houston, "The Critical Question," *Sight and Sound* 29, no. 4 (autumn 1960): 164.

33. *Channels of Discourse* suffers from this problem. See, for example, p. 227.
34. Kristin Thompson, "Report of the Ad hoc Committee of the Society For Cinema Studies, 'Fair Usage Publication of Film Stills,'" Society for Cinema and Media Studies, www.cmstudies.org/index.php?option=com_content&task=view&id=60& Itemid=110 (accessed March 12, 2009). See also, Kristin Thompson, "Fair Is Still Fair, And More So," David Bordwell's Website on Cinema, April 23, 2008, www. davidbordwell.net/blog/?p=2127 (accessed March 12, 2009).
35. Fair use of images by television educators and scholars was given a recent boost by the publication of "The Code of Best Practices in Fair Use for Media Literacy Education," Center for Social Media, American University, November 2008, www. centerforsocialmedia.org/resources/publications/code_for_media_literacy_education (accessed March 18, 2009), but for a recent incident of copyright extortion, see Justin Mittell, "Fair Use Held Hostage by ABC-Disney," Just TV, February 14, 2009, justtv.wordpress.com/2009/02/14/fair-use-held-hostage-by-abc-disney (accessed March 12, 2009).
36. Noël Carroll, "Film Form: An Argument for a Functional Theory of Style in the Individual Film," in *Engaging the Moving Image* (New Haven: Yale University Press, 2003), 141.
37. Bordwell, *Figures Traced in Light*, 33–4.
38. Ibid., 33.
39. Ibid., 34.
40. Ibid.
41. See, for example, Elizabeth M. Perse, *Media Effects and Society* (Mahwah: Lawrence Erlbaum, 2001), 146–8; and Byron Reeves and Clifford Nass, "Media and Form," in *The Media Equation: How People Treat Computers, Television, and New Media Like Real People and Places* (Cambridge: Cambridge University Press, 1996), 193–247.
42. Shuhua Zhou, "Effects of Visual Intensity and Audiovisual Redundancy in Bad News," *Media Psychology* 6 (2004): 237–56.
43. "Facial EMG measures minute changes in the electrical activity of facial muscles, which reflects minute muscle movements. This technique has been shown to be capable of measuring facial muscle activity to even weakly evocative emotional stimuli." Gallup & Robinson, Inc., "Welcome," FacialEMG, 2009, www.facialemg. com (accessed March 17, 2009).
44. Bordwell, *Figures Traced in Light*, 34.
45. Karen Lury, *Interpreting Television* (London: Hodder Arnold, 2005), 47.
46. Bordwell, *Figures Traced in Light*, 34.
47. John Thornton Caldwell, *Televisuality: Style, Crisis, and Authority in American Television* (New Brunswick: Rutgers University Press, 1995), 152.
48. Fiske, *Television Culture*, 260.
49. Ibid., 250.
50. Ibid., 249.
51. Paul Messaris, *Visual Persuasion: The Role of Images in Advertising* (Thousand Oaks: Sage, 1997).
52. Louis Althusser, "Ideology and Ideological State Apparatuses," in *Lenin and Philosophy and Other Essays*, trans. Ben Brewster (New York: Monthly Review Press, 1970), 174, www.marxists.org/reference/archive/althusser/1970/ideology.htm, Louis Althusser Archive (accessed June 12, 2008).
53. A significant body of work in film studies has been devoted to understanding how style might signify ideological undercurrents in 1950s melodrama. The key to this notion is the principle of irony, which has not found extensive application in television studies.
54. Rick Altman explicates six functions of television sound style in "Television Sound," in *Television: The Critical View*, 4th edn, ed. Horace Newcomb (New York: Oxford University Press, 1987), 566–84.

55. Christine Geraghty, "Aesthetics and Quality in Popular Television Drama," *International Journal of Cultural Studies* 6, no. 25 (2003): 26, 27.
56. Jason Jacobs, "Issues of Judgement and Value in Television Studies," *International Journal of Cultural Studies* 4, no. 4 (December 2001): 433.
57. Ibid., 434.
58. Greg M. Smith, *Beautiful TV: The Art and Argument of Ally McBeal* (Austin: University of Texas Press, 2007), 4.
59. Ibid., 197.
60. Smith relies on Russian Formalist methods ("devices," "functions") to describe and analyze style. Ibid., 9.
61. Ibid., 197.
62. According to Google Book Search, "beauty" is used only five times in reference to *Ally McBeal*, the program, in *Beautiful TV*. Of course, "beautiful" turns up many more times as it is in the title of the book. "Preview This Book," *Beautiful TV*, Google Book Search, books.google.com (accessed March 20, 2009).
63. Geraghty, "Aesthetics and Quality," 41–2.
64. Sue Turnbull, "The Hook and the Look: *CSI* and the Aesthetics of the Television Crime Series," in Allen, *Reading CSI*, 15–32.
65. Ibid., 27.
66. For more on stylistic mysticism, see Barrett Hodsdon, "The Mystique of Mise-en-scene Revisited," *Continuum: The Australian Journal of Media and Culture* 5, no. 2 (1990), wwwmcc.murdoch.edu.au/ReadingRoom/5.2/Hodsdon.html (accessed March 26, 2009).
67. Andrew Sarris, "Notes on the Auteur Theory in 1962," in *Auteurs and Authorship: A Film Reader*, ed. Barry Keith Grant (Malden: Blackwell, 2008), 43.
68. Ibid. Even Sarris's description of the shot is inaccurate. He writes that Renoir turns to his *right*, but actually he turns in the other direction.
69. Charlotte Brunsdon, "Television: Aesthetics and Audiences," in *Logics of Television: Essays in Cultural Criticism*, ed. Patricia Mellencamp (Bloomington: Indiana University Press, 1990), 61.
70. Ibid., 63.
71. David Bordwell, *Ozu and the Poetics of Cinema* (Princeton: Princeton University Press, 1988), 1. Available online at quod.lib.umich.edu/c/cjs/images/0920054-0001.001.pdf. The evolution of Bordwell's thinking is well chronicled in Colin Burnett, "A New Look at the Concept of Style in Film: The Origins and Development of the Problem-Solution Model," *New Review of Film and Television Studies* 6, no. 2 (August 2008): 127–49.
72. Bordwell, *Poetics of Cinema*, 17–18.
73. Bordwell, *Ozu and the Poetics of Cinema*, 1.
74. Bordwell, *Figures Traced in Light*, 265.
75. See E.H. Gombrich, *Art and Illusion: A Study in the Psychology of Pictorial Representation* (Princeton: Princeton University Press, 1960), 146–78. Regarding Bordwell's use of Gombrich, see Burnett, "A New Look," 139–40.
76. David Bordwell, *On the History of Film Style* (Cambridge: Harvard University Press, 1997), 152.
77. Ibid., 150.
78. See "Exceptionally Exact Perceptions: On Staging in Depth," in ibid., 158–271.
79. Ibid., 158.
80. Burnett, "A New Look," 143.
81. Jason Mittell, *Genre and Television: From Cop Shows to Cartoons in American Culture* (New York: Routledge, 2004), 121.
82. Mittell, *Genre and Television*, 122.
83. Bordwell, *On the History of Film Style*, 8.
84. Caldwell, *Televisuality*, 352.

1.

Television and Zero-Degree Style

It is commonly presumed—especially among film scholars—that daytime soap operas have no style, that their harried production schedule does not permit the luxury of stylistic embellishments. How could it when soap-opera production companies must churn out 30–60 broadcast minutes five days a week, with no breaks for holidays and, more significantly, with no reruns? But this attitude toward style views it as something extra that is added to a television program, an accouterment that might aid the signification process but is not central to it. In this book, I have argued that all television texts have a style born of a confluence of economic necessity, industry trade practices, aesthetics, and network standards. In this context, soap opera becomes a particularly interesting test case, because it illustrates narrative-television production under extreme time constraints. In a sense, it is narrative production without pretense, designed to present the maximum amount of narrative as efficiently as budget, time and technology will allow. Analyzing soap-opera style offers an opportunity to examine Caldwell's "zero-degree style," to see just how efficiently diegetic spaces may be constructed.[1]

Soap opera analysis is also important because of its position in media studies at the end of the twentieth century. At the time, the study of television soap opera lured scholars from cinema studies, myself included, to consider how melodrama might cross over from one medium to another. Film melodrama as a genre and directors such as Douglas Sirk, John Stahl, and Frank Borzage attracted heightened interest in the late 1970s. Feminists were particularly interested in unpacking the ideology of the "woman's picture." Several of these film scholars subsequently became interested in the equivalent television genre—the soap opera.[2] Consequently, soap opera was the first television genre to receive sustained attention from cinema scholars. In the 1980s critical commentaries on soap opera's narrative structure—modeled on cinema studies and literary criticism—became as commonplace as child custody conflicts in the genre itself.

In Charlotte Brunsdon's assessment of "The Role of Soap Opera in the Development of Feminist Television Scholarship" (1995) she incidentally chronicles the vanguard role of feminist film theorists in the deconstruction of television soap opera as a signifying system.[3] The work done by feminist television scholars up until that time, she maintains, can be grouped into four categories:

26

1. Studies of the position of women within television industries.
2. "Content analyses"—as they are called within the tradition of mass-communication research—of women in soap opera programs.
3. Considerations of the soap opera as semiotic text.
4. Research on soap-opera viewers and their relationship to the text.[4]

Of these four, textual studies has the greatest pertinence to stylistic analysis. Tania Modleski's relatively early (1979) essay, which sparked much of the feminist rethinking of the genre, is typical of this approach.[5] She contends that soap opera may prove to be the most (only?) feminist television form. Invoking Roland Barthes' hermeneutic code, Modleski sees feminist potential in three aspects of the soap opera: its disrupted narrative form, its avoidance of narrative closure, and its construction of a fragmented spectatorial viewpoint. Consequently, her argument is not concerned so much with what might be called a feminist television style of sound and image, but with a feminist form of narrative actions (and the feminine spectator's relationship to that form). She thus spends very little time on the actual use of sound and image. Modleski shares this concentration on narrative structure with many of the textual-studies writers drawing on literary and cinematic analytical traditions. The idea of an endless story has captivated those accustomed to narrative closure, largely because narrative aperture—the open text—is a trait normally associated with modernist or progressive texts, not forms of popular culture as seemingly conservative as soap opera. Ellen Seiter, for example, comments on the significance of soap opera's eternally disrupted and eternally reconstructed narrative:

> The importance of small discontinuous narrative units which are never organized by a single patriarchal discourse or main narrative line, which do not build towards an ending or closure of meaning, which in their very complexity cannot give a final ideological word on anything, makes soap opera uniquely open to feminist readings.[6]

This feminist concern with ideological paradoxes in soap opera narrative dominated the reevaluation of the genre in the 1980s and the emphasis on narrative form persists to the present day in textual studies.[7]

By the turn of the century, soap-opera analytical work could be found in publications as diverse as the *Journal of Employment Counseling* and *Screen*—much of it from a feminist perspective.[8] Moreover, as Brunsdon chronicles in *The Feminist, the Housewife, and the Soap Opera* (2000) and Louise Spence reviews in *Watching Daytime Soap Operas: The Power of Pleasure* (2005), feminist work on soap opera in the late twentieth century was dominated by new, ethnographic, audience-oriented research.[9] Central to our concerns, most of this audience-oriented work took for granted the positioning of the spectator through sound and image, through style. These studies rarely, if ever, asked their interviewees for their opinions about the characteristics of soap-opera videography, *mise-en-scène*, or sound design.

Further, in textual-studies work that was done during this time, narrative form was the primary draw and little attention was paid to the work of image-sound style in the construction of these never-ending narratives. To date, there has been no comprehensive study of soap opera as a system of signification, a text of sound and image constructed in a highly convention-alized fashion.[10]

Sampling the Ever-Expanding Text

To begin this work, the detailed analysis of the soap-opera text is necessary, but it quickly becomes obvious that this text is enormous and ever-expanding. Consider *As the World Turns* (commonly abbreviated as *ATWT*). Its continu-ing narrative text began at 1:30 p.m. EST on April 2, 1956 and has since broadcast over 13,000 episodes. Taking into account its expansion from 30 minutes to 60 minutes on December 1, 1975 and its approximately 250 annual episodes,[11] we can estimate that over 11,000 hours of broadcast time have been generated.[12] This makes for a rather unwieldy diegetic text when com-pared to the standard theatrical film or even a season's worth of episodes on prime-time television.

When I began this research in 1984, I adopted the strategy of narrowing my study to a sample containing one week's worth of *ATWT* episodes: July 18–24, 1984, episode numbers 7,296–7,300, Wednesday through the follow-ing Tuesday. A Wednesday-to-Tuesday week—instead of Monday to Friday—was chosen to investigate how *ATWT* handles the weekend interruption of its ongoing narrative. I wished to test the common assumption that, as Maryjo Adams explains,

> Daily, there is a minor climax—the incentive to tune in tomorrow letting each day build to a major climax on Friday which is ample bait to hook even the most casual viewer into tuning in on Monday to begin the cycle again.[13]

As a follow-up to the original study, I have sampled another Wednesday-to-Tuesday week from *ATWT*: January 30–February 5, 2008, episode numbers 13,194–13,198.[14] Clearly, ten episodes taken from over 13,000 is still not a sufficient amount of material on which to build a comprehensive study of *ATWT*'s visual style, let alone the entire genre's. However, the sty-listic "schema" governing these samples from 1984 and 2008 has remained relatively stable, suggesting that this genre's "standardized craft practices" have not changed much in the past 24 years—to put it in Bordwell's terms.[15] I would hazard to say this schema most probably extends even further back, to the mid-1970s when soap opera's craft practices underwent two signific-ant changes: the expansion to 60-minutes and the conversion from live broadcasting to videotape recording. *ATWT* was one of the last two pro-grams to convert from live broadcasts to taped ones (in 1975), but it was the first CBS soap opera to expand to one hour (the extra length made live telecasting untenable, according to Adams).[16] Additionally, *ATWT* led the way for CBS soap operas making the shift from black-and-white to color—starting on February 20, 1967, eight years before the program expansion.[17] After the shift to color, taped recordings of 60-minute programs, the mode of production of *ATWT*, in specific, and soap opera, in general, stabilized and so did its schema. It is difficult to test reliably this historical theory, because soap operas are so very ephemeral. No comprehensive archive of soap-opera episodes—particularly those broadcast live—is available to the researcher. Unlike prime-time television, soap operas are not distributed on DVDs and it is only recently that soap-opera episodes have begun to find a public life after their initial broadcast—through reruns on a cable-television network (SOAPnet) and streaming on the networks' websites.[18] And, according to Adams, the networks themselves are poor chroniclers of their programs:

> When *As the World Turns* was a live broadcast, the only records available for historical research were kinescopes made of a few episodes. Despite the videotaping of today [1980], the tapes are kept only 30 days and then erased. Special events, weddings, deaths, and flashbacks are kept in special files for future use.[19]

I must rely on my own informal viewing of *ATWT* before 1984, therefore, to substantiate the claim of schema stability. Also, the soap-opera's mode of production from that time lends credence to a theory of stability. There was little financial, technological, or aesthetic incentive to change this schema during this time period as the soap opera's ratings and ratings-based advertising revenue were unassailable. Only in the past few years has this begun to erode, which may well foment revolutions in the genre's mode of production. We will return to this question of schema change at the end of the chapter.

Stylistic schema, it should be clarified, signifies the *patterning* of techniques, the syntagmatic and paradigmatic relationships of one element to other elements within a textual system. Only these relationships generate meaning. My specific approach will be to discuss the soap opera schema in terms of space (*mise-en-scène* and videographic properties), time (editing), and sound (dialogue, music, and noise or "sound effects"). To best understand the single-shot schema and shot-to-shot relations within a scene I will narrow the ten-episode sample even further, concentrating on a scene from the program aired Friday, February 1, 2008.[20] The selected, 91-second scene between Katie (Terri Colombino) and Brad (Austin Peck) begins the episode's fourth act, at approximately 30 minutes into the broadcast. (See Table 1.1. TVStyleBook.com provides a video clip of the scene.) It contains 20 shots, with an average shot length of 4.55 seconds and a median shot length of 3 seconds. The setting is Al's Diner, where Brad is attempting to propose to Katie. Although he fails in this episode, he will eventually succeed and on the April 17, 2008 broadcast, they are married.

Table 1.1 As the World Turns scene *découpage*

Shot Number, Scale, and Length	Figure	Dialogue	Action/Camera Movement
1 long shot 3 secs. (*Figures 1.1–1.2*)		Katie: The backdoor's locked, too. We're trapped.	Fade in (from the commercial break). Camera zooms back to a long shot as Katie enters the diner.
2 medium close-up 3 secs. (*Figure 1.3*)		Brad: Maybe it's a sign that this was meant to be. Katie: No, it's a sign…	
3 longshot 3 secs. (*Figure 1.4*)		Katie: …that my friends are out to get me.	

Shot Number, Scale, and Length	Figure	Dialogue	Action/Camera Movement
4 medium close-up 5 secs. (*Figure 1.5*)		Brad: Our dinner may have been ruined, but that doesn't mean we can't have dessert.	
5 medium close-up 3 secs. (*Figure 1.6*)		Katie: I'm not really in the mood.	
6 medium close-up 1 sec. (*Figure 1.7*)		Brad: It's your favorite.	
7 medium close-up 3 secs. (*Figure 1.8*)		Katie: Oh, that's not fair. [Music begins.]	Promotional announcement chromakeyed over the lower fifth of the frame: "You're watching AS THE WORLD TURNS. CSI:NY WEDNESDAY 10/9C." Continues over shots 8–11.

continued

Table 1.1 continued

Shot Number, Scale, and Length	Figure	Dialogue	Action/Camera Movement
8 medium close-up 2 secs. (*Figure 1.9*)		Brad: Strawberry cheesecake.	
9 medium close-up 3 secs. (*Figure 1.10*)		Katie: Oh, no, no, no … The good one, with the little chopped up strawberries? Brad: Oh, yeah…	
10 medium close-up 2 secs. (*Figure 1.11*)		Brad: …yeah, just the way you like it.	
11 medium close-up 5 secs. (*Figure 1.12*)		Katie: Okay. We're stuck here. We might as well enjoy ourselves.	

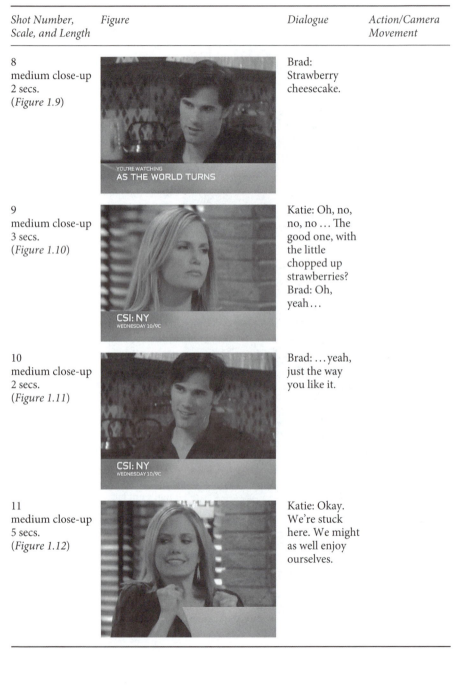

Shot Number, Scale, and Length	Figure	Dialogue	Action/Camera Movement
12 long shot 10 secs. (*Figures 1.13–1.14*)	 	Brad: Sit. Close your eyes.	Katie walks off frame left. The camera zooms in to a medium shot of Brad. [re-establishing shot]
13 medium shot 6 secs. (*Figure 1.15*)		Katie: Why? It's not exactly a surprise. Brad: Oh, yes, it is. Close your eyes. [Only full line spoken off camera.]	
14 medium shot 11 secs. (*Figure 1.16*)			

continued

Table 1.1 continued

Shot Number, Scale, and Length	Figure	Dialogue	Action/Camera Movement
15 extreme close-up 4 secs. (*Figure 1.17*)	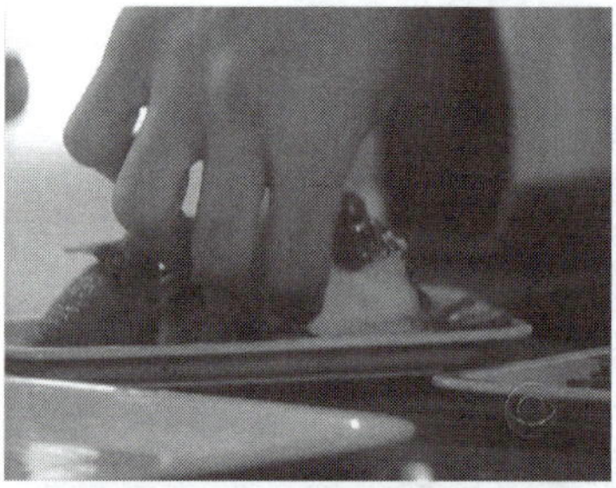		
16 medium shot 14 secs. (*Figures 1.18–1.20*)	  	Brad: Okay.	Brad hobbles out from behind the counter, because his foot is in a cast. Camera follows Brad.

Shot Number, Scale, and Length	Figure	Dialogue	Action/Camera Movement
17 medium shot 3 secs. (*Figures* *1.21–1.23*)		Brad: Ta-da!	Brad begins to sit.
18 long shot 2 secs. (*Figures* *1.24–1.25*)		Katie: Ooh, that…	Brad continues to sit. Camera zooms out to reframe the two of them.

continued

Table 1.1 continued

Shot Number, Scale, and Length	Figure	Dialogue	Action/Camera Movement
19 extreme close-up 5 secs. (*Figures 1.26–1.31*)		Katie: . . . looks delicious. [Sighs]	Camera starts on a tight shot of her fork, follows it up to a close-up of her face.

Shot Number, Scale, and Length	Figure	Dialogue	Action/Camera Movement

20 medium close-up 4 secs. (*Figure 1.32*)			[Cut to the first shot of the following scene.]
First shot, following scene. (*Figure 1.33*)			

Soap Opera *Mise-en-scène*

The *mise-en-scène* of soap opera is the aspect of its production that is most affected by so-called "below-the-line" costs: "Scenic Design, Scenic Construction and Painting, Studio Stagehands and Artists, Costume Design, Technical Personnel and Equipment, Studio Space, Support Crew (stage manager, wardrobe, makeup)," as listed in Francis B. Messmore's study of soap-opera production in New York City.[21] In contrast, "above-the-line" costs include salaries for producers, directors, scriptwriters, the starring performers, and so on. Below-the-line costs deal mostly with the primary elements of *mise-en-scène*, the physical elements of a production: sets, costumes, lighting, and so on. Consequently, to minimize below-the-line costs, soap opera's *mise-en-scène* has had to adapt certain craft practices that have had a major impact on the genre's signifying practices. The implications of these craft practices can be observed in the scene we are examining.

First, and most obviously, the setting is an interior one—as are the bulk of soap-opera scenes. Soap operas are shot on a limited number of mostly interior sets and in controlled, studio environments where shooting time can be minimized and below-the-line costs can be kept in check. *ATWT* typically uses ten or fewer sets from the dozens they hold in storage.[22] The February 1, 2008 episode, for example, uses eight, of which one is an exterior set. No actual location shooting was done, which is standard practice for the genre. In Natan Katzman's content analysis of the genre, he found, "of 884 locations coded, only 9 were clearly not indoors, while 690 were in homes, offices, or hospitals."[23] Beyond the pragmatic demands of production economics there are certain aesthetic reasons for the genre's abundance of interior settings. Soap-opera thematics find their most facile expression indoors. Charles Derry writes:

> Given this emphasis on interiors, it is not surprising that the soap opera has developed a stable of specific interiors—each of which serves a metaphorical function which allows the genre to deal with one or more of its themes.[24]

Derry identifies the hospital, the courtroom, the newspaper office, the restaurant or nightclub, and the private home—and their respective thematic concerns of life and death, guilt and innocence, gossip, socializing, and personal obsessions.[25] This *ATWT* scene is set in a restaurant, which normally allows for the maximum interaction among characters, but in this instance Al's Diner has been closed so that Brad can propose to Katie—transposing a scene of socializing into one of one-on-one intimacy. With the lack of other patrons, the restaurant becomes an arena for personal politics. In Brunsdon's terms, "the action of the soap opera is not restricted to familial or quasifamilial institutions but, as it were, *colonizes* the public masculine sphere, representing it from the point of view of the personal."[26] Brad pursues Katie and she resists his advances. In soap operas as in film melodramas, private homes are more commonly the settings for such scenes, but, in this case, Al's Diner substitutes for the private home.[27]

The articulation of space in soap opera sets tends to be shallow and confined, although this has changed over the years as soap-opera set design has grown increasingly elaborate, despite the severe financial constraints. At the beginning of the genre, in the early 1950s, set design was remarkably, even absurdly, minimalist. A black velvet curtain could be hung in a broadcast studio and windows and doors could be positioned in front of it—like something out of a Samuel Beckett play—in order to create the most basic illusion of a room. The studios were not large and thus blocking was limited to side-to-side movement. Even today's soap-opera studios do not permit much deep-space set design as five or six sets are commonly erected semi-permanently in a single studio, lining the walls so that camera equipment can be placed in the center of the room (Figure 1.34).[28] *ATWT*, in particular, currently shoots in JC Studios, Brooklyn, New York, which has two studio spaces: 163' by 70' and 131' by 75'.[29] Unlike *ER*, for instance, in which actors

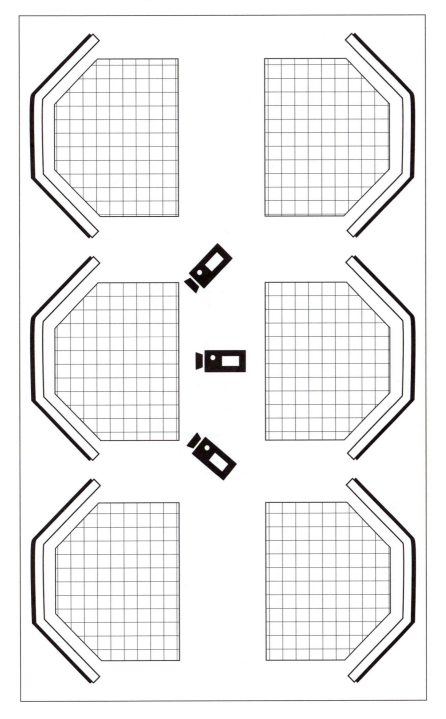

Figure 1.34 Studio layout for soap-opera production, with sets arrayed against the walls and cameras positioned in the middle.

and cameras can move forward and backward through the sets, *ATWT* sets are designed to accommodate their placement around the perimeter of a studio. An extremely deep set would protrude into the middle of the room, into space reserved for the cameras. As a result, soap-opera sets strongly resemble conventional sets designed for a theater with a proscenium: three walls, shallow space, no ceilings, and so on.

ATWT's set construction supports conversation, not dynamic movement. Ken Lewis, an *ATWT* scenic designer in the 1970s, comments:

> The sets are designed for the very limited physical movement that occurs on soaps. Shots are basically close-ups … or medium shots, with rarely a glimpse of a floor. Our attention is with the dialogue, not with the "action" so furniture is generally grouped in small clusters that make cu's (close-ups) of talking heads easily accessible. Because of the attention paid to

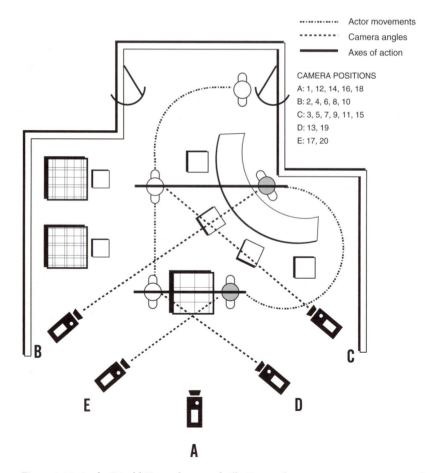

Figure 1.35 As the World Turns: layout of Al's Diner, showing camera positions and actor blocking of the scene where Brad proposes to Katie.

"interior movement," even the simplest movements—sitting, standing, walking—frequently appear stilted compared to prime-time action series.[30]

Although Lewis' insights take us forward into the realm of videography, which I will return to below, I want to emphasize here how craft practice facilitates the genre's emphasis on emotion over action.

The scene under analysis is one principally of interior movement, of Brad's barely concealed ardor, but director Michael Eilbaum's use of space in the scene departs from the emphasis on restricted, side-to-side movement that predominates in the genre. Herbert Zettl terms this typical movement across the width of the screen as being along the x-axis.[31] The height of the screen in this sense is the y-axis and movement toward or away from the camera runs along the z-axis. The Al's Diner set was built to permit movement in some depth, along the z-axis. Katie enters the set from the back of the diner (shot 1, Figure 1.1), not from the side, and then she and Brad make their way to the front of the set, as can be seen in shot 18 (Figure 1.25) and the diagram of the set with camera and actor positions (Figure 1.35). In essence, the scene is played out in two zones within the set. The first is near the counter (Figure 1.4) and the second is at the table (Figure 1.20). This blocking illustrates that the genre is able to innovate within its technological/economic restrictions. It also proves that individual directors and actors can create variations within standard craft practices.

Lighting is a second highly conventionalized element of *mise-en-scène*. Since the 1920s, film and then television lighting patterns have been dominated by three-point lighting: key light, fill light, and back light. It is possible to manipulate light in a broad variety of ways, according to position and intensity. Moreover gels may be used to change its color. Although there is some variation among individual soap operas, most do not stray far from a high-key norm exemplified in shot five (Figure 1.6), doubtlessly due to the necessity of lighting so many sets every working day. Katie's face is lit with a strong key light on her left side, a fill light to soften the shadows on her right and a back light to highlight her hair and separate her from the background. Although this effect is actually achieved with more than just three single lights, the basic three-point principle remains in effect. Only in the most extreme circumstances do soap operas deviate from this convention. Even in this nighttime, "candle-lit" scene, there are few shadows on the actors' faces and the restaurant, as a whole, is broadly lit, although some accent lights have been placed within the set to create a sense of depth (see shot 12, Figure 1.13).

Any consideration of soap opera's *mise-en-scène* would be incomplete without some mention of performance, of the gestures and movement through these diegetic spaces by human bodies. By popular consensus, the style of soap-opera acting differs markedly from that on nighttime television and in feature films. Jane Feuer suggests that it is in acting style that the concept of excess truly applies to soap opera. She writes that although acting on television serials seems quite sedate when compared with nineteenth-century theatrical conventions, nevertheless it appears excessive in comparison to the more naturalistic mode currently [1984] employed in other forms of television and in the cinema, just as the overblown "bad acting" in Sirk's films did for its time. Yet both forms of melodramatic acting are in keeping with related conventions for distilling and intensifying emotion.[32]

Jettisoning the evaluative baggage that "excessive" normally carries when applied to acting, Feuer argues that the stylized "over-acting" in melodrama is certainly appropriate to the intensity of the emotions portrayed. Indeed, it is here that one may most clearly see the "return of the repressed" that has been posited as residing in the visual style of 1950s melodrama. The *ATWT* scene chosen for analysis is a poor one to illustrate melodramatic acting as it is one of emotional constraint, of two characters resisting their attraction for each other. However, the scene I broke down in 1984, which features an argument between two characters, does indeed contain "excessive" facial expressions. (Video clips of this scene and similar ones are available on TVStyleBook.com.) Marisa Tomei's performance in that scene transgresses contemporary conventions of "realistic" acting—exemplified, possibly, in the work of Meryl Streep. More important, the style of Tomei's performance serves as a marker, a signifier, of an extraordinary emotional experience. Obviously, what she says and how she says it communicate distilled, intensified emotion to the sympathetic viewer. For some unsympathetic viewers, this emotional signifier represents something else entirely. "Melodramatic" acting exists on the edge of self-parody.[33] Persons unfamiliar with the genre or accustomed to other acting conventions may be distanced from Tomei's performance and find it amusing. The acting in soap operas, as with all acting, brings up the problem of reception, for one person's realism is another's melodrama. Feuer's article assumes that there is general agreement upon the conventions of contemporary acting when, indeed, they are still quite indeterminate.[34]

Soap Opera Videographic Properties

These three aspects of *mise-en-scène* (sets, lighting, performance) cannot exist in a vacuum. They are always articulated through the video camera and related technology. The regime of videography greatly influences our understanding of the television image. We may see this in at least four videographic properties: the use of video as a recording medium, framing and camera position, focal length and the zoom lens, and post-production special effects (including dissolves, fades, chroma key, and so on).

Because they are recorded on video, soap operas more closely resemble television news "actualities" (video of news events), reality-television programs, and talk shows than they do nighttime dramas and theatrical films, which are, for the time being, shot on 35 mm film. The advent of high-definition digital-video recording is quickly changing this reliance upon film stock, but it remains true that soap operas—even those shot in HD video—are not presented in as high a resolution as theatrical films and television dramas such as *Law & Order* (1990–) and *CSI: Crime Scene Investigation* (2000–). This resemblance to what television marks as "reality" supports John Ellis' contention: "Television presents itself as an immediate presence.... Television pretends to actuality, to immediacy; the television image in many transmissions (news, current affairs, chat shows, announcements) behaves as though it were live and uses the techniques of direct address."[35] Ellis believes that television lacks Barthes' photo effect, that sense of "presence-yet-absence" which is generated by the photographic and cinematic images.[36] Television, instead, is an "immediate presence"—seemingly live and personally directed at the viewer in news, talk shows and similar genres.[37] Ellis' argument appears particularly germane to soap opera. After all, the genre originated in live broadcasts and *ATWT* persisted in that format until 1975. In its present, recorded-video form soap opera strongly resembles those broadcasts that we know to be live presentations: local newscasts, sports programs, *Saturday Night Live*, and so on. Soap operas *seem* live and, indeed, can choose to be live again. On August 4, 1983, *Search for Tomorrow* reverted to a live broadcast because the show's tape had gone missing and for the week of May 13, 2002, *One Life to Live* was also broadcast live, in what at least one reporter called a "ratings stunt."[38]

For Ellis this immediacy is part of his analysis of the text–viewer relationship, but I would like to stress that this sense of "live-ness" is evident in the videographic properties of the text itself, not just the presumed text–viewer situation. Consider soap-opera framing, for example. The genre's reliance on the close-up has often been noted, but what is seldom perceived is the comparative haphazardness of these close-ups. *Cinematic* codes of framing operate to maximize narrative propulsion, to drive the story forward with maximum diegetic effect and minimum diegetic effort. Soap-opera videotaping, due to the exigencies of multiple camera production, creates framing that does not achieve this maximum effect. This is especially apparent in shots of accelerated figure movement. Shot 18, for example, begins with Brad mostly out of frame as he sits down (Figure 1.24). In the following shot, when Katie lifts her fork to her mouth, the camera is unable to keep up with her (Figures 1.26–1.31) and Brad partially blocks the shot (Figure 1.27). In pejorative terms—terms which assume cinematic conventions as *the* standard—the compositions of these shots are clumsy and awkward. I wish to avoid those terms, however, and suggest that this "awkwardness" functions to confirm the immediate presence of the television image. Furthermore, it is as if the character controls the framing rather than the framing controlling the character. The camera doesn't fully anticipate the figures' movements. Hence, the framing on soap opera closely resembles framing in sports and news actuality, with the camera operator struggling to keep up with the events that transpire before her or him. This slackness of framing consequently marks the scene as if it were "reality" (immediate presence) rather than "fiction" (photo effect).

The imprecision of soap-opera framing of action has an additional impact. It skews the genre's close-ups toward medium close-ups. As we previously noted in scenic designer Ken Lewis' comments on set design, the soap opera is considered to be a genre built on "close-ups of talking heads," but my examination of two weeks' worth of *ATWT* episodes contradicts this presumption. Far more common is the medium close-up, as may be observed in the analyzed scene (Figures 1.5 and 1.6). This aspect of soap-opera craft practices has both pragmatic and aesthetic implications. Pragmatically, a medium close-up is easier for camera operators to frame. Barry Salt interprets this avoidance of tight close-ups within the aesthetic standards and craft practices of contemporary television and film:

> under the fast-shooting regime of TV, there is a considerable danger of producing ugly looking pictures of the actors' heads in BCU ["big close-up," more commonly known as "extreme close-up" in the U.S.] if a slight error is made in framing by the operator. In looser framings, slight framing errors do not draw attention to themselves quite so much.[39]

Additionally, relying on medium close-ups for the majority of the close shots means that when close-ups, or extreme close-ups, are employed they will have more impact. For example, a subsequent scene in the February 1, 2008 episode escalates Brad and Katie's emotional state as she refuses his proposal. For that scene, director Michael Erlbaum brought the camera in closer—signifying the characters' heightened emotional state (Figures 1.36 and 1.37). In soap opera, as in most television, directors use the tightness of the framing to signify the level of intimacy and emotional impact of a shot—as can be varied in the zoom shot.

In terms of focal length, soap opera's norm is a slightly wide-angle lens, used ostensibly to make the small sets look larger. This focal length combines with high key lighting and camera positions relatively far from the actors to generate large depth of field. Shallow focus is consequently difficult to achieve. The most significant aspect of camera focal length in the soap opera is the genre's tendency to employ the zoom lens—that is, the variable focal length lens—to mark shots of particular emotional importance.[40] Feuer writes of its use in nighttime serials: "For coding moments of 'peak' hysteria, *Dallas* and *Dynasty* will employ repeated zooms-in to close-ups of all actors in a scene."[41] Feuer suggests that this device follows a convention of daytime soap opera and exaggerates it to the point of excess. Clearly, the zoom-in is used to signal key emotional moments, but my observation of daytime serials suggests that *Dynasty* and *Dallas* have exaggerated this device very little, if at all, beyond how it is used in daytime soap opera. Moreover, rather than a distinction based on degree of "exaggeration," I would argue that the daytime serial's zooms differ

Figure 1.36 As the World Turns: tighter close-ups signify the heightened emotions of Katie and...

from the nighttime serial's zooms only on the basis of the former's apparent lack of control. This distinction arises from the differences in filming/taping procedure of daytime and nighttime, and results in a discernible contrast between the two styles *in the images themselves*. The single, film-camera shooting style of *Dallas* and *Dynasty* produces a much more controlled, precise articulation of zooming codes than does the multiple-camera videotaping of *ATWT*. The soap opera's lack of "precision" links it with news events and their illusion of uncontrolled, unmediated "reality."

Figure 1.37 ...Brad. In this later scene, she rejects his proposal.

Visual Style and Editing

Television space—*mise-en-scène* articulated through videographic properties—is manipulated through highly conventionalized editing patterns that comprise "continuity editing," that editing system which initially developed in classical-era Hollywood.[42] Central to continuity editing is the shot-reverse shot or shot-counter shot structure, which is illustrated in two separate segments of the analyzed scene: shots 4–11 (Figures 1.5–1.12) and 19–20 (Figures 1.31–1.32).[43] In shot-reverse shot editing, crisscrossing camera angles alternate with one another, presenting first one character and then the other, or, in other terms, one spatial field and then another. "Scenographic space," according to Bordwell, Janet Staiger, and Kristin Thompson, is built through this alternation and other techniques of continuity editing.[44] Brunsdon, drawing on an unpublished paper by Andy Lowe, makes the following comments about the use of editing and television space in the British soap opera, *Crossroads*: "Generally, sets have two distinct spaces arranged laterally to each other—that is, there are two distinct camera fields, and it is the articulation of these fields which constructs the space."[45] In the analyzed scene, two laterally arranged spatial zones are developed around each body once Katie fully enters the diner, as can be seen in the diagram of camera positions on the Al's Diner set (Figure 1.35). During the scene's dessert-eating segment, the scenographic zones shift to the front of the set, to a table that was not previously visible. Most "action"—in this case, Brad and Katie's dialogue—occurs on two planes, or what can be called "axes of action."[46] As illustrated in the diagram, there's one axis toward the back of the set and a second in the front, cutting across the table. By having first Katie and then Brad move to the table, Eilbaum is able to establish this second axis. Considering the scene was likely shot live-on-tape (aka, direct-to-tape), there must have been some nimble repositioning of cameras to avoid one camera being shot by another. (The diagram shows five camera positions, but the scene was probably shot with four cameras, which, obviously, are not in fixed positions and can be moved on their dollies.)

Note also that camera A is positioned at a 90-degree angle to each action axis and the shot-counter shot cameras (B and C) are positioned at a roughly 45-degree angle to each axis. This crisscrossing, 45-degree angle is preferred for close-ups over a 90-degree angle because it generates three-quarter views of the actors' faces instead of profiles and three-quarter views reveal more of the actors' faces (e.g., Figures 1.5 and 1.6). Current craft practices hold that this better displays the emotions registering on actors' faces and emphasizes the words that come from their mouths.

In soap opera's specific use of the shot-counter shot pattern we can see still another instance in which the seemingly live nature of television is signified. Soap-opera editing leaves out "significant" action that conventional—that is, classical film-influenced—editing would include. This is illustrated by two aspects of shots 12 and 13 in the analyzed scene (Figures 1.13–1.15). Katie walks out of shot 12 and is not seen while Brad reaches behind the counter. We cut to her, seated, at the start of shot 13. Classical film editing—adhering to craft practices during the 1930s–1950s—might have included a medium shot in which both characters are visible as she changes location and goes from standing to sitting (and picks up a glass of wine). Conventional editing wisdom dictates that we return to a character in the same state in which we left her or him. In other words, Katie should be standing, without a glass of wine, at the start of shot 13, as she was in shot 12. Once again, soap-opera style seems closer to the haphazardness of reality television or *cinéma vérité* than to the precisely orchestrated style of prime-time television and theatrical fiction films. One can easily picture a cut like this, missing a small bit of action, in a program such as *The Real World* (1992–), but not in a classical film such as *Casablanca* (1942).

A second "violation" of continuity editing is a result of the serial nature of soap opera. Bordwell, Staiger, and Thompson, drawing on Thierry Kuntzel, describe the scene's semi-autonomous nature:

> the autonomy of the classical scene is a mixed one; the scene is both a detachable segment and a link in a chain. As such, the scene can be taken as having two roughly distinct phases, the exposition and the development.[47]

The expository phase establishes the characters involved, the space they will inhabit during the scene and the temporal position of the scene's events (presumably after those of the preceding scenes unless it is marked as a flashback or flashforward). Serial narrative, however, is based on the premise of *in medias res*, of beginning in the middle of the action and thus eschewing exposition on a general level. This genre-defining lack of exposition reveals itself in microcosm in individual scenes. Our analyzed scene begins 30 minutes into the episode, with Katie and Brad in the midst of a conversation that is previously established in six separate scenes that day—starting at :09, :10, :12, :16, :22, and :24. We have thus skipped the expository phase of the scene and moved directly into its development phase. Moreover, this conversation occurs in a space that was previously established in those earlier scenes.

The first shot of the scene captures Katie and Brad in the middle of the diner (Figure 1.2), and does not show us the candle-lit table that was introduced previously (at nine minutes into the episode) through a conventional establishing shot (Figure 1.38). This scene does not even offer us a re-establishing shot as we go from shot 12 to 13—although if you look closely at the bottom of Figure 1.13 you can just barely see the flowers that are on the table. Shot 16 (Figures 1.18–1.20) serves as a retroactive re-establishing shot as it shows us where the counter is in relation to the table and ends with a long shot of the table in the room. Thus, taken in isolation, this scene does not

Figure 1.38 As the World Turns: establishing shot of the diner, from earlier in the episode. The scene analyzed in detail skips the establishing shot since the space has already been established.

follow continuity editing's rules for establishing scenographic space—moving Katie into an area of the set that we have not seen in this scene (and moving her there while off screen). However, the truncation of exposition is a defining characteristic of the genre and is reflected in this scene's elision of an expository phase. Since it is the seventh scene to be set in that space on that particular day, an establishing shot of the diner would clearly be redundant.

Bordwell, Staiger, and Thompson are less expansive in their consideration of the ending of classical scenes, but we may surmise that many scenes have dénouement phases that mirror their expository phases. Once again, soap-opera editing reflects its larger, never-ending diegetic structure. The most common end to a soap-opera scene is some variety of a close-up, of a character about to respond to an event or in contemplation of what has just occurred. For example, our analyzed scene ends on a medium close-up of Brad as he watches Katie eat and anticipates her discovery of the ring he's hidden next to her piece of cheesecake (Figure 1.32). Anticipation is the key here, as it is in so much of soap-opera narrative. The finish of this scene does not conclude the scene's action, as it might in a classical scene. Rather, it anticipates the conclusion in a future scene—which occurs at :34 of the episode, less than three minutes later. That later scene begins without an establishing shot, starting instead with a tight close-up of Katie's cheesecake as she continues to eat it (Figure 1.39—the first frame of that scene) and then chokes on the ring. Brad then shows her the ring and, not surprisingly, that later scene ends on a medium close-up of her (Figures 1.40–1.41), similar to the scene-ending one of Brad, that anticipates what her reaction to the ring will be. Thus we may see that soap-opera editing constructs scenes without exposition or dénouement, scenes which signify in microcosm the larger project of the narrative. Or, as Louise Spence observes,

> The zoom in to the extended close-up of the character's face at the end of
> the sequence is a close look at the expression to enable the viewer to

gauge a character's mental or emotional activity, forecasting new possibilities. A climax may have been reached, but it is always undermined by the promise of new climaxes, the potential for and prospect of more problems ... and pleasures [ellipsis in the original].[48]

Soap Opera Time and Rhythm

Time on soap operas is quite unlike that in theatrical film and only minimally related to that of the nighttime television series. The amount of diegetic time in soap opera dwarfs that of the cinema and that of prime-time television. A 11,000-hour text, such as *As the World Turns*, must presumably incorporate temporal structures quite different from feature films or television's evening series. If it didn't, soap opera would collapse beneath the weight of its own, ever-enlarging storylines. How, then, are these mammoth time frames structured?

Television shares with the cinema the potential ability to manipulate time through editing, but it seldom makes use of that potential—at least, not within the individual scene. Shots are joined together in a seamless continuum that

Figure 1.39 *As The World Turns*: three minutes later in the episode, a follow-up scene begins with a tight close-up of cheesecake, which...

Figure 1.40 ...contains a ring on which Katie chokes.

Figure 1.41 The last shot of the scene shows Katie in close-up, much as the previous scene ended on Brad in close-up.

Figure 1.42 *As the World Turns*: a later scene resumes the action with Brad still holding the ring, as if no time has passed.

preserves real time rather than manipulating or distorting it. A soap-opera scene is normally taped straight through and simultaneously recorded by three or more cameras. Scenes in prime-time dramas and classical films are created from small fragments that are recorded one piece at a time by a single camera on set. These craft practices have implications for the visual representation of time through editing. In a multiple-camera, live-on-tape production the recorded scene exists as a totality the moment the actors cease performing it, because the cameras are typically switched—i.e., cut from one to the next— while the scene is performed.[49] The scene's temporal continuum exists a priori, during the performance, and is *preserved as performed* when recorded.[50] In contrast, a single-camera production records bits and pieces of performance time, which must be assembled in order to *construct* the scene's temporal continuum. What implications does this have for the representation of time in the text? The inter-shot malleability of single-camera editing allows its editors to lengthen or shorten shots—within the constraints of other editing conventions—in ways that multiple-camera editors cannot. Shot 13, in the analyzed scene, ends with Katie moving the wine glass toward her lips, but it cuts before it gets there. If this were a single-camera production, the editor could choose to lengthen the shot to include her taking a sip; but the multiple-camera editor cannot as he or she has no additional material with which to work. Similarly, if Brad's arrangement of the ring on the cheesecake seemed to be taking "too long," the single-camera editor could shorten it. The multiple-camera editor could, too, but the time constraints of editing 250 programs per year militate against making such minor adjustments.[51] In sum, in a live-on-tape, multiple-camera production the "real" time of the performance equals the diegetic time of the scene.

Stephen Heath and Gillian Skirrow contend that the equivalence of real time and story time in television reconfirms its immediacy. All television programs are in effect identified with the *"live"* television program. They borrow the following scheme from M. Tardy, comparing the temporal structures of the novel, the film, and the television program (= indicates equivalence, ≠ indicates non-equivalence):

> *Novel*: time of literary creation ≠ time of reading ≠ diegetic time
> *Film*: time of cinematic creation ≠ projection-viewing time ≠ diegetic time
> *TV program*: time of television creation = transmission-viewing time = diegetic time (time of event).[52]

From this they conclude:

> The immediate time of the image is pulled into a confusion with the time of the events shown, tending to diminish the impression of the mode of presence in absence characteristic of film, suggesting a permanently alive view on the world; the generalized fantasy of the television institution of the image is exactly that it is *direct*, and direct for *me*.[53]

Thus, the editing style of the individual scene confirms what has already been noted in the context of soap-opera framing: the immediate presence of television. This immediate presence serves the ideological function of naturalizing the representation. It invokes the illusion of a "reality" presented immediately and expressly for the viewer. Heath and Skirrow's comments are directed to a news program, *World in Action*, but they apply equally well to soap opera.

Soap-opera scenes preserve a real-time temporal structure, but the length of individual shots is modulated according to certain conventional rhythms—regardless of whether those rhythms are created with live switching or in post-production. *ATWT*'s and other American soaps' scenes typically contain at least one alternating pattern of approximately equal shots-counter shots, where each shot is three seconds or less. Longer re-establishing shots interrupt these alternations. This alternation-longer shots-alternation pattern may be observed in the example from *ATWT*. After the opening shot shows both Katie and Brad, we launch into alternating shots of them that are three-to-five seconds each. Then, shot 12 breaks that rhythm with a 10-second shot that allows Katie to move toward the candle-lit table and Brad to start preparing his surprise. Shots 13–16 slow the pace with two shots lasting over ten seconds and shot 16, in which Brad hobbles to the table, is the scene's longest shot: 14 seconds. After this 14-second shot, the scene returns to short, alternating shots of two-to-five seconds each. In this typical, 20-shot scene we observe a fundamental pattern: alternation of two visual fields with shots approximately three seconds long, longer shots re-establishing the scene or developing the action, and temporary resolution.

One broad indication of the temporal rhythm of soap opera editing is average shot length (ASL). The ASL of our five-episode sample of 2008 *ATWT* episodes is 4.84 seconds.[54] That number alone is not very revealing, but it is useful to compare it with the ASLs of other times and other forms of film/television production. Salt, one of the leading advocates of statistical analysis of style, has begun work on prime-time television dramas—including several from the 1990s.[55] Compared with those 1990s prime-time programs, *ATWT*'s 4.84 ASL is very fast, although, notably, the prime-time melodrama serial, *Melrose Place* (1992–9), was cut faster (4.0 ASL). Until further research is done, however, it's impossible to know if that is also true of 2000s prime-time programs or theatrical films. Preliminary work has been accomplished by the CineMetrics project, in which volunteers use software to calculate ASLs and contribute them to a central database, and Shot Logger, a similar service that calculates shot length from time-stamped frame captures.[56] In the CineMetrics analysis of 46 U.S. theatrical films released 2000–8, it has found a median ASL of 4.8—meaning that an equal number of films are faster and slower than 4.8 ASL. And in data combined from CineMetrics and Shot Logger of 24 television programs from the same time period the median ASL is 5.25—indicating that *ATWT* is edited faster than most of those programs. (See TVStyleBook.com for more detailed data tables.)

One can see from Salt's analysis of hundreds of theatrical films that ASL has consistently decreased since 1946. The median ASL of films from the post-

World War II decade was over ten seconds, but by 1999 it had decreased to 5.92 seconds.[57] My analysis of *ATWT* ASLs from 1984 and 2008 confirms this general decrease. The median ASL of my five-episode sample from 1984 is 7.77 seconds, or 53 percent slower than the median ASL of 5.07 calculated from my five 2008 episodes. I suspect that the decrease would be even more radical if *ATWT*'s live broadcasts from the 1950s and 1960s were generally available. Preliminary analysis of television programs from the 1950s finds ASLs over 10 seconds are quite common and an episode of *The Honeymooners* broadcast October 1, 1955 was shot at the relatively leisurely pace of 17.7 seconds per shot.[58] An incomplete analysis of one live, 1960s *ATWT* episode in the Shot Logger database clocks in with a 12.6 ASL, but, more notably, this episode includes long takes of 30 seconds and more, and some scenes are played in a single shot.

Even though the time frame of the individual scene is firmly rooted in real time (albeit modulated real time), the temporal relationship among scenes and among the daily episodes is much more ambiguous. Derry provides a starting point for the analysis of time in soap operas. He contends that there are basically two, sometimes contradictory time schemes: "Extended Time" and "Landmark Time." He explains:

> First there is what can be termed a Landmark Time: that is, the episode broadcast on Thanksgiving is generally represented as Thanksgiving, likewise with Christmas. Landmark Time is complicated by the intrusion of Extended Time, whereby one day of soap opera story can be extended into a week or more of half-hour or hour episodes.[59]

These are further complicated, Derry notes, by the idiosyncratic time schemes of certain diegetic lines. He points out that the time frames of pregnancies are frequently drawn out, while those of children aging are compressed.[60] Indeed, the latter is so common that the soap-opera press and fans have dubbed it "SORAS"—soap opera rapid aging syndrome.[61] Time, it would appear, is constructed rather casually on soap operas.

The implausible, occasionally contradictory time schemes of soap opera are evident in my *ATWT* samples. In the episode that contains the Brad and Katie scene analyzed above, the subsequent scene of her choking on the ring comes to a conclusion with Brad saying, "I was trying to propose." He holds the ring in a close-up (Figure 1.40) and then the scene fades to black, at :34 in the broadcast, with a shot of Katie appearing shocked (Figure 1.41). After the shot of Katie, the act ends, going to commercials. Following the commercial break and *five* intervening scenes, including one just outside Al's Diner, we return to a close-up of the ring at :42 (Figure 1.42)—as if Brad were frozen in this position for that entire time. He begins the scene with the line, "I wanted this to go so much better." Within the logic of the story, Brad's two lines should only be a few seconds apart, but they are separated by eight minutes of broadcast time and, more significantly, four minutes of diegetic time occurring in five other locations.

Temporal extensions and gaps may not be large in soap opera, but they do indicate a more general component of the genre's temporal style: time is manipulated, but only between scenes and, especially, between episodes. This temporal manipulation may result in either extended or compressed time. On the one hand, diegetic time may be drawn out (as we see above); entire scenes may even be repeated shot for shot. On the other hand, diegetic time may also be elided. One segment might end with the characters heading for bed; the very next scene following the commercial break could be the following day. Indeed, soap opera may even construct a time frame that is apparently contradictory when examined closely, but which seems to make sense while viewed. Thus, even though the time within a scene adheres strictly to real time constraints, the time between scenes and between episodes is quite malleable, shaped to fit conventional dramatic demands.

This intersegment malleability is facilitated by television's highly segmented nature. Though there must be absolute consistency within a particular segment—as in the temporal structure of the individual scene—there may be considerable variation in the time scheme between scenes. Television assumes pragmatically that the viewer may not have seen the previous segment and may not see the succeeding one.[62] Consequently, the relationship between scenes is less causal than the classical cinema, where the narrative is assumed to be "*a chain of events in cause-effect relationship occurring in time and space*" (Bordwell and Thompson).[63] In television, the narrative "links" are very loosely soldered together, forming a chain that is more dependent upon simple succession than causality. In this regard, soap opera is the apotheosis of television. Its numerous diegetic lines (approximately 20 on *ATWT* currently) demand a flexible time scheme in order to facilitate the many activities that are occurring at the same diegetic time; i.e., within a similar present tense. As Brunsdon notes regarding *Crossroads*, "There is no single linear time flow." She continues, "The different present tenses of the narrative co-exist, temporally unhierarchised."[64] Individual scenes—small parcels of present tenses, as it were—marshal the viewer's attention for the scene's duration, setting her or him in a rigid real-time scheme. The next scene, however, is still another small parcel, and one which may bear little relationship to the previous one. Indeed, it may well contradict the present tense of the past scene. No present tense is given greater priority in the world of soap opera, because the hierarchy that exists in classical cinema has been mostly dismantled.[65]

The hour-long episodes of *ATWT* in 2008 are broken down into largely self-sufficient scenes—each typically lasting between 50 and 70 seconds.[66] Scenes are considerably shorter now than they were in 1984, when the average was above two minutes per scene. In one extreme example, a scene from our sample week is just five seconds long (and a single shot). Using the week from 2008 for some specific figures, one can note that median number of 38 scenes per day are distributed in six segments of commercial-separated narrative action, which are often called "acts." Acts average six minutes, one second each—ranging from four to ten minutes, with the second act usually being the longest and the fourth act the shortest. Out of each 58.5-minute daily program (from the first shot of the first pre-credit scene to the end of the copyright credit), 22 minutes and 14 seconds, on average, are devoted to non-narrative material. Hence, some *38 percent* of each program "hour" is actually extra-diegetic material. It is small wonder that soap operas were sponsored by soap manufacturers and proved to be the financial backbone of the television networks for decades. Even though the length of the programs has stabilized at 58.5 minutes, there have been significant changes in how that time is allocated. In 1984, there were seven narrative acts, not six as there are today. And in 1984 *ATWT* broadcast over 40 diegetic minutes every day. Today, that number is down to 36 minutes and 20 seconds. Or, viewed from another perspective, the percentage of time per episode devoted to non-narrative material has substantially increased over that time, from 30 percent to 38 percent.

Soap opera time is compartmentalized into self-sustaining individual units of scene, segment (diegetic acts and extradiegetic commercial breaks), and single day's episode. The relative strength of the division between each of these units is signified by the device used for the transition. Transitions from scene to scene within an act are almost invariably achieved with straight cuts, while the conclusion of an act is marked with a fade to black—to facilitate movement from a diegetic segment to an extra-diegetic one or vice versa. The end of the day's program is marked with a copyright notice. Dissolves are seldom if ever used between units though they do occur occasionally within a scene for an "artistic" effect. In making use of these various transitions to make temporal breaks, soap opera is employing conventions inherited from the cinema. Depending on the context, a cut can signify immediate succession of the two images joined—or it can mean an indeterminate amount of time has passed. A fade, in contrast, signifies a substantial ellipsis. As we shall see, certain audio elements work to pull the viewer across those boundaries, but the basic principle remains one of segmentation.

Soap Opera Sound

The soundtrack is a crucial component of soap opera. As radio soap opera has already proven, the genre can do quite well without any visual accouterments. Even today it is entirely possible to "view" television soap opera without actually seeing it; indeed, there are many who listen rather than watch. In an intriguing throwback to radio days, CBS has made available audio-only podcasts of *ATWT*, which it touts thus: "As *As the World Turns* prepares to celebrate its 50th year on television, this the show that has delighted fans for so long has something new to offer: a podcast of the complete audio track of each episode."[67] Unlike *Guiding Light*, *ATWT* never existed in a radio format, but its podcast closely resembles a radio broadcast—down to an announcer introducing the scenes and explaining the action. For instance, the podcast of the analyzed scene includes this commentary: "Katie tries the door, but it won't open." (The *Television Style* website contains an excerpt from the podcast.) Soap opera's emphasis on dialogue is evidenced in most of its scripts, which contain very little specific action and few, if any, camera positions. In a practical sense, the images are constructed to illustrate the words, rather than vice versa. Heath and Skirrow have noted, "The problem for television as institution of images is then the constraint of the image, its ideological currency constantly to be maintained: the commentary must be accompanied, the screen *filled*."[68] In this regard, sound "precedes" the television image. As Ellis has argued, television appeals more to our desire to hear than our desire to look: "In psychoanalytic terms, when compared to cinema, TV demonstrates a displacement from the invocatory drive of scopophilia (looking) to the closest related of the invocatory drives, that of hearing."[69] Instead of demanding the sustained gaze of the cinema, Ellis continues, television requests only that its viewers occasionally glance in its direction, when summoned to do so by signals from the soundtrack.

Assuming the primacy of sound in soap opera, we can articulate specific stylistic patterns that characterize the genre's use of dialogue, music, and sound effects. Of these three, dialogue has proven to be the dominant concern for those who have written on the genre. Most of this material has focused on dialogue's preponderance at the expense of physical activity. Ellis's comment typifies thinking on the subject: "It [soap opera] is massively composed of talk; conversation, speculation, confrontation, chat."[70] This has been borne out by content analyses, such as Natan Katzman's 1970 study of "Characters and Conversations": "Almost everything that happens in soap operas takes the form of verbal activity.... The characters talk, and talk, and talk."[71] Although since the 1980s those soap operas which seek a more youthful audience have incorporated more adventure stories and less talk, the basic principle remains the same: characters suffer and discuss their suffering. If we accept the dichotomy between doing and suffering, action and passion that Geoffrey Nowell-Smith traces from classical tragedy in his discussion of film melodrama, then soap opera has inherited the legacy of "passion" from the cinema.[72] In our analyzed scene from *ATWT*, Brad and Katie do not actually do much of anything beyond eating a little cheesecake and talking about whether they should eat that cheesecake—the dessert serving as a metaphor for their on-again-off-again romance. The unspoken subtext is Brad's love for Katie, which they'll talk about later in the episode. The "actions" they discuss (Brad wanting to propose) are themselves principally verbal actions rather than physical ones. In soap opera, talk is the main topic of conversation.

An analysis of the content of soap-opera dialogue is well outside the purview of this study, but I would like to offer a few observations on the interdependent relationship of dialogue style, editing, and syntagmatic narrative form.[73] Dialogue functions as one of the most common and most significant devices for overcoming the segmental nature of television and concatenating one scene to another—"hooking" together links in a chain, as Bordwell maintains.[74] As a result, it strongly affects the operation of television style. Dialogue constructs a question-and-answer pattern. It may be as explicit as one character asking where another might be, followed by a cut to that character. More often, a character will simply mention another in a style that suggests there is some question surrounding what that character might do. Dialogue continually acts as the catalyst for new enigmas in the never-ending narrative chain that is at the very heart of the genre. This eternally confounded hermeneutic works its way into soap opera's smallest narrative unit, the single scene. Small questions are answered while larger ones are held in abeyance. Thus the soap opera does not so much continuously withhold resolution, as it does parcel out incomplete pieces of closure. And, as we can see in the way dialogue is manipulated, those pieces of closure always construct the foundations of new enigmas.

Melodrama has been as closely associated with music as it has with words. The term itself derives from the eighteenth-century theatrical tradition of *melos* (music) drama. Judging from the parodies of soap opera such as "As the Stomach Turns" of *The Carol Burnett Show*, circa 1969, organ music is as closely identified with the genre as is the mountain of verbiage. In many parodies, the type of music and the style of narrative are actually those of radio and 1960s television soap opera much more than those of contemporary television programs. (A sample of 1960s *ATWT* audio is on the TVStyleBook.com.) Rising organ and resonant announcer voicing queries (from *Our Gal Sunday*: "The story asks the question, Can this girl from a mining town in the West find happiness as the wife of a wealthy and titled Englishman?")[75] have been replaced by pseudo-rock rhythms, plaintive solo guitars and pianos, and copyrighted popular songs. The music is digitally synthesized and added during post-production, although until recently the music cues were inserted as *ATWT* was shot. Rock music as performed by its original artists began to be used in narrative television in the later 1970s and our sample week from 1984 does include a Pat Benatar tune.[76] Previously, rock-style music performed by studio musicians had been the standard on the rare occasions when rock music was necessitated by the narrative—say, when characters visited a discotheque. Indeed, until the late 1970s soap operas generally avoided rock music, considering it inappropriate for their older, conservative audience.[77] The frequent use of rock music on today's soap operas, as well as on traditionally conservative sports programs, indicates that this musical style has achieved general acceptance. It also reflects the interest of the networks in more youthful consumers.

Even though the style of soap-opera music has evolved, its function has largely remained the same. Music, more than any other element of *mise-en-scène*, is responsible for setting the mood and marking intense emotions. The analyzed *ATWT* scene begins without music, but it starts under Katie's line, "Oh, that's not fair," in shot seven (Figure 1.8) and then continues to the end of the scene. It has no distinct melody in this case, but rather vamps synthesized notes with a (digitized) electric guitar playing over it. At the end of the scene, a deep bass note grows louder, mirroring Brad's rising emotions in the scene, as he waits for Katie to discover the ring he's hidden in her dessert (Figure 1.32). The music's crescendo at the end accompanies the final shot of Brad contemplating Katie and serves to heighten the suspense of what will happen next. It then *continues* across the cut to the next scene (Figure 1.33), where it segues into a new musical theme. The rising musical theme, a conventional, stylistic use of music, serves a dual narrative function, signifying both the segment's conclusion (as it gains volume) and drawing the viewer into the next segment (as it continues into the next scene).[78] As with the dialogue, music generates narrative momentum—in an attempt to counteract segmentation. Just as there is music "left over" when the scene ends, so do several narrative elements remain unresolved: will Katie find the ring? Will she accept Brad's proposal? It is critical to the soap opera form that emotions are never quite fully discharged; traces always linger. As Laura Mulvey has written about film melodrama, a certain excess remains—"an excess which precludes satisfaction."[79] Some emotion has been drained off, but, as the music suggests, emotional undercurrents continue to flow throughout the day's program.

Small Oases of Closure

In Sandy Flitterman's consideration of soap-opera commercials, she argues, "Far from interrupting the narrative flow of stimulated yearning for a just conclusion and perpetual indication of its impossibility, commercials are small oases of narrative closure, homogeneous and systematic units of unproblematized meaning."[80] Further, she characterizes the soap-opera's "technical execution" of its narratives as tending toward "relative poverty"— or what we have been calling zero-degree style—while commercials are imbued with stylistic riches, one might say.[81] Flitterman's insight is an important one that is borne out by our sample *ATWT* weeks, where commercials do indeed offer 30-second oases of closure in vast deserts of narrative aperture. The stylistic significance of commercials is considered fully in a later chapter, but it is worth briefly considering here how the style of commercials stands in stark contrast to the style of soap operas discussed above.

As Flitterman notes, commercials make use of camera movement and angles, special effects, and music in ways that are not to be found in the standard soap-opera dialogue scene and its reliance upon shot-counter shot. What is particularly intriguing, however, is how narrative commercials use a compressed and maximized articulation of classical style—or what Bordwell calls "intensified continuity"—to present their didactic stories of a product's success in its alleviation of pain, hunger, low self-esteem, and so on.[82] "The new style amounts to an *intensification* of established techniques," Bordwell argues in 2006, "Intensified continuity is traditional continuity amped up, raised to a higher pitch of emphasis."[83] Because the commercial has only 30 seconds or less to make its point, it must do so with extremely efficacious sound and image. Take as an example, a 15-second Pillsbury Crescent rolls commercial that aired repeatedly during the 2008 sample week. (See Table 1.2. The commercial itself is included on the TVStyleBook.com.) It rapidly tells the story of two girls at a family dinner. They stare each other down over the last roll in a basket. Ennio Morricone's theme from *The Good, the Bad and the Ugly* (1966) accompanies their competition—a common use of intertextuality to signal quickly the story's meaning. After staring for 11 shots, the first girl shown grabs the roll, but a mother figure simultaneously arrives, proclaiming, "I've got more." A narrator then delivers the pitch over a shot of the product and the Pillsbury Doughboy: "Pillsbury Crescents. Do you have enough?" Thus in 15 seconds, we have exposition (the opening long shot, lasting just over one second; Figure 1.43), conflict (the girls staring each other down; Figures 1.48–1.49), climax (girl one grabbing the roll; Figure 1.55), and dénouement (after the mother brings more, one girl giggles; Figures 1.56). Further, one need not dig deeply to expose the "unproblematized" consumerism and sexual politics of this narrative as it is the mother who serves the rolls and it is her anxiety that is invoked in the ad's tagline, "Do you have enough?" The "you" being addressed is doubtlessly the mothers in the viewing audience.

As Flitterman contends, this commercial clearly features blunt narrative closure to support its consumerism, but it is more than that. It is a short, intensified chunk of the continuity system and single-camera production breaking up soap opera's attenuated, zero-degree style and multiple-camera, live-on-tape shooting. Fourteen shots comprise the commercial, cut so quickly that a fine-grained average shot length calculation is necessary—using video frames instead of seconds (based on video's frame rate of 30 per second). The commercial's ASL is a mere 32 *frames* (one second, two frames), with one shot lasting just ten frames (one-third of a second). Roughly four times faster than *ATWT*'s diegetic scenes, it exceeds the cutting rate of all the feature-length films in CineMetrics', Shot Logger's and Barry Salt's data-bases.[84] Although the editing is much faster than feature-length films or prime-time television could sustain, it remains a textbook example of con-tinuity editing. There is no dialogue until the mother's line at the very end and so the editing is motivated solely by the looks of the two girls—at each other and at the roll in the basket. In shot one, the first girl looks across the table at the second, which cues the cut to the second girl (an eyeline match cut; Figure 1.43 to 1.44). The second girl then looks down (Figure 1.45), whereupon the camera cuts to a subjective shot of the biscuit (Figure 1.46)—in shot three. What is notable about shot three is that it would be impossible to attain in live-on-tape, multiple-camera shooting. To achieve that precise shot, the camera would have to be positioned where the second girl is sit-ting—right on the axis of action—and would then be visible in shot five of that girl (Figure 1.48), which comes just one second later. The cut from a second subjective shot—the extreme close-up in shot 11 (Figure 1.54)—to the long shot in shot 12 (Figure 1.55) has the same issue. Point-of-view (POV) shots such as these are extremely rare in soap operas. Exceptions do exist, but those shots must be achieved after the main scene has been shot, making them costly and expendable. The analyzed scene above includes a shot that comes close, when Brad arranges the ring next to the cheesecake (Figure 1.17), but even that tight close-up is not from his POV. Other aspects of this commer-cial's style also do not fit with the craft practices of multiple-camera produc-tion. As Salt has noted, the extreme close-up of the first girl (Figure 1.54) would typically be avoided in multiple-camera shooting, because it would be difficult to frame her eyes so tightly.

Table 1.2 Pillsbury Crescent rolls commercial *découpage*

Shot Number, Scale, and Length	Figure	Sound	Action/Camera Movement
1 long shot 39 frames (*Figure 1.43*)		[Ennio Morricone's theme from *The Good, the Bad and the Ugly* (1966), begins. Ambient sounds of the dinner party can be heard.]	All shots are handheld.
2 medium shot 26 frames (*Figures 1.44–1.45*)	 		
3 close-up 26 frames (*Figure 1.46*)		Voiceover: Flaky on the outside, soft on the inside.	

Shot Number, Scale, and Length	Figure	Sound	Action/Camera Movement
4 close-up 31 frames (*Figure 1.47*)			
5 medium shot 36 frames (*Figure 1.48*)			
6 medium shot 37 frames (*Figure 1.49*)		[Ambient sounds fade out.]	
7 close-up 53 frames (*Figure 1.50*)			

continued

Table 1.2 continued

Shot Number, Scale, and Length	Figure	Sound	Action/Camera Movement
8 close-up 21 frames (*Figure 1.51*)			
9 close-up 10 frames (*Figure 1.52*)			
10 close-up 17 frames (*Figure 1.53*)		Small zoom in.	
11 extreme close-up 16 frames (*Figure 1.54*)	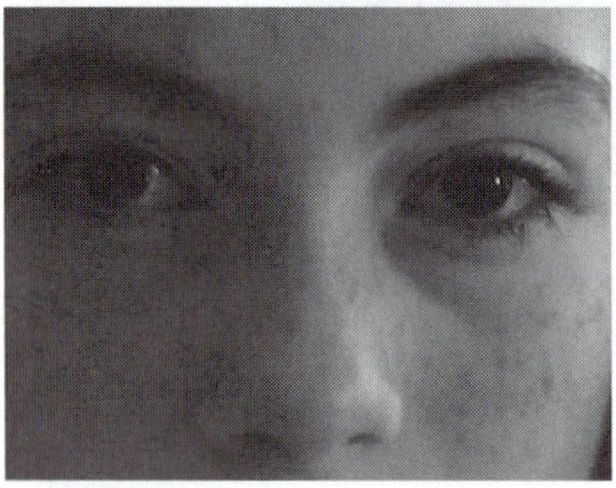		

Shot Number, Scale, and Length	Figure	Sound	Action/Camera Movement
12 long shot 48 frames (*Figure 1.55*)		Mother figure: I got more. [Ambient sound fades up.]	
13 close-up 34 frames (*Figure 1.56*)			
14 long shot 54 frames (*Figure 1.57*)		Voiceover: Pillsbury Crescents. Do you have enough?	

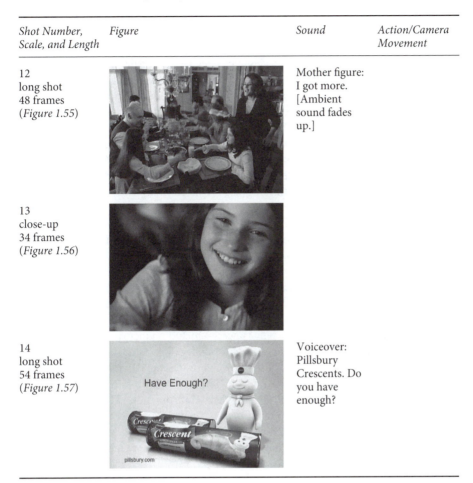

The economic and physical imperatives of soap-opera production prevent it from being able to create a commercial like this, but the aesthetics of soap-opera craft practices also enter into the equation. For instance, the commercial is entirely shot with a handheld camera—signifying the tension between the two girls, perhaps. Soap operas have access to handheld cameras and there is nothing economic or physical preventing them from using them in every scene. Indeed, on rare occasions, soap operas do use them—including an *ATWT* scene within our sample week of Lily and Holden in a hospital stairwell. But these exceptions merely prove that the *ATWT* directors are able to shoot in this manner, but that it does not fit the aesthetic conventions of soap-opera craft practices for day-to-day shooting. Similarly, *ATWT* could conceivably shoot scenes with minimal or no dialogue—as in this commercial—but soap opera's aesthetics would not "allow" it. Thus, we may see that economics, pragmatic production concerns, and aesthetics blend together to form the craft practices of the genre.

A Conclusion that Precludes Satisfaction

Style is a fundamental component of the soap-opera apparatus—a significant and signifying element. Style validates television's illusion of immediate presence and hence certifies the world presented as "natural" and naturally for the viewer. Soap-opera style also transcends television's segmentalized nature. Although editing patterns construct self-sufficient narrative units, a specific manipulation of dialogue and music propels the story forward, beyond segmental boundaries, and beckons to the viewer to stay tuned. Small, almost self-contained narrative pieces are revealed, while larger issues remain in limbo. In this fashion, style serves the critical function of nurturing and maintaining the genre's diegetic enigmas. A close analysis of soap-opera texts reveals a consistency to this style, which I label the multiple-camera proscenium schema and summarize in Table 1.3.

The future of the soap opera, in general, and soap-opera style, in particular, is in question. After decades of reliable ratings and income production the genre finds itself losing viewers at a rate that alarms network executives, soap-opera producers and media buyers alike.[85] As Rino Scanzoni, chief investment officer for media buyer, GroupM, commented, "Daytime ratings are bleeding and it's a problem for advertisers."[86] Soap-opera producers have employed a number of strategies to woo new viewers—including increased online offerings (e.g., podcasts) and contests designed for college-aged students. And CBS executives, such as Barbara Bloom, senior vice president of daytime, have reportedly advised their lower-rated programs to "'evolve' their production process,"[87] or, in other words, to significantly alter their craft practices. The most radical of these efforts in terms of soap-opera style is the approach taken by CBS's *Guiding Light* (commonly abbreviated as *GL*), the oldest television soap opera and the only remaining program to have made the transition from radio.

Table 1.3 Multiple-camera proscenium schema

Mise-en-scène	*Editing (live-on-tape)*
Interiors and in-studio exteriors	Stable axis of action
Limited number of recurring sets	Shot-reverse shot
Proscenium set design	Gaps; missing action
Lateral (*x*-axis) blocking, some limited diagonal movement	Theatrical-scene time
	Malleable time between segments
High-key lighting	Few POV shots
"Excessive" performance style	
Videography	*Sound*
Video (not film) recording	Dialogue intensive
Imprecise framing	Functional music, supports narrative
Reliance on medium shots	
Zoom in for emphasis (especially at scene ends)	
Cameras outside fourth wall/proscenium	
Large depth-of-field	

After residing at the bottom of soap-opera ratings for months, *GL* sought to reverse its bad fortune by adopting a radically different mode of production that rejected fundamental elements of multiple-camera, live-on-tape production. As of the episode aired February 29, 2008, handheld digital cameras are used to record scenes that are either shot on location (using Peapack, New Jersey, to represent the show's fictional town of Springfield) or on 40 newly constructed, four-wall sets. The medium close-ups that are still the standard on *ATWT* have been replaced with tight close-ups and frequent extreme close-ups. And the conventions of continuity editing have been so relaxed that they're practically non-existent. The 180-degree rule is often broken and standard shot-counter shot editing has nearly been eliminated. (See a sample on TVStyleBook.com.) This radical restructuring of the soap opera's craft practices was done, according to *GL*'s executive producer, Ellen Wheeler, to bring "realism" to the genre: "Now we are able to tell stories that are much more real life. People wanted to see the realness and that's what we are giving them."[88] However, as one perceptive *GL* fan noted in an online bulletin board, the claims to realism are rather specious:

> I also am getting a headache with your hand held camera work. It's like *Blair Witch Project* now. Your camera work is very bad for a soap. Low angle, extreme close ups, birds eye view, etc., makes it too stylized for me.... The new look can be outside, but at least don't have so many jump cuts and extreme close ups that ignore the mise en scene that is so important. How does an eight year old boy show up all over the place all the time. He doesn't get stopped, ever. It is too unrealistic. You have gone to less realism, not more.[89]

Mixed in with the claims to realism are also aspirations for a "more cinematic feel,"[90] which it does if one equates the cinematic with *cinéma vérité* (as in *The Blair Witch Project*) and not with classical style. Additionally, *GL*'s new editing schema owes a good deal to prime-time shows such as *24* (2001–) and their rejection of continuity editing. As *24*'s cinematographer, Rodney Charters, explains, "We don't worry about the line [of axis]. We don't believe in it. We cross the line all the time."[91]

The ongoing changes in today's soap operas sharply illustrate the pressures placed on craft practices and their motivations for change—summed up in Wheeler's defensive comment: "This is not a desperate survival move. This is a creative, financially efficient way to move soap operas into the future. *GL* has always led the way."[92] In *GL*'s audacious use of sound and image we may be witnessing a significant shift in soap-opera's stylistic schema, with new implications for how style signifies. Or, we may be witnessing a genre in its death throes, as could have been observed in *radio* soap operas—including *Guiding Light* in radio format—in the late 1950s.[93] In either case, the contemporary soap opera offers a telling case study for stylistic analysis.

Notes

1. John Thornton Caldwell, *Televisuality: Style, Crisis, and Authority in American Television* (New Brunswick: Rutgers University Press, 1995), 56.

2. See especially (cited below) Allen, Brunsdon, Derry, Dyer, Ellis, Feuer, Flitterman, Geraghty, Heath, Kuhn, Lovell, Modleski, Seiter, and Skirrow. And, on a personal note, I perceive television through the filter of a graduate education in cinema studies and several years experience teaching the same, as well as courses on soap opera.

3. Charlotte Brunsdon, "The Role of Soap Opera in the Development of Feminist Television Scholarship," *To Be Continued...: Soap Operas Around the World*, ed. Robert C. Allen (New York: Routledge, 1995), 49–65. Developments in this area were documented earlier by Jane Feuer and Annette Kuhn. See Jane Feuer, "Melodrama, Serial Form and Television Today," *Screen* 25, no. 1 (January/February 1984): 4–16; and Kuhn, "Women's Genres," *Screen* 25, no. 1 (January/February 1984): 18–28.

4. Brunsdon, "The Role of Soap Opera," 52–5.

5. Tania Modleski, "The Search for Tomorrow in Today's Soap Opera: Notes on a Feminine Narrative Form," *Film Quarterly* 33, no. 1 (fall 1979): 12–21. Incorporated in Tania Modleski, *Loving with a Vengeance: Mass-Produced Fantasies for Women* (New York: Methuen, 1982).

6. Ellen Seiter, "Eco's TV Guide—The Soaps," *Tabloid* 6 (1981): 43.

7. In this theoretical context even soap-opera commercials may be analyzed in terms of their narrative effect. See Sandy Flitterman's use of Christian Metz's "Large Syntagmatic Category"—Sandy Flitterman, "The *Real* Soap Operas: TV Commercials," in *Regarding Television: Critical Approaches—An Anthology*, ed. E.M. Kaplan (Frederick: University Publications of America, 1983), 84–95.

8. See, for example, E.M. Gade, "Representation of the World of Work in Daytime Television Serials," *Journal of Employment Counseling* 8 (1971): 37–42; Charlotte Brunsdon, "*Crossroads*—Notes on Soap Opera," *Screen* 4, no. 22 (1981): 32–7. For an annotated bibliography of writings on soap opera, see Patricia Tegler, "Bibliography," in *Life on Daytime Television: Tuning-In American Serial Drama*, eds. Mary Cassata and Thomas Skill (Norwood: Ablex Publishing, 1983), 187–202. In addition, a variety of dissertations on soap opera have been written—for example, Ronald James Compesi, "Gratifications of Daytime Television Serial Viewers: an Analysis of Fans of the Program *All My Children*" (PhD diss., University of Oregon, 1976), available from www.proquest.com (publication number AAT 7704707; accessed April 25, 2008). ProQuest Digital Dissertations (AAT 7704707).

9. Charlotte Brunsdon, *The Feminist, the Housewife, and the Soap Opera* (New York: Oxford University Press, 2000) examines the usefulness of ethnographic methods by interviewing five television scholars (Christine Geraghty, Dorothy Hobson, Terry Lovell, Ien Ang, and Ellen Seiter) about their research experiences with viewers. Louise Spence, *Watching Daytime Soap Operas: The Power of Pleasure* (Middletown: Wesleyan University Press, 2005) develops her own variation on ethnographic and psychological methods.

10. The BFI's informative, but short, monograph on *Coronation Street* also concentrates predominantly on narrative form. Richard Paterson does provide some thoughts on the "stylistic rhetoric" of the serial, but the brevity of his article does not allow for sufficient elaboration. See Richard Dyer, Christine Geraghty, Marion Jordan, Terry Lovell, Richard Paterson, and John Stewart, *Coronation Street* (London: British Film Institute, 1981).

11. "'As World Turns' on CBS Will Expand to Hour Dec.1," *New York Times (1857–Current file)*, September 10, 1975, www.proquest.com (accessed April 24, 2008) and Ralph Tyler, "Can Soap Actors Find Happiness In a Full Hour?" *New York Times (1857–Current file)*, November 30, 1975, www.proquest.com (accessed April 24, 2008). The expansion to hour-long shows began with *Another World* in January 1975.

12. At a time when television soap opera, like its radio antecedent, was broadcast in 15-minute episodes, *As the World Turns* was the first 30-minute soap opera and, later, among the first programs to expand to 60-minute episodes (in 1975). The expansion to half-hour television programs proved to be a crucial development in the demise of the *radio* soap opera. Fifteen-minute television programs were not cost effective, but 30-minute programs, on a per-minute basis, were much more profitable than radio programs of that era. Consequently, the expansion to 30 minutes was the death knell for radio soap opera. Similarly, the expansion of popular television soap operas to 60 minutes in 1975 was prompted by industrial needs. Ratings declined in the early part of that decade, leading to a decline in profitability. An hour of a popular program could bring in more revenue than two mediocre 30-minute shows.

13. Maryjo Adams, "An American Soap Opera: *As the World Turns* 1956–1978" (PhD diss., The University of Michigan, 1980), 121. Moreover, Adams states, "Today, Monday's episode is usually a recap of what happened the week before" (122).

14. CNET Networks, "*As the World Turns* Episode Guide," TV.com, www.tv.com/as-the-world-turns/show/162/episode_guide.html?season=52 (accessed May 29, 2008).

15. David Bordwell, *Figures Traced in Light: On Cinematic Staging* (Berkeley: University of California Press, 2005), 4, 15.

16. Adams, "An American Soap Opera," 132.

17. "CBS at 75," *CBS*, 2007, www.cbs.com/specials/cbs_75/timeline/1960.shtml (accessed June 10, 2008).

18. Even these resources are rather hit or miss. Currently, the networks' websites only present a limited number of past episodes. And SOAPnet, which is owned by ABC, carries just a few non-ABC programs.

19. Adams, "An American Soap Opera," 140. David R. Jackson has compiled a list of episodes in archives, which confirms the haphazard preservation of the program. See "ATWT: Where the Old Episodes Are," *Classic As the World Turns*, www.geocities.com/TelevisionCity/Studio/5185/sources/vidsources.html (accessed May 26, 2008).

20. The initial 1984 study breaks down a scene from the July 20, 1984 broadcast. Although I make few direct references to that breakdown here, it does inform my approach to the 2008 scene.

21. Francis B. Messmore, "An Exploratory Investigation of Below-the-Line Cost Components for Soap Opera Production in New York City" (DPS diss., Pace University, 1988), 20, retrieved from ProQuest Digital Dissertations (AAT 8914658). Messmore also includes a table of actual below-the-line costs (40).

22. According to Adams, writing in 1980, "Today, *As the World Turns* has over 82 permanent sets in the storage shop, though usually no more than nine or ten sets are used in a normal day's shooting." Adams, "An American Soap Opera," 148.

23. Natan Katzman, "Television Soap Operas: What's Been Going on Anyway?" *Public Opinion Quarterly* 36, no. 2 (summer 1972): 209.

24. Charles Derry, "Television Soap Opera: Incest, Bigamy, and Fatal Disease," *Journal of the University Film and Video Association* 35, no. 1 (winter 1983): 8.

25. Ibid., 9.

26. Brunsdon, "*Crossroads*," 34.

27. The significance of setting has informed much work on cinematic melodrama—beginning with Thomas Elsaesser's observation that certain 1950s melodramas use "setting and decor so as to reflect the characters' fetishist fixations" (Thomas Elsaesser, "Tales of Sound and Fury: Observations on the Family Melodrama," *Monogram* 4 [1973]: 10). It has also informed Jane Feuer's analysis of nighttime soap opera, specifically *Dynasty* (Feuer, "Melodrama, Serial Form," 8–10). Although some daytime soap operas have aspired to the glamour of conspicuous consumption in their decor, the genre's settings remain relatively barren—using only the necessities to preserve naturalism.

28. Messmore provides studio schematics for *Search for Tomorrow* and *Another World*, which illustrate the deployment of sets within the studios. Messmore, "An Exploratory Investigation," appendix Q.

29. In addition, they have 31 dressing rooms, two control rooms and one edit suite. City of New York, "Studios and Stages," Mayor's Office of Film Theatre & Broadcasting, www.nyc.gov/html/film/html/resources/studios.shtml (accessed June 3, 2008).

30. Interviewed in March 1978. Adams, "An American Soap Opera," 149.

31. Herb Zettl, *Sight Sound Motion: Applied Media Aesthetics*, 4th edn (Belmont: Wadsworth, 2005), 153.

32. Feuer, "Melodrama, Serial Form," 10.

33. Douglas Sirk's films have this problem.

34. The image of actors/characters in soap opera is discussed further in Jeremy G. Butler " 'I'm Not a Doctor, But I Play One on TV': Characters, Actors and Acting in Television Soap Opera," *Cinema Journal* 30, no. 4 (summer 1991): 75–91. Reprinted in *To Be Continued ... Soap Operas Around the World*, ed. Robert C. Allen (New York: Routledge, 1995), 145–63.

35. John Ellis, *Visible Fictions* (Boston: Routledge & Kegan Paul, 1992), 106.

36. Ibid., 38.

37. Ibid., 106.

38. Richard L. Eldredge, "Soap Opera 'Life' Visiting Live Territory" [Home Edition]. *The Atlanta Journal—Constitution*, May 13, 2002, D1, www.proquest.com (accessed June 4, 2008).

39. Barry Salt, *Moving Into Pictures: More on Film History, Style and Analysis* (London: Starword, 2006), 337.

40. In most instances, this effect is achieved with a zoom in and not through physical movement of the camera closer to the actor. A dolly-in is more difficult to shoot than a zoom in, making it less cost-effective.

41. Feuer, "Melodrama, Serial Form," 11–12.

42. For a more detailed explication of film editing and the 180-degree system, see the chapters, "Space in the Classical Film" and "Shot and Scene" in David Bordwell, Janet Staiger, and Kristin Thompson, *The Classical Hollywood Cinema: Film Style & Mode of Production to 1960* (New York: Columbia University Press, 1985), 50–69. For a broader application of these film-based concepts, see Zettl, "Structuring the Four-Dimensional Field: Continuity Editing," in *Sight Sound Motion*, 285–309. And for an overview of the Hollywood production process, see Thomas Schatz, *The Genius of the System: Hollywood Filmmaking in the Studio Era* (New York: Pantheon, 1988).

43. In cinema studies, shot-counter shot has been at the center of highly controversial Lacanian incursions into textual analysis—ultimately evolving into the "system of the suture." Key texts include Daniel Dayan, "The Tutor-Code of Classical Cinema," *Film Quarterly* 28, no. 1 (fall 1974): 22–31; and William Rothman, "Against 'The System of the Suture,' " *Film Quarterly* 29, no. 1 (fall 1975): 45–50. A recent overview of the controversy may be found in Edward Branigan, *Projecting a Camera* (New York: Routlege, 2006), 133–45.

44. Bordwell *et al.*, *Classical Hollywood Cinema*, 58.

45. Brunsdon, "Crossroads," 35.

46. See David Bordwell and Kristin Thompson, *Film Art: An Introduction*, 8th edn (New York: McGraw Hill, 2008), 231–4. Zettl refers to the axis of action as the "index vector line" (294).

47. Bordwell *et al.*, *Classical Hollywood Cinema*, 63. The elements of classical narrative have been extended into contemporary cinema in Kristin Thompson, *Storytelling in the New Hollywood: Understanding Classical Technique* (Cambridge: Harvard University Press, 1999).

48. Spence, *Watching Daytime Soap Operas*, 93.

49. This is more true of soap operas than another multiple-camera genre, the sitcom. In multiple-camera sitcoms, the feeds of all cameras and several takes of each scene are all recorded. In post-production, the editors assemble all that material into the final product. In multiple-camera soap operas, the post-production period is much shorter and so the editors must rely largely on the scene as switched live.

50. Utilizing a content analysis of "characteristics of form," Gretchen Barbatsis and Yvette Guy come to a similar conclusion, but frame it in different terms: "In soap opera's similarity to the intensification of live television, it is 'as if' there were an actual event, existing in real time and possessing a rhythm of its own, which determined the screen event created from it." Gretchen Barbatsis and Yvette Guy, "Analyzing Meaning in Form: Soap Opera's Compositional Construction of 'Realness,'" *Journal of Broadcasting & Electronic Media* 35, no. 1 (1991): 59–75, *Communication & Mass Media Complete*, EBSCOhost, www.ebscohost.com (accessed June 11, 2008).

51. Around 2005, *ATWT* changed editing systems to the Sony Xpri, a non-linear editor. This greatly accelerated their editing process and may facilitate small editing tweaks such as this one. Ken Lewis, "As the World Turns Nonlinear," *Editors Guild Magazine* (May–June 2006), www.editorsguild.com/v2/magazine/archives/0506/features_article02.htm (accessed June 5, 2008).

52. Stephen Heath and Gillian Skirrow, "Television, a World in Action," *Screen* 18, no. 2 (summer 1977): 53.

53. Ibid., 54.

54. The length of every shot in the sample, along with frame captures from each shot, is available on Shot Logger: www.shotlogger.org.

55. Salt, "The Stylistic Analysis of Television Drama Programs," in *Moving Into Pictures*, 259–76.

56. CineMetrics, "Movie Measurement and Study Tool Database," CineMetrics, www.cinemetrics.lv (accessed June 5, 2008); Shot Logger, "Frame Captures and Stats," Telecommunication and Film Department, University of Alabama, www.shotlogger.org (accessed June 5, 2008).

57. Salt, "The Stylistic Analysis," 320.

58. Shot Logger, "TV or Not TV," Telecommunication and Film Department, University of Alabama, www.tcf.ua.edu/slgallery/shotlogger/TitleListDetailPage.php?recordID=23 (accessed June 5, 2008).

59. Derry, "Television Soap Opera," 6–7.

60. Ibid.

61. Daniel R. Coleridge, senior producer at SOAPnet, attributes the term to Mimi Torchin, editor-in-chief of *Soap Opera Weekly*. See his comment to the online article at "Is the Evil Sheila Returning to *Young and the Restless?*" *TV Guide.com*, community.tvguide.com/blog-entry/TVGuide-Editors-Blog/Soaps-News/700000046/700008741 (accessed June 6, 2008). A Wikipedia article provides numerous SORAS examples. Wikipedia contributors, "Soap Opera Rapid Aging Syndrome," *Wikipedia, The Free Encyclopedia*, en.wikipedia.org/w/index.php?title=Soap_Opera_Rapid_Aging_Syndrome&oldid=217241280 (accessed June 6, 2008).

62. Ellis observes,

> The segment is self-contained in TV production partly because of the fragmentary nature of much broadcast TV (especially if it carries spot advertising), but also because of the attention span that TV assumes of its audience, and the fact that memory of the particular series in all its detail cannot be assumed.
>
> (*Visible Fictions*, 148)

63. Emphasis in original, Bordwell and Thompson, *Film Art*, 75.

64. Brunsdon, "*Crossroads*," 34.

65. The erosion of scene-to-scene diachronic causality in soap opera leads to a narrative form quite distinct from (some would say inferior to) classical film and the

traditional novel. Robert C. Allen has argued, however, that although this syntagmatic structure of soap opera may be seen as one-dimensional, the genre articulates a surprisingly "elaborate paradigmatic structure." Indeed, a synchronic
consideration of character relationships reveals a dense layering of potential
meaning that is fully decipherable to only the most dedicated viewer. (See Robert
C. Allen, "On Reading Soaps: A Semiotic Primer," in *Regarding Television*, 102–3.)
Moreover, drawing on Lévi-Strauss, one may posit thematic oppositions structuring these paradigmatic relationships. Richard Paterson and John Stewart, for
example, maintain that the British soap opera *Coronation Street* emphasizes three
structural oppositions: inside/outside, male/female, and work/no-work (Richard
Paterson and John Stewart, "*Street* Life," *Coronation Street* [London: British Film
Institute, 1983], 84).

66. The average length of an *As the World Turns* scene during July 18–24, 1984 was
one minute, 55 seconds. The longest scene ran five minutes, 53 seconds; and the
shortest, 13 seconds.
67. CBS Netcast, "As the World Turns," CBS Broadcasting, www.cbs.com/netcast/
archive/atwt_archive.shtml (accessed June 6, 2008).
68. Heath and Skirrow, "Television," 19.
69. Ellis, *Visible Fictions*, 137.
70. Ibid., 157.
71. Katzman, "Television Soap Operas," 209.
72. Geoffrey Nowell-Smith, "Minnelli and Melodrama," *Screen* 18, no. 2 (summer
1977): 115.
73. Dialogue is also an integral component of Allen's intricate paradigmatic structure
of character relationships (Allen, "On Reading Soaps," 103).
74. David Bordwell, "The Hook: Scene Transitions in Classical Cinema," *David Bordwell's Website on Cinema*, January 2008, www.davidbordwell.net/essays/hook.php
(accessed June 10, 2008).
75. Quoted in Madeleine Edmondson and David Rounds, *From Mary Noble to Mary
Hartman: The Complete Soap Opera Book* (New York: Stein and Day, 1976), 45.
76. As late as 1978 and *WKRP in Cincinnati*, the inclusion of songs by their original
artists was considered innovative.
77. Although 18 to 34-year-olds (the target audience for rock music) also constitute a
large segment of the soap opera audience, more than 50 percent of the genre's
viewers are over 35 according to studies done in 1970 and 1980. See Katzman "Television Soap Operas," and Mary Cassata and Thomas Skill, "Television Soap
Operas: What's Been Going on Anyway?—Revisited," in *Life on Daytime Television: Tuning-In American Serial Drama*, eds. Mary Cassata and Thomas Skill
(Norwood: Ablex Publishing, 1983), 160–3.
78. This is what Bordwell refers to this as the "hook." Bordwell, "The Hook."
79. Laura Mulvey, "Notes on Sirk and Melodrama," *Movie* 25 (winter 1977/8): 56.
80. Flitterman, "The *Real* Soap Operas," 94.
81. Ibid.
82. Bordwell, *Figures Traced in Light*, 23.
83. David Bordwell, *The Way Hollywood Tells It: Story and Style in Modern Movies*
(Berkeley: University of California Press, 2006), 120.
84. The six-minute short by Guy Maddin, *The Heart of the World*, may well be cut
faster. Its CineMetrics ASL is 0.9 seconds.
85. Jennifer Ordoñez, "A Real Cliffhanger," *Newsweek* 151, no. 4 (January 28, 2008):
58–9.
86. John Consoli, "Soaps on the Ropes," *MediaWeek* 17, no. 14 (April 2, 2007): 7, *Academic Search Premier*, EBSCOhost (accessed April 8, 2008).
87. James Hibberd, "Changes Planned to Save 'Turns' and 'Light,'" *TVWeek*, October
15, 2007, www.tvweek.com/blogs/james-hibberd/2007/10/changes_planned_to_
save_turns.php (accessed June 10, 2008).

88. A.C. Powers, "*Guiding Light* Producer Dishes on Changes," *The Soap Dispenser*, March 6, 2008, www.thesoapdispenser.com/2008/03/guiding-light-producer-dishes-on-changes (accessed June 10, 2008).

89. Victoria Nikolov, in response to A.C. Powers, "Guiding Light Producer Dishes on Changes," March 6, 2008, *The Soap Dispenser*, www.thesoapdispenser.com/2008/03/guiding-light-producer-dishes-on-changes (accessed June 10, 2008).

90. Andrew Krukowski, "'Light' of Realism Shines on Veteran Soap Opera," *Television Week* 27, no. 7 (March 3, 2008): 4–4, *Academic Search Premier, EBSCOhost*, www.ebscohost.com (accessed April 8, 2008).

91. "The Clock Starts Ticking on Season 6," *Videography*, January 2007, 22.

92. Michael Logan, "Inside *Guiding Light*'s Extreme Makeover," *TV Guide* (February 25, 2008), community.tvguide.com/blog-entry/TVGuide-Editors-Blog/Soaps-News/Inside-Guiding-Lights/800034134 (accessed June 10, 2008).

93. On April 1, 2009, CBS announced that Guiding Light would be canceled as of September 18, 2009. Bill Carter, "CBS Turns Out 'Guiding Light'," *New York Times*, April 1, 2009, www.nytimes.com/2009/04/02/arts/television/02ligh.html?_r=2 (accessed September 4, 2009).

2.

Stylistic Crossover in the Network Era

From Film to Television

> The look, the style, of *Miami Vice is* its character, its spectacle is the source of its pleasure.[1]
>
> (John Fiske)

> *Miami Vice* displays an attention to style which, compared to the rest of TV, seems luxurious, extravagant. Some might even say "criminal," feeling that such an expenditure of style must, in some way, hide an attempt to defraud, to cover some bankruptcy of substance.[2]
>
> (R.L. Rutsky)

> The interplay between cinema and television is clearly complex, many-sided, and by no means one-way.[3]
>
> (Steve Neale)

In the time since *Miami Vice* debuted in 1984, the formerly unyielding boundary between television and film has been breached with increasing regularity. The two media have converged to the point now that they primarily serve as marketing vectors for one another. They have become what John Thornton Caldwell has called "semiotic cluster bombs."[4] Detonating in one context, they send polysemic shrapnel out into the general intertextuality of the modern cultural landscape. In so doing they participate in a "viral marketing scheme" (Caldwell) that promotes properties across numerous media, growing like a virus in media-related blogs, on Facebook/MySpace pages, in video games, and so on. In 1984, however, the videocassette had not yet achieved its eventual dominance over theatrical box office, the Internet did not exist, and the membrane separating television and film was much less permeable than now. In this context, *Miami Vice* was met with general astonishment. It seemed too "cinematic" for the small screen. Even film magazines that generally disdained television took note. In *Film Comment*, Richard T. Jameson exclaimed, "It's hard to forbear saying, every five minutes or so, 'I can't believe this was shot for *television!*' "[5] Strata of aesthetic status, the hierarchy of screen media, were brought into sharp relief by *Miami Vice*—highlighting normally unexamined assumptions about the essences of film and of television. In an interdiscipinary study of television, film, and video published two years before the program's debut, John Ellis sums the pecking order: "For broadcast TV, the culturally respectable is increasingly equated with the cinematic."[6] Presumably, broadcast television does not command our attention the way a film in a theater does. We gaze intensely at film but glance casually at television.[7] This widely held assumption about film and television is challenged by *Miami Vice*, which rewards the sustained gaze of the viewer that is normally reserved for the cinema. Consider the following television fragment.

A television anchorman appears and reminds you that he'll return in an hour to give you the day's news. The screen is then filled with a close-up of Carlos Mendez (Tito Goya), profiled in a field of bleached white (Figure 2.1); there is no music and very little ambient sound. A transparent drinking glass in his hand becomes visible as a clear fluid is poured into it from off screen. We are aware of the glass' presence mostly from the fluid's ambient sound, which is startlingly loud compared to the previous silence. The image disorients the viewer through absences: the lack of television's conventionally hyperactive imagery and the lack of television's noisy soundtrack. This disorientation is soon replaced by mild shock as the glass is slapped from the man's hand by police detective Ricardo "Rico" Tubbs (Philip Michael Thomas), whose face juts into the frame (Figure 2.2). Another episode of *Miami Vice* has just begun.

For Caldwell, *Miami Vice* was among the first programs to challenge the aesthetic bias toward film by incorporating a "cinematic air of distinction" into a television text.[8] Particularly notable for our purposes is that much of what Caldwell, Jameson, Ellis, and others presume to be cinematic characteristics exists within the realm of style. To Caldwell this is self-evident: "The cinematic refers, obviously, to a film look in television," by which he means "spectacle, high-production values, and feature-style cinematography."[9] Although I might demur that the cinematic could just as "obviously" refer to narrative structures as it does to a film look, I share his fascination with a stylistic schema associated with a specific cinematic genre, the film noir, and I wish to track that schema's journey from 1940s movie houses to 1980s television—thereby examining film noir's polysemy and the evolution of a schema. *Miami Vice* was not the first television program to adopt the film-noir schema, as I will detail later. I choose this program not as a necessarily typical example of the film–television relationship but because it poses unique

Figure 2.1 A tight close-up of an interrogated prisoner begins an episode of *Miami Vice.*

Figure 2.2 Ricardo Tubbs' face juts into the frame unexpectedly.

questions about genre and style. In so doing, it raises issues about the impact of style on narrative and theme in a highly stylized genre.

It would be hard to overestimate the impact of film-noir scholarship on genre studies, especially since the present chapter was originally published in 1985.[10] Since then, 111 film-noir Master's theses and PhD dissertations have been written—averaging nearly five per year.[11] A quick search of Amazon.com reveals 84 books with significant reference to film noir; all but eight were published after 1985. Can any other genre claim more scholarly activity in the past two decades?[12] More significantly for our purposes, the scholarly attention to film noir has had the collateral effect of drawing attention to the study of style. Indeed, some writers have gone so far as to insist that film noir is not actually a genre per se but rather a style or attitude. Paul Schrader, for example, has argued bluntly, "Film noir is not a genre…. It is not defined, as are the Western and gangster genres, by conventions of setting and conflict, but rather by the more subtle qualities of tone and mood."[13] Schrader's comments illustrate one major difference between film noir and his implicitly conventional genres (the Western and the gangster film); film noir's defining characteristics reside largely within style rather than within thematic and narrative structures. Moreover, content-heavy genres such as the Western, the gangster film, and the melodrama have made easy transitions to broadcast television, but because film noir depends so heavily on its cinematic visual style, it is unclear how well the genre might adapt to broadcast television's constraints. In an effort to understand the "televisualization" of a stylized cinematic genre, I focus on *Miami Vice*'s noir permutations, but I also offer some thoughts on noir's previous incursions into television and the legacy of *Miami Vice*'s unique implementation of the film-noir schema.

The Film-Noir Schema and the Meaning of Style

> Film noir is an abstract form of art that uses light and shadows to set the moods for stories.[14]
>
> (Vilmos Zsigmond)

Noir visual style is catalogued lucidly in J.A. Place and L.S. Peterson's "Some Visual Motifs of Film Noir."[15] They argue that film noir is fundamentally "antitraditional" in its visual style—that it consistently violates the schemas of classical film-making that had evolved through the 1930s. These "violations" are summarized in Table 2.1. To Place and Peterson's catalogue I would add only the use of black-and-white film stock, which is not antitraditional for the time, but is still an essential part of noir visual style.

Place and Peterson stress that stylistic elements such as lighting, camera position, and *mise-en-scène* construct meaning as much as noir iconography.[16] Further, they argue that these stylistic elements are as responsible for the films' meaning as are conventional components of plot and theme. They note, "The characteristic noir moods of claustrophobia, paranoia, despair, and nihilism constitute a world view that is expressed not through the films' terse, elliptical dialogue, nor through their confusing, often insoluble plots, but ultimately

Table 2.1 Place and Peterson's contrast of classical cinema and film noir

Classical Cinema	Film Noir
High-key (low-contrast) lighting	Low-key (high-contrast) lighting
Balanced, three-point lighting	Imbalanced lighting
Day-for-night	Night-for-night
Shallow focus	Deep focus
"Normal" focal length	Wide angle focal length
Symmetrical *mise-en-scène*	Dissymmetrical *mise-en-scène*
Eye-level camera	Extreme low and high angles
Open, unobstructed views	Foreground obstructions

through their remarkable style."[17] In effect, Place and Peterson (and many other writers on film noir) have created a metaphorical interpretation of cinematic style: imbalanced compositions equal an unstable worldview.[18] The key to Place and Peterson's position is that film noir is antitraditional; the significance of the genre is generated by its opposition to previous standards of visual style, to a previous schema, as I have been using the term. Meaning is constructed from the contrast of film noir with classicism. This meaning includes the principal themes of the genre: the hostile instability of the universe (especially women), the impossibility of moral purity, and questions of identity that often involve a *Doppelgänger*. Similar to noir style, noir themes are defined in terms of their break with tradition. More specifically, many writers on film noir assume that "post-war disillusionment"—displacing wartime faith in America—is expressed in the genre.[19] Thus, noir thematics become significant, generate meaning, in contrast to a presumed traditional ideology.[20] Noir thematics are assumed to be the dark side of the American dream, a negative image of the 1940s status quo. This "dark" ideology expresses itself in recurrent noir narrative structures and character relationships. Indeed, most writers on the genre approach visual style in terms of how that style affects the representation of characters in the films. Place and Peterson, for example, contend,

> in the most notable examples of film noir, as the narratives drift headlong into confusion and irrelevance, each character's precarious relationship to the world, the people who inhabit it, and to himself and his own emotions, becomes a function of visual style.[21]

Thus, style in film noir signifies character dynamics. It is not the presumably neutral or invisible style of the classical cinema.

Several generalizations can be made about the genre's conventional characters. Men are the ostensible heroes of most films noir. They are conventionally the protagonists, but there is seldom anything heroic about them. Most commonly they are men with an indiscretion in their past and unpleasantness in their future toward which the present rapidly carries them. The noir protagonist is alienated from a combustible, hostile world, driven by obsessions transcending morality and causality—according to Alain Silver and Elizabeth

Ward.[22] The obsessive noir protagonist is drawn into a destiny he cannot escape; he is impelled toward his fate by exterior forces beyond his power and interior forces beyond his control. The women of film noir have been divided by Janey Place into two categories: the "rejuvenating redeemer" and the "deadly seductress," also known as the "spider woman."[23] The redemptive woman, according to Place, is strongly associated with the status quo, moral values, and stable identities. Her love provides an escape route for the alienated protagonist, but he is seldom able to join her world of safety.[24] The rejuvenating redeemer exists as more of an ideal than an attainable reality. The spider woman is much more central to the genre. Rather than providing an escape or potential release for the protagonist—as does the redeemer—she usually contributes to his downfall. Indeed, she is the central disruptive force: disturbing narrative equilibrium, generating enigmas, and thus catalyzing the entire diegesis. As Mary Ann Doane notes, film noir "constitutes itself as a detour, a bending of the hermeneutic code from the questions connected with a crime to the difficulty posed by the woman as enigma (or crime)."[25] In many cases it is the woman who, as Annette Kuhn has observed, motivates the narrative—acting as "the 'trouble' that sets the plot in motion."[26] Consequently, the narrative can be closed off only when it solves the "problem" of the spider woman, when it neutralizes her (sexual) power.

Feminists have been attracted to the spider woman because she provides one of the few instances in classical American cinema in which the woman is strong and sexually independent. She manipulates and uses men rather than performing as the victim or plaything. To understand the source of her power, we must return to the genre's visual style. The spider woman's diegetic power is directly expressed in her stylistic dominance. She commands the gaze of the camera and occupies a privileged position in the composition.[27] Laura Mulvey argues that this show of spectatorial dominance invokes severe castration anxiety in the male protagonist.[28] In so doing, it corrodes the very foundations of the narrative. Woman is unknowable, unattainable, and lethal. She is an enigma that goes beyond resolution, beyond understanding. Indeed, the desire/threat that she embodies fissures the very foundations of the classical cinematic apparatus. In her analysis of *Gilda* (1946), Doane argues that the spider woman generates a "crisis of vision:"

> Since the epistemological cornerstone of the classical text is the dictum, "the image does not lie," film noir tends to flirt with the limits of this system, the guarantee of its readability oscillating between an image which often conceals a great deal and a voice-over which is not always entirely credible. Nevertheless, the message is quite clear—unrestrained female sexuality constitutes a danger. Not only to the male but to the system of signification itself. Woman is "the ruin of representation."[29]

According to Doane, the spider woman creates disturbances that are not merely on the level of narrative action but extend to visual style and the cinematic system of signification.

Miami Vice and Film-Noir Thematics

Miami Vice shares at least three principal themes with film noir: moral ambiguity, confusion of identities, and fatalism (caused by a past that predetermines the present). To examine in detail how they find expression in individual episodes, this chapter relies heavily on the first season, partially because this chapter was originally written in the midst of that season and partially because the program's impact diminished over the subsequent four seasons. And, from a practical analytical perspective, all of the first-season episodes are available online for further reference.[30] Additionally, I here drill down to the "Calderone's Demise" episode for some specifics.[31] Originally broadcast October 26, 1984 and rerun as the second half of "The Return of Calderone," a two-hour special presentation, this episode crystalized the program's stylistic ambitions early in the first season.

The shifting ambiguities of *Miami Vice*'s moral universe may well be its most salient thematic characteristic. Unlike, say, *Dragnet* (1951–9), the representatives of law and order in *Miami Vice* are quite similar to the sociopaths they stalk. There is no clear demarcation between forces of good and those of evil—or at least that distinction is constantly changing. In "Calderone's Demise," detectives Tubbs and James "Sonny" Crockett (Don Johnson) are betrayed by the St. Andrews' police chief who turns out to be corrupt and the evil Esteban Calderone (Miguel Pinero) has managed to convince his daughter, Angelina (Phanie Napoli), that he is an honorable businessman and kind and loving father. Such turnabouts and duplicities are common in the program. In one episode, Crockett's friend turns out to be a cop on the take. In another, Crockett himself is suspected of taking a bribe. I would argue that these deceptions are more than just "plot twists." They underpin a fundamentally unstable universe, one in which black is white and white black. As Place points out in regard to film noir, identities, like values, are ever changing and must constantly be re-established. The main technique of vice police is to work undercover—in a complicated masquerade. They look, talk, and act much like the criminals they pursue. In short, they assume the style of Miami's criminal element. The identities of Crockett and Tubbs change time and again, depending on their assignments. In "Calderone's Demise," they are out of their regular jurisdiction, forced to rely on a corrupt Bahamian official. When they must cut off their ties with him they lose all official status and are, in effect, acting completely as vigilantes. They have no authority in St. Andrews. As Crockett comments, "We're so 'under' we may as well be on another planet." Identity switches are not limited to the police either. In the pilot episode, the viewer is misled into believing that a woman is murdering several persons. When the "woman" is apprehended, she turns out to be a man. On more than one occasion, the "criminal" who is apprehended turns out to be another police officer or an FBI undercover agent. Identities, allegiances, and even sexualities are constantly shifting in *Miami Vice*, resulting in a morally ambiguous universe. This play of identity construction leads Douglas Kellner to conclude that "*Miami Vice* provides many insights into the fragmentation, reconstruction, and fragility of identity in contemporary culture and that it also provides insight into how identities are constructed through the incorporation of subject positions offered for emulation by media culture."[32]

This moral ambiguity also expresses itself in one of the program's main thematic oppositions: the conflict between performing police duties "by the book" and vigilante justice. In the latter, the police detective/officer's actions are motivated by an ambiguous mixture of public duty and personal vengeance. The supposedly neutral defender of society becomes an active participant in the breakdown of social order. *Miami Vice*'s police detectives are conversant in the language of the underworld, skilled in its practices, and prepared to use both for their own ends. Most of the time, these ends coincide with the public good. Sometimes, however, they are not quite congruent. Tubbs, at the end of "Calderone's Demise," defends the actions that led to the death of Angelina's father with a simple explanation: "I'm a cop." But Angelina correctly rejects his rationalization: "And that makes it alright for you, Richard? What brought you to this island was far more than just your job." Clearly, his duty as a police officer is not all that governs Tubbs' actions; it is also a more base desire for revenge. At the end of the fourth season, in an episode appropriately titled, "Mirror Image," one of the detectives fully surrenders to his criminal alter ego. Following a head injury, Crockett suffers from amnesia and wholly becomes Sonny Burnett, drug dealer, with no memory of his police detective identity. The defender of social order has become its transgressor. Crockett/Burnett remains on the wrong side of the law for three episodes into the fifth and final season—eventually, but never fully, recovering from his dissociative identity disorder in the "Redemption in Blood" episode.[33] Truth be told, redemption, even in blood, is a difficult commodity to find in *Miami Vice*.

The form of detection that goes on in *Miami Vice* owes less to Sherlock Holmes-style ratiocination than it does to the film noir and, more generally, American hard-boiled fiction, in which the private eye is implicated in the crime that he is supposed to solve. The police work in *Miami Vice* is based on masquerade—bordering on entrapment—rather than well-reasoned deduction. Indeed, the perpetrators of the crimes are often known from the beginning of the episode. When they are not, and Crockett and Tubbs are forced to actually solve a mystery, they perform quite badly as deductive reasoners. More often than not, they solve it incorrectly—as in "The Return of Calderone" and "Cool Running," in which they mistakenly believe they have captured the killer. Their ineptness as problem solvers emphasizes the fact that the true enigma in *Miami Vice* is not who killed whom or who set up the drug deal, but will the moral fabric of society remain intact? In this regard, each episode is a test of faith for the vice detectives.

Crockett and Tubbs are occasionally drawn out of the underworld by a redemptive woman. Crockett's dissolving marriage to Caroline (Belinda Montgomery) and his one-episode romance with Brenda (Kim Greist), a career woman, involve redemptive women who could appear in a film noir:

"She offers the possibility of integration for the alienated, lost man into the stable world of secure values, roles and identities."[34] In slightly different ways, Caroline and Brenda represent the morally stable world of the status quo. Each is outside Crockett and Tubbs' world. Each provides Crockett with an avenue of escape from the world of vice; they offer integration into the middle class. In each case, however, Crockett elects to return to the realm of vice after that realm threatens the redemptive woman. When Crockett attempts to spend time with his estranged wife and their child, for example, he lures Calderone's hitman to their home—a scene reminiscent of the car bombing of the police officer's wife in the film noir, *The Big Heat* (1953). Crockett's weary re-immersion in the underworld typifies the noir hero's attitude toward the "above-ground" world of the middle class: not only does he not belong there, he also can destabilize that world simply by his presence. Consequently, he is fated to remain on the dark side of human existence.

Other elements also nurture the noir-like alienation of Crockett and Tubbs. As with many noir protagonists, each is haunted by events from the past—indiscretions, acts demanding revenge, humiliation—that intrude on the present. In "Calderone's Demise," Tubbs's obsessive desire to avenge his brother's murder poisons his romance with Angelina, a redemptive woman, when it soon becomes apparent that the man responsible for the killing is also Angelina's father. In a sense, the past determines the future. This is true of many films noir, particularly *The Locket* (1947) and the appropriately titled *Out of the Past* (1947). It is small wonder, therefore, that the film noir so heavily favors the flashback, a cinematic technique that became fashionable concurrent with the emergence of the genre in the late 1940s. The flashback specifically suits film noir's fatalism because its ending is predetermined. The viewer knows—to a certain extent—how the narrative will close. The two flashbacks of "Calderone's Demise" serve different narrative functions. The first occurs while Crockett and Tubbs journey to St. Andrews. It includes shots from previous episodes involving Calderone, presented quickly and with no voiceover or, significantly, any sync sound. Instead, the entire sequence is accompanied by a rock song—Russ Ballard's "Voices:" "Don't look back, look straight ahead, don't turn away, then the voice it said/Don't look back, yesterday's gone, don't turn away, you can take it on." This flashback functions slightly differently from many cinematic flashbacks. The great majority of film flashbacks present diegetic material the viewer has not previously seen. Although this would be the case in "Calderone's Demise" for a viewer who has never watched the program before, *Miami Vice*'s regular viewers would have seen these shots previously. Thus, the reception of the flashback sequence would differ greatly between regular viewers and nonviewers of the program. For the former, this flashback functions as a quick review of past events. For the latter, it catalyzes an enigma: what do these events mean? For both viewers, however, the flashback connotes the influence of the past on the present. The second flashback (while Crockett and Tubbs return to Miami) serves an altogether different narrative function. It summarizes the episode, redundantly closing off the narrative that begins the first flashback—and could be traced back to the program's pilot. The enigma has been solved before the second flashback begins, so that it (the flashback) operates as a double closure. It emphasizes that the narrative that begins in the pilot and continues through two episodes is now finished.

The fact that Crockett and Tubbs' story continues the week following "Calderone's Demise" exemplifies a significant difference between cinema and television. A typical, classical film follows a conventional narrative progression: stasis, violence/disruption (the enigma posed), the process of solving the enigma through a cause-effect chain, and resolution or closure. A television series, in contrast, must never have complete narrative closure.[35] Instead, each week's episode must work through a set pattern, one which forestalls complete closure. Ellis notes, "Its [broadcast television's] characteristic mode is not one of final closure or totalising vision; rather, it offers a continuous refiguration of events."[36] According to Ellis, television adopts the ever-repeatable form of the dilemma—a "narrative problematic" that is stable in its instability, as it were.[37] Fresh incidents are continuously fed into the problematic to maintain viewer interest, but the problem at its heart is never totally resolved. To do so would obviate the purpose of the series. In this context, I suggest that the core narrative problematic of *Miami Vice* is whether or not the police officers will surrender themselves to the world of vice. Each time they go undercover there is the implication that they might *stay* undercover forever. Each investigation threatens to move beyond neutral police work into personal vendetta. With the resolution of the dilemma in a particular episode, Crockett and Tubbs' decision to enforce the law is reaffirmed, but the knowledge that they will face the same temptations next week prevents complete closure. In some respects the program is little more than a contemporary morality play, in which temptable men are immersed in a world of temptations. Over the course of each episode they resist their more ignoble impulses and return to the socially approved fold, prepared to renew this internalized conflict next week.

Broadcast television's lack of closure undercuts a crucial element of film noir: its arch fatalism. Narrative closure is critical to film noir because it fulfills the doom that is prophesied implicitly at the film's start. Noir protagonists are paranoid with good reason; the world is generally pitted against them and their fate is invariably an unpleasant one. As is noted in James Damico's model of the typical noir narrative, the conclusion involves "the sometimes metaphoric, but usually literal destruction of the woman, the man to whom she is attached, and frequently the protagonist himself" (see, for example, *Out of the Past*).[38] By purging these morally contaminated characters, the film noir is able to achieve closure. Such a resolution—Crockett or Tubbs dying—would be aesthetically and economically impossible for *Miami Vice*. Aesthetically, broadcast television must have certain recurring figures with which to renew the series' dilemma. Economically, broadcast television depends on recognizable, bankable, star actors to nurture the ratings system. Consequently, the fatalism of *Miami Vice* is never as cogent or as final as that of film noir.

The first season of *Miami Vice* also de-emphasizes one key noir character: the sexy, duplicitous woman. The sexually independent woman—who disrupts both narrative form and visual style—does not appear in a central, recurring role in early episodes of the program. Women who do try to exploit the detectives for their own gain typically exist as single-episode subplots, with no substantive narrative power. In season one's "The Great McCarthy," for example, Tubbs becomes involved with a gangster's woman, a murderer, but he controls their encounter and she offers no power over or threat to him. In fact, the episode spends more screen time on a speedboat race than it does on their short-lived romance.[39] Angelina, in "Calderone's Demise," may be the episode's central enigma and as the evil Calderone's daughter, a potential femme noir, but she is not part of his world and does not lure Tubbs into danger. In a reversal of noir dynamics, it is the man who manipulates the woman, bringing her into the world of vice from which her father has insulated her. Similar to Tubbs' encounters with women, Crockett's lovers typically do not deceive him; instead, most represent an escape from vice. Thus, it may surprise those looking to *Miami Vice* for its noir elements that most of the women with whom Crockett and Tubbs become involved function as redeemers or are themselves so damaged that they seldom endanger the detectives. However, certain periods or clusters of films noir also eliminate the seemingly crucial figure of the duplicitous woman. Andrew Spicer maintains, for instance, that the femme fatale was "conspicuously absent in modernist noir," by which he means films from 1967–76.[40] This trend was broken by the rise of "postmodern film noir" in 1981, signaled by *Body Heat* and a remake of *The Postman Always Rings Twice*—just three years before *Miami Vice*'s debut.[41] The deadly femme noir was back.

The significance of this lack of the "spider woman" during the program's formative episodes becomes most apparent when one considers the voyeurism in *Miami Vice*. Practically every episode includes a scene of police surveillance of a suspect. Indeed, many episodes begin with pre-credit surveillance sequences. These scenes frequently include shots of women in revealing attire and the men usually make a casually sexist remark about their attractiveness. Unlike the voyeurs of film noir, however, Crockett and Tubbs are never enthralled with the woman as spectacle. They are never consumed by an obsession to possess those women—as Johnny Farrell is with Gilda or Frank Chambers is with Cora Smith.[42] Thus, the *image* of a woman in *Miami Vice* does not have the same impact as it does in film noir. The woman is divested of her conventional power as spectacle and, consequently, she is no longer the narrative's central enigma, "the 'trouble' that sets the plot in motion."[43] Women continue to be displayed as specular objects, but they now attract the *glance* rather than the sustained gaze. As a result, they no longer exert an implicitly evil influence over men. As feminists have argued, this influence is the result of the woman's masquerade, of Gilda or Cora's manipulation of conventional feminine attractiveness to attain her own ends. The masquerade is thus the source of her power, giving her a sexual independence quite rare in classical cinema. In contrast, although women in *Miami Vice* are used for their masquerade (their conventional feminine attractiveness), they are denied the power and independence of the femme noir.

In *Miami Vice* we may, therefore, observe a narrative text in which the act of looking holds a central fascination, but in which, strangely enough, a woman is not the object of the gaze. Instead, the figures gratifying Crockett and Tubbs' visual pleasure are men—individuals involved with narcotics, prostitution, or other criminal activities. Rather than the women of film noir, these men are the "trouble" that inaugurates the plot. (The exclusion of women from most of *Miami Vice* opens the program up to an analysis of a homoerotic subtext, especially since one episode, "Evan," specifically addresses homophobia in Crockett and another detective. Such an analysis, however, lies outside the purview of this chapter.) The substitution of men for women as objects of the masculine gaze severely alters the voyeuristic apparatus. Rather than the unknowable and castration anxiety-provoking woman (according to Lacanian psychoanalysis), Crockett and Tubbs gaze at men who are very similar to themselves—mirror images, one might say. It is as if there were an imaginary unity between the vice detectives and the criminal element. John Fiske suggests:

> The feminine is written out, for the masculine is both the subject and the object of the look. That frozen moment when the subject and object of desire merge is the moment of *jouissance*, when power, pleasure and affect liberate the masculine self into its own masculinity, freeing it from the necessity of the feminine.[44]

This unity and the potential of *jouissance*, perhaps, are inevitably disturbed when the object on display commits an act of violence, which forces the subjects/spectators to leave their positions as viewers and engage the object as other. Thus, their voyeuristic pleasure is disrupted by the aggressive action of the object under observation. Rather than an ostensibly passive woman on display for the active gaze of the male spectator, *Miami Vice* presents displays of active men that elicit the response of the male spectator. To choose one example among many, in "Smuggler's Blues" Crockett and Tubbs use binoculars to observe a man making a narcotics payoff on a bridge (Figure 2.3). They then follow him to a boat, which violently explodes while Crockett watches (Figures 2.4–2.5). Because of this murder, he and Tubbs must place themselves on display, masquerading as drug dealers in Cartagena.

Just as conventional heterosexual voyeurism is disrupted, so is the conventional use of masquerade and an identity without fragmentation. Crockett and Tubbs' many undercover identities are just so many masquerades. Characteristically, the song, "This Masquerade," is used prominently in the program's second episode ("Heart of Darkness") and might well serve as a theme song for the entire run of episodes:[45]

> Thoughts of leaving disappear
> Every time I see your eyes
> No matter how hard I try
> To understand the reasons
> That we carry on this way.
> We're lost in this masquerade.

In a sense, the frequent masquerades of Crockett and Tubbs place them in a conventionally feminine position.[46] As Cathy Schwichtenberg argues, "Where he [Johnson] stands, he strikes poses not as threats but as seductive invitations to-be-looked-at and to be fetishized—a 'feminized' position invested with the male power to command the city for his staging as the white, illuminated fetish."[47] Crockett and Tubbs display themselves as narcotics dealers, as pimps, as derelicts for the benefit of the active gaze of the underworld figures they are attempting to lure into captivity—much as the spider woman lures her prey. Their masquerade is of legal necessity a passive one. If Crockett and Tubbs were to actively pursue criminals in this fashion, they would be guilty of entrapment. This passive masquerade cannot be maintained through an entire episode, however. Usually it is broken with an act of violence—for example, the car chase and subsequent dunking in "Calderone's Demise." The spectators of Crockett and Tubbs' masquerades respond violently when the truth is revealed. In turn, their violence triggers Crockett and Tubbs' retribution, making the detectives *active* forces in the repression of the violent figures. Crockett and Tubbs' final disavowal of the masquerade signals their shift from passivity to activity, allowing them to subjugate the forces of violence and restore the limited narrative equilibrium that television permits. Crockett and Tubbs must "unmask" themselves before the dénouement in order to re-establish their position as law enforcers and prepare for subsequent masquerades in episodes to come. There is no conclusion, only a refiguration of events.

Figure 2.3 A man is observed through binoculars. Surveillance is almost always of men, not women, in *Miami Vice*—confounding heterosexual voyeurism.

Figure 2.4 *Miami Vice*: Surveillance turns deadly as a boat blows up, causing...

Figure 2.5 ...Sonny Crockett to wince. The disruption of his vision leads to him performing a masquerade.

The Schema of Attenuated Continuity in 1980s Television

Thus far I have examined film-noir's stylistic schema and the ramifications of its thematic and narrative strategies. I wish to expand now on the notion of "antitraditional" style that Place and Peterson find in film noir. I contend that:

1. *Miami Vice* exemplifies antitraditional television style for its time period; and

2. parallels may be drawn between film-noir's antitraditionalism and *Miami Vice*'s.

The fundamental assumption here is that the respective traditions film noir and *Miami Vice* broke share stylistic similarities. That is, television before *Miami Vice* (1984) shares a stylistic schema with the classical cinema from the period before film noir (i.e. before roughly 1941). The danger here should be obvious. We are attempting to reduce decades worth of television and film— thousands of programs and films—into a rather narrow "traditional" schema. The conventions of Hollywood classicism have been well documented by Bordwell, Kristin Thompson, and Janet Staiger, among others; but less detailed attention has been spent on pre-1980s television.[48] Therefore, a brief consideration of the stylistic state of U.S. television circa 1980 seems prudent before moving on to *Miami Vice*'s rebellion against that style.

As the 1980s began, prime-time television in the U.S. was dominated by two things: sitcoms and *Dallas* (1978–91). In the season ratings for September 1979 to April 1980, fully half of the top-20 rated shows were sitcoms. *Dallas* was ranked sixth that season, but on March 21, 1980 it aired a cliffhanger—the shooting of J.R. (Larry Hagman)—that became a national obsession. When the mystery was finally resolved, in the November 21, 1980 episode, it garnered a 53.3 rating and a massive 76 percent share (meaning three out of every four televisions turned on at that time were tuned to *Dallas*), which still stands as the second highest rating of a single U.S. television episode.[49] Thus, examining the style of 1980s sitcoms and of *Dallas* provides an accurate representation of the stylistic schemas to which most viewers were exposed.[50] The sitcom's multiple-camera schema is discussed in detail in Chapter 5 and, further, the multiple-camera schema in the soap opera is considered in Chapter 1. For a quick summary of those schemas, see Table 1.3 and Table 5.6. Suffice to say here that these two multiple-camera schemas align themselves with the most conventional aspects of classical cinema, as listed in Table 2.1 above. In contrast, *Dallas* is a single-camera production, just like *Miami Vice*, and its craft practices are consequently more flexible than those of the multiple-camera mode of production. Despite this flexibility, *Dallas*—and most single-camera programs of the time—employs a spartan, near zero-degree style where Caldwell's "conventional production orthodoxy" obtains.[51] Of course, the dwellings that the wealthy Ewing family inhabit are quite opulent; the performances of *Dallas*' actors in those settings are not known for their subtlety and cannot be described as "zero degree;" and the program itself is often grouped with daytime soap operas and derisively labeled "melodramatic," by which is meant excessively emotional and which might well be the exact opposite of spartan. Nonetheless, the directors of *Dallas* did not construct an excessive visual and sound style to mirror the characters' excessive behavior. In other words, they did not transfer narrative excess into visual excess—as did Douglas Sirk, Vincente Minnelli, and other directors of 1950s melodrama. In that genre, Geoffrey Nowell-

Smith finds the equivalent of Freud's "conversion hysteria:" "The undischarged emotion which cannot be accommodated in the action, subordinated as it is to the demands of family/lineage/inheritance, is traditionally expressed in the music and, in the case of film, in certain elements of the *mise-en-scène*."[52] A similar argument could be made for film noir, but not for *Dallas*.

Dallas and, generally speaking, most early-1980s single-camera programs show very little evidence of the intensified-continuity style which, according to Bordwell, came to dominate theatrically released film in the 1980s.[53] As discussed previously in regard to the soap-opera commercial, in intensified continuity, classical-cinema techniques are hyperbolic, exaggerated, pumped up to excessive levels. More specifically, Bordwell contends, "Four strategies of camerawork and editing seem central to the new style: rapid editing, bipolar extremes of lens lengths, reliance on close shots, and wide-ranging camera movements."[54] For the most part, *Dallas* and its ilk rely on the polar opposite of intensified continuity, on what might perhaps be termed attenuated continuity. Classical-cinema techniques are attenuated, reduced to the bare, efficacious minimum for narrative signification. There are some exceptions to this, however, as can be seen by applying Bordwell's four points to *Dallas* and then examining additional aspects of the continuity system that he does not address in his analysis of cinematography and cutting.

Bordwell uses the average length of shots in theatrical films as a method for gauging the editing's rhythm. Although there are limitations to this approach, as he himself points out, it does give the analyst a general sense of a television program's or film's editing speed.[55] Bordwell notes that editing tempo increased in the 1980s, with most feature-length films containing average shot lengths (ASLs) of between five and seven seconds—although ASLs between four and five seconds were not uncommon and action pictures or "movies influenced by music videos" could be clocked under four seconds—e.g., *Road Warrior* (1981) and *WarGames* (1983).[56] According to Barry Salt—whose work inspired Bordwell—American films from 1976 to 1981 contain a mean ASL of 6.55 seconds, while those of the next six years were slightly faster, at 6.12 seconds.[57] Salt himself has begun the statistical analysis of *Dallas* with the examination of three episodes originally broadcast in 1978 and 1980—including "Who Done It?" the highly rated episode mentioned above. He finds that they have ASLs of 6.4, 5.8, and 6.0 seconds. My own analysis of *Dallas* episodes has found slightly higher ASLs—running closer to seven seconds.[58] Nonetheless, the editing rate is not significantly higher than that era's mean, as derived by Salt, and is still within the standard range that Bordwell notes, although at the upper (i.e., slower) limit. Thus, *Dallas* kept pace with the *average* editing rate of its time in television and theatrical film, but it was not on the cutting edge of the new, intensified editing which, by the beginning of the 1990s, resulted in ASLs below three seconds.[59] *Dallas*' conventional, slightly restrained pace was further reinforced by its strict adherence to the 180-degree rule and attendant continuity-editing conventions, particularly the prohibition of jump cuts. Jump cuts can accelerate editing, but narrative television would not make extensive use of them until the debut of *Homicide: Life on the Street* in 1993.

Another instance of attenuated continuity in *Dallas* may be found in its moderate choice of lens lengths, which contrasts with the bipolar extremes Bordwell sees in intensified continuity. *Dallas* rarely departs from the 50 mm, "normal" lens that became the standard during the early years of the classical era. That is, one does not typically see intensified continuity's extreme wide-angle or extreme telephoto shots in *Dallas*. However, the program does make considerable use of variable focal-length (i.e., zoom) lenses. Its directors frequently zoom in to heighten the emotional impact of a performance (e.g., Figures 2.6 to 2.7)—as is common in daytime soap operas to this day. However, this technique is never used to extreme. Figure 2.6 is not an extreme wide-angle shot and Figure 2.7 is not an extreme close-up. Moreover, the zoom in *Dallas* is an attenuated substitute for another intensified-continuity technique: "ostentatious" camera movements, particularly those which do not follow action.[60] According to Bordwell, there was a marked jump in the use of camera movement as the 1980s came to an end.[61] Previously, the camera might roam freely in a few shots in a film, but by 1990, the roaming camera was much more common. Tracking and dolly shots were slow to set up compared to zooming and consequently they were more expensive and less frequently used in episodic television—even in single-camera programs. Technologically speaking, handheld shots would have been an option when *Dallas* was on the air and they were a signature element of the contemporary show, *Hill Street Blues* (1981–7). However, handheld work at the time was exclusively associated with a documentary stylistic schema, which is why *Hill Street Blues*' producers chose it. Craft practices of the time would have declared it too gritty and "realistic" for a glossy soap opera such as *Dallas*. Other practical concerns militated against active camera movement. The relatively narrow studio sets were not designed to accommodate extensive lateral tracking shots—as was even more the case with sets for sitcoms and daytime soap operas. And the Steadicam and the freedom it affords camera operators would not gain acceptance within television craft practices until the mid-1990s when programs such as *ER* (1994–2009) made moving, Steadicam shots

Figure 2.6 Dallas relies heavily on zooms to punctuate scenes. Here, the camera starts on a medium close-up of Kristin and…

Figure 2.7 …zooms into a close-up. The lighting is notably high key.

de rigueur (see Chapter 4 for more on *ER*'s peripatetic camera).[62] Camera movement that does not follow action and extreme focal lengths were thus seldom a part of the attenuated-continuity stylistic schema—due to a mix of economic, technological, and aesthetic limitations.

As Bordwell points out, film and television practitioners have often suggested that television's small screen demands close-ups and that theatrical films which wish to accommodate television must scale down their shots.[63] This is certainly true to some extent as the broad vistas of, say, a Western such as *The Searchers* (1956) certainly suffer on a 19" television monitor. John Ford's lone horseman on the horizon line is barely visible on such a television screen. However, certain television craft practices mitigate the effects of the physical size of the screen and there is no one, single television schema by which the cinema has been influenced. Television's shot scale does not necessarily gravitate to very close framing, as is often presumed. Sitcoms, soap operas, and other multiple-camera shows frequently favor *medium* shots and *medium* close-ups and not true close-ups (see, for example, Figure 5.52, from *The New Adventures of Old Christine* [2006–]). Certain craft practices encourage this "medium" framing. Camera operators cannot obtain precise, tight framings while the actors move about the set in a live-on-tape multiple-camera production. And certain comedians—as established early on by Jackie Gleason and Lucille Ball—need loose framings so that they can freely improvise and so that their entire bodies can be seen doing physical comedy. Thus, blaming (or crediting) television for the rise of close-ups in intensified continuity is misguided. That said, television programs that do not employ the multiple-camera mode of production are quite likely to rely heavily on close-ups—as we can see in *Dallas* and as is born out by Salt's statistical analysis of shot scale in television drama programs.[64] Salt believes, however, that, "In general, television drama style has *followed behind* the changes in cinema film style" (my emphasis).[65] Consequently, increased frequency of close-ups in intensified-continuity films can not accurately be said to have been caused by the demands of the television medium.

Bordwell's discussion of intensified continuity favors techniques associated with the camera and editing, but attenuated continuity goes beyond those techniques into the realm of *mise-en-scène*—specifically, staging of actors, set design, and lighting.[66] For interior scenes, television craft practices in the early 1980s favored studio sets over location work and those sets were generally not designed to accommodate deep-space staging. Directors tended to block scenes laterally (side-to-side) and not in deep space (front-to-back). As can be seen in Figure 2.8, a *Dallas* scene involving Cliff (Ken Kercheval), Pam (Victoria Principal), Digger (Keenan Wynn), director Irving J. Moore arranges the actors perpendicular to the camera angle. Cliff could conceivably have been placed on the far side of the bed, in depth, but that would not adhere to craft practices of the time. Figure 2.8 also illustrates the standard, high-key lighting employed in attenuated continuity—all three actors and everything else in the room are broadly illuminated. Figure 2.9 illustrates high-key lighting even more clearly. It shows Sue Ellen (Linda Gray) leaving a typical *Dallas* studio set. Her body casts at least two shadows from light sources not seen within the frame. Even the one visible light source, the lamp on the bedside table, casts a shadow. The rest of the room is evenly lit, with a few highlighted spots on the walls. Most early 1980s programs also gravitate toward this lighting convention in their indoor scenes. In a *Magnum, P.I.* episode from 1983, for example, we see Magnum (Tom Selleck) in a punk nightclub, but even in this presumably low-light situation he is illuminated in perfect three-point lighting (Figure 2.10).[67] Even in outdoor scenes from the early 1980s, "silks" (large frames covered with silk-like material) diffused the sun's hard light and reflectors and auxiliary lights aggressively filled in shadows—resulting in virtually shadowless faces, as in the exterior shots from *Dallas* of J.R. and Pam in Figures 2.11 and 2.12, respectively.[68] The large cowboy hats worn by many characters must have been particularly challenging to the program's directors of photography. In the backlit shot of J.R. (Figure 2.11), his hat would cast a dark shadow over his face if that shadow were not filled by secondary lights or reflector boards bouncing sunlight. Evidence of the height of a reflector or fill light (just above the actor's eyes) can be seen in the shadow cast by the hat brim on J.R.'s forehead. Lighting was also notably high-key in exterior scenes at the Ewing family's ranch (Southfork), many of which were shot on a sound stage or studio back lot—as is indicated in the lighting and set design of the front porch in Figure 2.13. Whether outside or inside, characters in narrative television of this time were captured in aquarium-style, markedly high-key lighting.

In sum, attenuated-continuity style in single-camera television programs circa 1980 manifests itself in conventions of *mise-en-scène*, cinematography, and editing. The *mise-en-scène*'s foundation is built on studio sets with high-key lighting and actors arrayed in shallow space. The *mise-en-scène* is recorded with normal focal-length lenses (not extremely telephoto or extremely wide angle) that frame the actors in close-up and medium shots (not extreme close-ups or extreme long shots). If there is no movement within the scene, there will be no movement of the camera; camera movement only occurs to follow action. In some instances, short zooms substitute for camera movements. And finally, the pace of the editing adheres to the era's average and editing

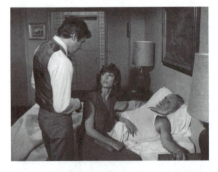

Figure 2.8 Dallas: director Irving J. Moore arranges Cliff, Pam, and Digger like clothes on a line, in shallow space.

Figure 2.9 Typical high-key lighting in *Dallas*, with Sue Ellen casting at least three shadows.

Figure 2.10 *Magnum, P.I.*: even in a punk nightclub, the lighting is high key.

Figure 2.11 In outdoor scenes from *Dallas*, reflectors fill in any shadows, including those cast by J.R.'s hat.

Figure 2.12 *Dallas*: Pam on the beach is similarly devoid of shadows.

Figure 2.13 *Dallas*: "Exterior" scene at Southfork that appears to have been shot in a studio or on a back lot, with shadows filled in.

flourishes (e.g., jump cuts) are avoided. In short, television's implementation of attenuated continuity in 1980 would not violate any of the craft practices of the Hollywood studio system of the mid-1930s.[69]

Miami Vice and the Film-Noir Stylistic Schema

> Impact on *Miami Vice* is, first and foremost, a matter of style.[70]
>
> (Richard T. Jameson)

> [Style] is perhaps the strongest element in glamorizing the margin and representing a dream world of the unconscious. In *Miami Vice*, image and music take the place of language.[71]
>
> (Kathleen Karlyn)

Many, many claims have been made for the significance of style in *Miami Vice*. Some of them now appear quite overheated: "The surface of *Miami Vice* is sensualized through a proteinics realized in the plasticity of the medium itself."[72] The enthusiasm and vigor with which 1980s television critics and

scholars hailed (or assailed) the program provides clear evidence for its depar-
ture from the attenuated-continuity stylistic schema and craft practices that
obtained at the time. Caldwell sums its revolutionary impact:

> almost every aspect of the show—direction, cinematography, lighting,
> cutting, and sound design—was both expressionistic and, according to
> conventional production orthodoxy, excessive. Each production depart-
> ment regularly broke a cardinal rule of classical Hollywood or television.
> Rather than subordinating themselves to an overarching narrative, each
> craft drew attention to itself. From a traditional perspective, that is, the
> series was overphotographed, overcostumed, overmixed, and overcut.[73]

In short, the program's "overdone" style—drawn from a cinematic genre—
embodies intensified continuity. Bordwell even specifies Michael Mann-
directed films as examples of intensified-continuity's schemas, although he
does not mention his work on *Miami Vice*.[74] Nonetheless, it is important to
resist the hyperbole that infected mid-1980s writing on *Miami Vice*. We must
look for textual evidence to support these claims for the breaking of television's traditions and cardinal rules. I divide this evidence into aspects of the
program's *mise-en-scène*, cinematographic qualities, and visual effects—considering briefly the program's stylized sound.

The *mise-en-scène* of *Miami Vice* is largely determined by its chosen setting
of Miami and South Florida. Just as film noir is strongly associated with the
image of squalid city streets, glistening from recent rain, *Miami Vice* depends
on the imagery of Miami: bleached white beaches, pastel mansions on the
water, wide boulevards, crowded urban streets, ultra-modern office complexes,
and various bodies of water (the ocean, canals, rivers, concrete swimming
pools). Indeed, the program's opening and closing credits serve as a catalogue
of Miami iconography (Figures 2.14–2.18), constructing the city itself as a
major figure in the narrative. This links *Miami Vice* to film noir in two ways.
First, the paranoia of film noir is specifically associated with *urban* violence,
the violence on a metropolis' mean streets and back alleys. Noir cities are most
commonly Eastern cities, but the genre does expand to include the Western
decadence of Las Vegas and, most pertinently to *Miami Vice*, Los Angeles. The
palm trees of southern California in, say, *Kiss Me Deadly* (1955) are closely
allied with those of *Miami Vice*. Calling *Miami Vice* a key example of such
"sunshine noir," Steven M. Sanders discusses the importance of *mise-en-scène*s
anchored in very specific and evocative cities, which are implicated as "buzzing
hives of criminality and corruption, places whose disruptive and destructive
elements can only be partially contained but not avoided."[75] Second, films noir
were among the first Hollywood films to reject the studio in favor of extensive
location shooting, especially in post-World War II, semi-documentary films
noir such as *The House on 92nd Street* (1945) and *The Naked City* (1948). To
be sure, *Miami Vice* inherited this impulse toward location shooting, although
it is far from unique in this respect. Several 1970s and 1980s detective television programs use location shooting in a specific, evocative setting—for

Figure 2.14 *Miami Vice*'s titles sequence contains iconography associated with the city—connoting…

Figure 2.15 …leisure activities…

Figure 2.16 …sensuality…

Figure 2.17 …conspicuous consumption…

example, San Francisco in *The Streets of San Francisco* (1972–77) and Hawaii in *Magnum, P.I.* (1980–88). None of these programs would resort to an exterior set such as the one from *Dallas* (refer Figure 2.13). The distinctiveness of *Miami Vice* lies in its choice of Miami and its stylization of a lively and diverse cultural mix.

Miami Vice's settings and costuming contribute to a marked visual scheme. Blindingly bright whites and translucent pastels dominate the daytime imagery (Figure 2.19)—quite unlike most films noir (except, perhaps, the sunlit *The Postman Always Rings Twice*). As Sanders notes,

Figure 2.18 …and postmodernism (in architectural design).

> The signal achievement of *Miami Vice* is to have conveyed a noir sensibility despite its representation of metropolitan space as, in the words of the poet Morgen Kapner, an "amphetamine theatre," a highly colored, brightly lit zone of fast-paced activity.[76]

Most interiors are decorated in white with occasional patches of color, as can be seen in a variety of settings: Calderone's home (Figure 2.20), detective Switek's apartment (Figure 2.21), and the police department's interrogation room (Figure 2.22). Most of the color saturation is leached out, leaving very light, pastel colors. In some scenes the blacks and whites contrast so strongly that one forgets one is watching a color program—as when Crockett, dressed in white, questions an informant with two-toned shoes hiding in a bathroom stall (Figure 2.23), or a thug is propelled across black and white tiles by the force of a shotgun blast (Figure 2.24). As in film noir, blacks contrast starkly with whites in *Miami Vice*. In 1980s television, true black-and-white cinematography was used only as an isolated gimmick—as in a black-and-white *Moonlighting* (1985–9) episode, "The Dream Sequence Always Rings Twice," aired October 15, 1985, while *Miami Vice* was in its second season. The episode is introduced by Orson Welles proclaiming,

> Tonight broadcasting takes a giant leap backward. In this age of living color and stereophonic sound, the television show, *Moonlighting*, is daring to be different and share with you a monochromatic, monophonic hour of entertainment.... Tonight's episode is an experiment.[77]

However, *Moonlighting*'s black-and-white cinematography is actually less distinctive than *Miami Vice*'s black-and-white set design. *Moonlighting*'s episode begins in color and clearly marks its black-and-white segment as a dream sequence—with low-key lighting and characters dressed in 1940s garb and hair style (Figure 2.25). Its black-and-white cinematography signals a conventional narrative shift into dream, just as a rack focus might in classical cinema. *Miami Vice*'s emulation of black-and-white film through its set design, however, is an unconventional rejection of color production design—perversively using color film to shoot black-and-white objects. Its closest analogue in feature film-making is the Coen brothers' latter-day noir, *The Man Who Wasn't There* (2001). Cinematographer Richard Deakins shot that film on color film stock, but it was desaturated in post-production to convert it to black-and-white. Release

Figure 2.19 Miami Vice often eschews film noir's darkness in favor of brilliantly lit beaches and pastel-colored buildings.

Figure 2.20 Miami Vice: white decor, accented with pastel colors, in Calderone's home...

Figure 2.21 …Detective Switek's apartment and…

Figure 2.22 …the interrogation room.

Figure 2.23 Miami Vice emulates black-and-white cinematography through set design and costume. Crockett confronts an informant in a bathroom stall and…

Figure 2.24 …a thug is propelled across black-and-white tiles by a shotgun blast.

prints were created on a monochromatic stock—lending it an authentic noir look despite its color roots.[78] *Miami Vice* does not go to that extreme, but its impulse is very similar.

In contrast to the sunshine noir of the daytime scenes, nighttime scenes are dominated by deep blacks. Scenes are shot night-for-night and employ unconventional noir-style lighting positions. Emily Benedek evocatively describes one such scene:

Figure 2.25 The film noir dream sequence in *Moonlighting*.

following a long shot of Crockett and Tubbs in the Ferrari, the car rolls to a stop under an arching pink and blue neon sign that reads "Bernay's Cafe." Beneath the sign is a lone, lit telephone booth. Everything else is blacked out. Sonny gets out of the car and steps to the phone. Edward Hopper in Miami.[79]

Figure 2.26 Miami Vice: a slightly low angle shot reveals the set's ceiling and "practicals" (functioning lights).

Rejecting standard "three-point" lighting, *Miami Vice* makes full use of lighting positions to create unusually dynamic, imbalanced compositions. The wan color spectrum of a show such as *Dallas* is rejected in favor of deeply saturated blacks and whites and ephemeral pastels. Scenes in the police station contain another unconventional aspect of set design and lighting technique: the set's ceiling and neon light fixtures are revealed in low angle shots (Figure 2.26). In classical, 1930s cinema and attenuated-continuity single-camera television programs such as *Dallas* (as well as all multiple-camera productions), sets were lit from lighting grids suspended above—making it difficult to hang ceilings above sets. In this shot from *Miami Vice*, where a prisoner sits with a bag on his head, the neon lights are likely "practicals"—functioning lights that help illuminate the set. As noted previously, in *Dallas* the lights are seldom practicals; they cast shadows instead of radiating light (see Figures 2.8 and 2.9).

Lighting is, of course, largely a function of where the actors are positioned on the set. Attenuated-continuity schemas conventionally position the actors for the most efficient transmission of narrative information and little more. *Miami Vice*, in contrast, often places the actors in such a way as to confuse viewers, to deny them immediate narrative gratification. The opening shot of Mendez in "Calderone's Demise" is one such example (see Figures 2.1–2.2). Positioned as he is, we have no sense of his location or narrative situation. Contrast this with Figure 2.6, where a conventional over-the-shoulder shot provides a three-quarter view of Kristin's face and Bobby's shoulder clearly indicates where she is relative to him. Another shot later in the same *Miami Vice* episode also obfuscates diegetic space. When Crockett poses as a hired killer and goes to meet Calderone's man, the sequence opens with a long shot of both men in profile, silhouetted, with a large table occupying the foreground leading up to them and a roof cutting off the upper portion of the frame (Figure 2.27). Instead of performing the customary opening shot function of exposition, this shot conceals who the characters are and where they are located. The main visual pleasure of these two shots is their compositional arrangement; they perform inefficiently as narrative signifiers. They disconcert the viewer, delaying the progression of the narrative.

The blocking of the shot above would not seem unconventional if it weren't for the position of the camera relative to the actors. In this case, the camera is farther back than standard craft practices would favor and is perpendicular to the actors, thus showing them in profile which reveals less of their faces and expressions than a standard three-quarter shot (contrast with Figure 2.6). *Miami Vice*'s directors (notably, John Nicolella, Abel Ferrara, and Paul Michael Glaser) constructed a broad variety of unconventional camera positions for the program.[80] Rather than rely on standard eye-level camera height, the program is peppered with extreme low-angle shots (for example, shooting through Crockett's arm while he is doing push-ups [Figure 2.28]) and, less frequently, high-angle shots (Figure 2.29). Instead of a shallow depth of field, spatial relationships are constructed in deep focus—as when Tubbs approaches Angelina on the beach (Figure 2.30). Foreground objects often cramp the frame, obscuring our view of the scene. While Calderone dines in front of a captive Crockett, the foreground is filled with an unidentifiable object (Figure 2.31).

Figure 2.27 Miami Vice's style conceals as much as it reveals, as in this ambiguous shot of Crockett trying to make a deal.

Frames within the frame also constrict figure movement, confining characters in claustrophobic compositions, as in a shot in "The Maze" where a fleeing suspect is framed within a window within another window (Figure 2.32). A mattress in the foreground is more visually prominent than the human figure in the background. Several of these shots exemplify an aggressive, intensified-continuity implementation of the principle of thirds by Miami Vice directors. Borrowed from still photography by cinematographers, the principle of thirds (aka, rule of thirds) divides the frame into a nine-part grid of three sections horizontally and vertically—like a tic-tac-toe board laid over an image, as may be applied to the shot of Tubbs discussed above (Figure 2.33). The most expressive layout, it is argued by numerous photography textbooks, places the main subject of the photograph not in the frame's center but at one of the grid's intersecting points—as is Tubbs in Figure 2.33 (see also Angelina's position in the frame's right third in Figure 2.30, discussed below).[81] Attenuated continuity eschews expressiveness in favor of narrative efficacy—often resulting in dead-center compositions with enough surrounding space to avoid confusion (see Figures 2.11 and 2.12).[82]

Many of the framings discussed above depend upon a wide-angle focal length, which is necessary for both the angle of view and the deep focus in most of those shots (see Figures 2.18, 2.19, 2.27, 2.28, 2.30, 2.32). At a time when attenuated continuity favored a "normal" focal length of approximately 50 mm and zooms in for emphasis (for example, see Figures 2.6–2.7), Miami Vice's directors moved the camera close to the actors and opened the frame with a short, wide-angle lens (focal lengths closer to 25 mm). However, they did not use extremely long lenses—unlike what Bordwell calls "bipolar extremes of lens lengths" in intensified continuity. Miami Vice typically went to one extreme (short lenses) but not the other (long lenses). The program was also very judicious in its use of zooms, preferring camera movement over lens movement—as was typical in the work of intensified-continuity directors in the 1980s who were reacting against the zoom's overuse in 1970s film and television. The dependence upon wide angle and the reluctance to zoom are also traits of film noir (see, for instance, the opening shot of Touch of Evil [1958]), thus linking Miami Vice to the genre once again.

In sum, set design, blocking, camera position, and cinematography combine to create angular forms in strange, asymmetric, closed compositions—imagery that could function well in film noir, but which is quite uncommon in early 1980s, attenuated-continuity broadcast television.

Figure 2.28 Extreme low-angle shot: Crockett does push-ups in *Miami Vice*.

Figure 2.29 High-angle shot: floating bathers in *Miami Vice*.

Figure 2.30 Deep focus and deep space in *Miami Vice*. Angelina paints in the foreground while Tubbs approaches from the background.

Figure 2.31 Miami Vice: an out-of-focus foreground object blocks our vision as Calderone questions Crockett.

Figure 2.32 A frame within a frame within the *Miami Vice* frame creates a claustrophobic composition of a suspect fleeing with a hostage.

Figure 2.33 In the rule of thirds, the strongest points of visual interest are said to be where these lines intersect, as in the intersection on Tubbs' face.

Variations on a Style

One of the most radically unconventional stylistic techniques in *Miami Vice* is its use of visual effects—in particular, slow motion. The program resorts to

conventional slow motion for scenes of violence, but it twists those conventions slightly. Slow motion will frequently begin well before the violence does, creating a spooky foreshadowing of things to come. In "Calderone's Demise," for instance, Crockett and Tubbs are attacked while driving in a car. The slow motion starts well before the gunfire, foreshadowing the impending violence. Additionally, slow motion sometimes continues after the violent act has concluded. When Calderone is machine gunned by Crockett (Figure 2.34), his death is (conventionally) presented in slow motion as he twists in agony. We cut away to a reaction shot of Angelina and Tubbs (Figure 2.35). Then we cut back to Calderone—still in slow motion even though the violence is over—as he sits at the side of the swimming pool (Figure 2.36). Once he sits down, and without cutting away, the shot shifts into regular speed and he falls backward into the pool. The use of slow motion is echoed in some non-violent scenes that would not customarily incorporate slow motion. In "Return of Calderone," several shots of Crockett turning his head are done in slow motion, sometimes leading into the conventional freeze frame before a commercial break. In other episodes, shots of his car will be slowed into a hesitant slow motion—for no conventional reason. Slow motion in *Miami Vice* breaks the conventions of film noir, broadcast television, and classical cinema.

Figure 2.34 Miami Vice's unconventional use of slow motion is illustrated by a scene in which Crockett machine-guns Calderone while...

Figure 2.35 ...his daughter and Tubbs watch. We cut from her horror to...

Perhaps the greatest seeming difference between *Miami Vice* and film noir lies not in any particular element in the imagery but instead in the soundtrack. *Miami Vice*'s audio style and its relationship with image are much closer to music video than they are to film noir. In a story that received

Figure 2.36 ...Calderone on the side of the pool, dead. He collapses into the pool in slow motion, even though the action of the scene is over.

wide circulation in the popular press at the time, the president of NBC's entertainment division, Brandon Tartikoff, is said to have conceived the program through two simple words jotted in a memo to executive producer Michael Mann: "MTV cops."[83] Contemporary musical trends clearly influenced the program's non-diegetic sound, as can be heard in Jan Hammer's pulsating synth music tracks, but it is in the show's incorporation of copyrighted songs—with lyrics—that the greatest debt to music video's mode of production is located. Despite earlier attempts such as Soundies and Scopitones to provide visual illustration of popular music, it was not until MTV's debut in 1981 that short, song-based promotional films had a significant impact on popular culture and the selling of musical recordings in the U.S. They quickly developed a relatively rigid stylistic schema: shots of the band members (performing or not); little additional sound beyond the song, to which the performers often lip synced; "excessive" cinematography; film, not video, recording; rapid editing; and so on. And, perhaps it goes without saying, music videos were rarely based on instrumental recordings; lyric-based songs dominated. At the time that *Miami Vice* premiered, such copyrighted songs were still a rarity in narrative television. The sitcom, *WKRP in Cincinnati* (1978–82), was a pioneer in this regard—lauded for its decision to include authentic rock music instead of the generic substitutes that were standard craft practice in the late 1970s. This sitcom, set in a radio station, seldom used songs to comment on the narrative action; rather, they were just part of the radio station's atmosphere. Thus, in *Miami Vice* there are two distinctive aspects which qualify it as "MTV cops:"

1. popular music—both recognizable hit songs and Hammer's very contemporary score—fill the soundtrack; and
2. certain sequences are presented using music-video's presentational format.

For instance, in "Calderone's Demise," the two flashbacks are done without any dialogue or ambient sound whatsoever. In each, a rock song fills the soundtrack and suggests an interpretation of the images. As Crockett and Tubbs travel to the Bahamas, Russ Ballard sings "Voices." This song, with lyrics about looking to the future, accompanies images from past episodes. In "Smuggler's Blues," the entire narrative was suggested by a song written by Glenn Frey. In that instance and in others less literally, the song precedes the image. Images are constructed to "fill in," as it were, the soundtrack.

Several critics have remarked on this as one of *Miami Vice*'s main innovations. In one respect, however, it is just the logical extension of television's heavy reliance on sound. Because the television viewer does not gaze at the screen with the intensity of the film viewer, television must use the soundtrack to invoke the viewer's attention, to hail the viewer.[84] As Ellis maintains, "Sound carries the fiction or documentary; the image has a more illustrative function."[85] He contends that the visual poverty of television's images is compensated by the invocatory soundtrack—manipulating and demanding the viewer's attention. Thus, the "Smuggler's Blues" episode is the apotheosis of television: images redundantly restating the meaning of the sound. However, not all of the program's music video-style segments operate in this fashion. The images in the flashback in "Calderone's Demise," for example, do not so much illustrate the song as they operate in obscure counterpoint. The images are cut together quickly and enigmatically so that viewers are forced to gaze intently at them at the same time they try to make some connection between them and the song. Here and elsewhere in *Miami Vice*, the images are more allusive than illustrative. This is not only because the first "Calderone's Demise" flashback occurs toward the episode's beginning and thus is part of the construction of an enigma. Even the episode's concluding flashback—accompanied by Tina Turner's "What's Love Got to Do with It?"—points to no one specific meaning. Rather, sound and image interact with one another to create an elusive signification. Consequently, *Miami Vice* places demands on the viewer that are normally reserved for the cinema. We are invited to gaze—not glance—at the images and listen intently to the sounds.

The devoted gaze is further necessitated by the rapid editing of the images. The pace of *Miami Vice*'s editing was often commented on when it initially debuted. Andrew Ross, in a highly critical piece published in 1986, dismisses *Miami Vice*'s quickly cut scenes as mere faddishness, a superficial attempt to cash in on the trend of music video. He singles out Mann for scorn as he excoriates the program:

> Director Michael Mann pretentiously claims to be working in the tradi-
> tion of audio-visual counterpoint established by Eisenstein in films like
> *Alexander Nevsky*. This innovation, however, is more directly a response
> to the dictatorial pressure exercized by the ratings, in an attempt to win
> back an audience lost to cable programming, and particularly, the poten-
> tial high-level consumer MTV audience who are now too visually literate
> to react favourably to the domestic look of network TV.[86]

Is the editing of *Miami Vice* truly Eisensteinian in its speed? Is it cut as quickly as *Alexander Nevsky*, or, more pertinently, does it measure up to early 1980s music videos? And how does it compare to attenuated-continuity programs such as *Dallas*?

If we turn to data on average shot length, we can begin to answer these questions. Table 2.2 arrays a few *Miami Vice*-related data from fastest to slowest. Preliminary work on *Miami Vice*—provisionally based on a limited sample of just three episodes—suggests that the program's mean ASL is just under six seconds.[87] This puts it in the general neighborhood of attenuated-continuity programs of the 1980s, as illustrated by *Dallas*' mean ASL of 6.6 seconds.[88] It is also right on target for feature film releases of this time period, which, according to both Bordwell and Salt, hover around six-second ASLs, too. And, to respond to Ross's snide comment about *Alexander Nevsky*: Eisenstein would approve; *Miami Vice* is cut slightly faster than the former's ASL of 6.8 seconds, but only by a statistically insignificant 0.2 seconds.[89]

However, the average shot lengths for entire episodes of *Miami Vice* only present part of the picture. Fiske timed the shot lengths of two music-video style excerpts within an unspecified *Miami Vice* episode. There he found ASLs close to three seconds—twice as fast as the ASL for the full episode and equal to the intensified-continuity editing of contemporary feature films.[90] Following Fiske's lead, I have broken down the first music-video montage in "Calderone's Demise" and found an even shorter ASL of 2.27 seconds.[91] ASLs under three seconds indicate that the program, in spurts, is cut more quickly than the feature-film, intensified-continuity version of *Miami Vice* that was released two decades later. (That 2006 film's ASL is 4.9 seconds.)[92] The segments' quick editing corroborates Fiske's contention that the music montages in the program are qualitatively different from the rest of the show and that they disrupt narrative progression. He argues, "The style, the music, the look, the interruptions of the narrative remain open, active, disruptive and linger on as the pleasures of *Miami Vice*."[93] In his view, narrative interruption by image and sound supports a postmodern interpretation of the program. I am not prepared to step into a full postmodern analysis of *Miami Vice*, but the ASL data and the quickness of the program's music montages do signal its demand for an attentive viewer's gaze. And that qualifies the program as anti-traditional television, if not necessarily postmodern television.[94]

Television Noir Before *Miami Vice*

Miami Vice was not the first television program to incorporate a noir visual style borrowed from the cinema. It would be an incomplete account, therefore, to present it as a revolutionary, antitraditional television program born fully grown from the head of Zeus, or at least the heads of Anthony Yerkovich and Michael Mann. Before leaving my consideration of film noir's impact on television, I would like to offer a few thoughts on television noir before *Miami Vice*.

If we cast a broad net for any television program containing crime and some form of ratiocination—by private and police detectives, the FBI, defense attorneys, Texas Rangers, and so on—we find remarkably few have been popular enough to be included within the top-30 programs as rated by A.C. Nielsen. The earliest Nielsen ratings (covering October 1950–April 1951) include just two detective shows in the top 30: *Martin Kane, Private Eye* (1949–54) and *Man Against Crime* (1949–56). During the 1950s, *Martin Kane*, *Dragnet* (1952–9, 1967–70) and *The Lineup* (1954–60) were the lonely standard bearers for this broadly defined umbrella genre, which nearly became extinct in the early 1960s. From 1961 to fall 1966, the only ratiocinative, top-rated program was *Perry Mason* (1957–66) and that program weighted courtroom drama over detective work. It wasn't until the 1970s that the genre captured the imagination of the viewing audience, with five-to-seven top-rated shows each year—peaking in 1974–5 when nine ratiocinative programs were in the top 30. The genre went into decline again in the late 1970s, but was staging a comeback in 1984 when *Miami Vice* debuted. The most popular crime drama in the 1984–5 season was not *Miami Vice*. Instead, it was *Murder, She Wrote* (1984–96), which would continue strongly in the ratings even as the genre hit a dry spell in the 1990s. *Murder, She Wrote* was the only crime drama in the top-30 programs in the 1991–2 season, but the genre soon rebounded on the strength of *NYPD Blue* (1993–2005) and the phenomenally successful *Law & Order* (1990–) franchise—

which, as of this writing, is entering its eighteenth season. Since the mid-1990s, there have consistently been four or five crime dramas in the top 30—including the *CSI* programs discussed in the Introduction. Of course, not every crime drama is a film noir.

The earliest crime dramas on television had limited film-noir potential. As Jason Mittell notes,

> The production values on programs like *Man Against Crime* and *Treasury Men in Action* (1950–54) were limited by their live format, with action confined to fourth-wall interior sets, camerawork privileging long takes and distant shots, and scripts requiring lengthy scenes to avoid set changes.[95]

Figure 2.37 The brightly lit, primitive sets of early television, as seen in *Martin Kane*.

Live crime dramas could have average shot lengths as high as 20 seconds, over three times slower than *Miami Vice*—as an analysis of *Martin Kane* from circa 1951, reveals.[96] Inexpensive studio sets were often lit very brightly, to accommodate television cameras that were not sensitive to light (Figure 2.37). However, even in these very early days of television, one can see directors aspiring to cinematic noir lighting. *Martin Kane* begins with a silhouette of a man lighting a pipe—a quintessential noir image (Figure 2.38) and surprising examples of low-key lighting occasionally crop up in the program (Figure 2.39). For instance, in Figure 2.39 we can see how director Frank Burns incorporates low-key chiaroscuro lighting and has even blocked the actors in depth, using deep focus to reveal the building outside the window. Mittell and other broadcast historians presume that the exigencies of live telecasts preclude any visual stylization, but close

Figure 2.38 Despite the limitations of early television technology, *Martin Kane* created low-key images of the detective and his pipe and…

Figure 2.39 …chiaroscuro lighting of an apartment room, with the actors blocked in depth.

analysis provides some exceptions to this stylistic schema. As more kine-scopes of these programs find their way onto DVD, television historians and genre scholars should revisit the programs' visual schemas.

Nonetheless, there is general agreement among film-noir scholars that tel-evision noir needs to be shot on film—black-and-white film—in order to achieve a true noir look. James Ursini claims that a "classic period" of noir existed in 1950s and 1960s television, before the medium shifted to color pro-duction.[97] He marks its beginnings with *China Smith* in 1952—distinguished by "dark, labyrinthine streets; burning sampans dotting the harbor at night; shadowy patterns over the faces of villains."[98] Mittell might quarrel with Ursini and make an argument for *Dragnet* (also debuting in 1952) as the pre-eminent early noir, but he (Mittell) is interested in *Dragnet* as a hybrid blend of genres rather than a "pure" noir. He specifically explores "how the generic categories of police show, documentary, film noir, and radio crime drama were all activated within and around the program."[99] Moreover, there is little doubt that *Dragnet* contains none of the moral ambiguity or identity confu-sion central to film noir. And the series' visual style disdains stylistic excess as detracting from the quotidian stories of these morally unambiguous police detectives—resulting in a preponderance of high-key close-ups and medium close-ups of Joe Friday (Jack Webb) and the perpetrators he pursues.

The most significant television noirs of the late-1950s, from Ursini's perspec-tive, are *Peter Gunn* (1958–61) and the short-lived *Johnny Staccato* (1959–60). Blake Edwards, who created and produced *Peter Gunn*, had an established fea-ture-film career when the show debuted—providing one explanation for the show's indisputable borrowing of noir visual style from the cinema. Urban ico-nography (Figure 2.40); unusual low-angle shots, some of which reveal ceilings (Figure 2.41); night-for-night shooting (Figure 2.42); and angular, low-key com-positions (Figure 2.43) define the program's *mise-en-scène* and shot-on-film cin-ematography. And, unlike Sgt. Friday, Peter Gunn (Craig Stevens) is a *private* investigator who feels comfortable among the criminal element and is una-shamed to use illegal methods to protect his clients. *The Fugitive* (1963–7), which Ursini figures to be the "most self-conscious noir series" of the 1960s, contains another quintessential noir protagonist.[100] Richard Kimble (David Janssen) is alienated, disenfranchised from proper society, living on the run, wrongly accused of murder. And the show's fundamental narrative problematic (will he find the true killer, the one-armed man?) ensures that he is repeatedly doomed to this lot in life. Although *The Fugitive* maintains clear connections to noir themes and narratives, its visual style is actually less noir than previous programs. Further research is necessary, but some scenes incorporate the attenuated con-tinuity style that came to dominate television in the late 1960s and 1970s—espe-cially once color became standard.[101] A scene in a hallway of a boxing arena, from the October 22, 1963 episode, is lit broadly and evenly and contains a practical light does not appear to be functioning (Figure 2.44). One can only imagine how a noir director such as Edgar G. Ulmer would have shot such a scene. For Ursini, *The Fugitive* concludes television noir's classic period. Color film and attenuated-continuity style did not make for compelling noir television. He concludes,

Figure 2.40 *Peter Gunn* brought film noir imagery to television—with urban streets illuminated by neon lights...

Figure 2.41 ...low camera angles...

Figure 2.42 ...night-for-night shooting...

Figure 2.43 ...and angular shadows.

Noir did not really come into its own again until the success of the movie *Body Heat* (1981) and Michael Mann's TV series *Miami Vice* (1984–9). As a result of these neo-noir milestones, TV noir has resurfaced with a vengeance.[102]

Conclusion: Intensified Television and the Possible Illumination of Abysses

All of the unconventional stylistic techniques articulated above work against models of classical narrative and attenuated continuity. They undermine the efficient

Figure 2.44 Some claims have been made for *The Fugitive* as television noir, but high-key scenes such as this one in a boxing arena belie those claims.

presentation of narrative and by so doing they offer the viewer a pleasure that is not normally available on television: the pleasure of gazing, of considering the image as image. In this regard, one might apply Michel Mourlet's description of noir director Fritz Lang's post-1948 work to *Miami Vice*:

Lang's climactic period began in 1948 with a *mise-en-scène* which ceased being a prop for the script or a superficial decoration of space to become intense and inward, calling people and settings into question, predicated upon such fundamental problems as eyes, hand movements, the sudden illumination of abysses. Here the script supports the *mise-en-scène*, which becomes the end.[103]

Miami Vice's foregrounding of *mise-en-scène*, its antitraditional slow-motion shots, and even its stress on music that, ironically, heightens viewer awareness of the image, are elements that may be traced back to film noir—some more directly than others. The intensity that Mourlet sees in Lang's *mise-en-scène* may be found intermittently in *Miami Vice*'s—interrupting the narrative and entreating us to enjoy style as style. As Roland Barthes has argued, narrative delay such as this may well be a source of narrative pleasure. It allows the viewer the time to *look*, to grasp the image as image, rather than merely a signifier used to obtain a signified. Schwichtenberg is prepared to take this argument one step further. Declaring *Miami Vice* "an exemplification of Baudrillardian postmodernist theory," she contends, "As a commodity catalogue of surfaces informed by late capitalism, *Miami Vice* makes no moral pretense about its narrative vacuity or lack of depth: a stylish surface is all there is."[104]

It would be misleading and inaccurate, however, to assume that *Miami Vice* is nothing but style and that style is the only factor connecting *Miami Vice* to film noir. Viewed over 20 years later, after so many of its stylistic innovations have become commonplace, the program's conventional, genre-based elements become clear. Crockett and Tubbs, alienated heroes in a hostile universe of shifting identities, are the Phillip Marlowes of the 1980s. The diminished presence of the spider woman and the ever-repeatable nature of the television narrative form may eviscerate the fatalism of film noir, but the genre struggles on, attracting a new audience and developing new mechanisms to deal with the demands of the electronic medium. These variations on the original genre place *Miami Vice* into a loosely defined category that has been termed "neo-noir," which, at its most expansive, refers to any noirish artifact created after film noir's initial period (approximately 1941–58, although its boundary years are contested). Robert Arnett, in a recent re-evaluation of 1980s neo-noir, summarizes the show's significance to the genre: "*Miami Vice* became an important point in an evolution of '80s noir visual style, one with its own codes and one that questions the complacency of the image."[105] The program's innovations in image and sound function to intensify its themes of moral ambiguity and identity confusion, in addition to providing pure visual *jouissance*. Thus, close analysis of the *Miami Vice* text does not support claims that it is *sui generis* or that its narrative is wholly vacuous. Rather, it illustrates how conventions of a cinematic genre, when teamed with 1980s intensified continuity, can produce provocative, antitraditional television.

Notes

1. John Fiske, *Television Culture* (New York: Methuen, 1987), 260.
2. R.L. Rutsky, "Visible Sins, Vicarious Pleasures: Style and Vice in *Miami Vice*," *SubStance* 55 (1988): 77.
3. Steve Neale, "Widescreen Composition in the Age of Television," in *Contemporary Hollywood Cinema* (New York: Routledge, 1998), 140.
4. John Thornton Caldwell, *Production Culture* (Durham: Duke University Press, 2008), 307.
5. Richard T. Jameson, "Men over Miami," *Film Comment*, April 1985, 66.
6. John Ellis, *Visible Fictions: Cinema: Television: Video* (Boston: Routledge & Kegan Paul, 1982), 116. Perhaps this trend no longer "increases." Caldwell recently argued that, in the 2000s, "the content on television is regularly edgier, more cinematic, and more compelling" than in feature-length, theatrical films. See John T. Caldwell, "Welcome to the Viral Future of Cinema (Television)," *Cinema Journal* 45, no. 1 (fall 2005): 91.
7. "Gazing is the constitutive activity of cinema. Broadcast TV demands a rather different kind of looking: that of the glance," writes John Ellis. Ellis, *Visible Fictions*, 50. He revisits the issue nearly 20 years later, but argues new, dynamic graphic designs still "seem to suit a glance-like mode of attention which is all that television can assume of its audiences." John Ellis, *Seeing Things: Television in the Age of Uncertainty* (New York: I.B. Tauris, 2000), 100.
8. John Thornton Caldwell, *Televisuality: Style, Crisis, and Authority in American Television* (New Brunswick: Rutgers University Press, 1995), 12.
9. Ibid.
10. Jeremy G. Butler, "*Miami Vice*: The Legacy of Film Noir," *Journal of Popular Film and Television* 13, no. 3 (fall 1985): 126–38. Reprinted in *Film Noir Reader*, eds. Alain Silver and James Ursini (New York: Limelight, 1996), 289–305.
11. From 1985 to 2007, according to a ProQuest search conducted on September 1, 2008. Edward Dimendberg performed a similar survey in 1998—finding six dissertations up until 1982 and 46 from 1983–98. Edward Dimendberg, *Film Noir and the Spaces of Modernity* (Cambridge: Harvard University Press, 2004), 3, n.1.
12. One possible competitor is the horror film. A ProQuest thesis/dissertation search conducted on September 24, 2008 returned 79 responses for the phrase "horror film," and other horror theses/dissertations might exist without that specific phrase in their titles or abstracts. In contrast, "Western film" returns only 32 theses/dissertations and "gangster film" a mere 15 theses/dissertations.
13. Paul Schrader, "Notes on *Film Noir*," *Film Comment*, spring 1972, 8.
14. "Vilmos Zsgimond, ASC: *The Black Dahlia*," *The International Cinematographers Guild Magazine*, October 9, 2008, www.cameraguild.com/awards/oscars-07/zsigmond.htm (accessed February 17, 2009).
15. J.A. Place and L.S. Peterson, "Some Visual Motifs of *Film Noir*," *Film Comment*, January–February 1974, 30–5. Reprinted as J.A. Place and L.S. Peterson, "Some Visual Motifs of *Film Noir*," in *Movies and Methods*, ed. Bill Nichols (Berkeley: University of California Press, 1976), 325–38.
16. Cf. Lawrence Alloway, *Violent America: The Movies 1946–1964* (New York: The Museum of Modern Art, 1971); Colin McArthur, *Underworld U.S.A.* (New York: Viking Press, 1972); and Edward Buscombe, "The Idea of Genre in the American Cinema," *Screen* 11, no. 2 (March–April 1970): 33–45.
17. Place and Peterson, "Some Visual Motifs," 30.
18. This is a legitimate link to make, as long as one recognizes that this signified (unstable worldview) has been associated with this stylistic signifier (imbalanced compositions) through arbitrary or, at best, culturally determined, symbolic codes. Imbalanced composition need not necessarily signify disruption and instability.

19. Characteristically, Schrader writes,

> For fifteen years the pressures against America's amelioristic cinema had been building up, and, given the freedom, audiences and artists were now eager to take a less optimistic view of things. The disillusionment many soldiers, small businessmen and housewife/factory employees felt in returning to a peacetime economy was directly mirrored in the sordidness of the urban crime film.
>
> ("Notes on *Film Noir*," 9–10)

20. This can be observed best when the noir/"normal" contrast is articulated within a single film—as Pam Cook and Joyce Nelson have shown in *Mildred Pierce* (1945). See Pam Cook, "Duplicity in *Mildred Pierce*," in *Women in Film Noir*, ed. E. Ann Kaplan (London: British Film Institute, 1978), 68–82; and Joyce Nelson, "*Mildred Pierce* Reconsidered," *Film Reader* 2 (1977): 65–70. See also Janey Place's comments on *The Big Heat* (1953) and *Night and the City* (1950): Janey Place, "Women in *Film Noir*," in Kaplan, *Women in Film Noir*, 35–67. Andrew Spicer calls into question the ability of contemporary, postmodern film noir to function in opposition to today's status quo. Film noir's look, he contends, was turned into a commodity in the 1980s and 1990s and is "no longer clearly an oppositional form of filmmaking;" "Neo-Noir 2: Postmodern Film Noir," in *Film Noir* (Harlow: Pearson Education, 2002), 149.
21. Place and Peterson, "Some Visual Motifs," 32.
22. Alain Silver and Elizabeth Ward, eds., *Film Noir: An Encyclopedic Reference to the American Style* (Woodstock: Overlook Press, 1979), 4–5.
23. Place, "Women in *Film Noir*," 42–54.
24. Ibid., 50.
25. Mary Ann Doane, "*Gilda*: Epistemology as Striptease," *Camera Obscura* 11 (fall 1983): 10.
26. Annette Kuhn, *Women's Pictures: Feminism and Cinema* (Boston: Routledge & Kegan Paul, 1982), 34.
27. See Place, "Women in *Film Noir*," 45.
28. Laura Mulvey, "Visual Pleasure and Narrative Cinema," *Screen* 16, no. 3 (1975): 6–18.
29. Doane, "*Gilda*," 11, quoting Michele Montrelay.
30. See www.hulu.com/miami-vice.
31. The episode may be found online, in high resolution, www.hulu.com/watch/12477/miami-vice-calderones-demise#x-0,vepisode,1 (accessed February 17, 2009).
32. Douglas Kellner, *Media Culture: Cultural Studies, Identity and Politics Between the Modern and the Postmodern* (New York: Routledge, 1995), 239.
33. "This condition, formerly known as multiple personality disorder, is characterized by 'switching' to alternate identities when you're under stress." "Dissociative Disorders: Symptoms," *Mental Health*, March 1, 2007, www.mayoclinic.com/health/dissociative-disorders/DS00574/DSECTION=symptoms (accessed February 17, 2009).
34. Place, "Women in *Film Noir*," 50.
35. Except for those very rare instances in which a program is deliberately brought to a halt (for example, *The Fugitive* [1963–7]).
36. Ellis, *Visible Fictions*, 147.
37. Ibid., 154.
38. James Damico, "Film Noir: A Modest Proposal," *Film Reader* 3 (1978): 54.
39. Steven M. Sanders discusses how the femme fatale does play a role in later episodes. Steven M. Sanders, "Sunshine Noir: Postmodernism and Miami Vice," in *The Philosophy of Neo-Noir*, ed. Mark T. Conard (Lexington: The University Press of Kentucky, 2007), 189.
40. Andrew Spicer, "Neo-Noir 2: Postmodern Film Noir," in *Film Noir*, 162.

41. Ibid., 149. In contrast, Robert Arnett maintains, "The femme fatale was not prominent in '80s noir. She was a prominent character in soap operas of the time, especially on primetime soaps like *Dynasty*." Robert Arnett, "Eighties Noir: the Dissenting Voice in Reagan's America," *Journal of Popular Film & Television* 34, no. 3 (fall 2006): 126.

42. Johnny (Glenn Ford) and Gilda (Rita Hayworth) are in *Gilda*; Frank (John Garfield) and Cora (Lana Turner) are in *The Postman Always Rings Twice*—both from 1946.

43. Kuhn, *Women's Pictures*, 34.

44. John Fiske, "*Miami Vice*, Miami Pleasure," *Cultural Studies* 1, no. 1 (1987): 117.

45. George Benson's performance of the Leon Russell composition was chosen.

46. John Fiske suggests that Crockett and Tubbs might themselves be objects of desire—the desire of the female viewer. Echoing 1980s feminist criticism, he states that television of that time period "is capable of turning the male body into the object of gaze, not the subject of action, thus feminizing it, opening it to feminine desire." Fiske, "*Miami Vice*, Miami Pleasure," 117.

47. Cathy Schwichtenberg, "Sensual Surfaces and Stylistic Excess: The Pleasure and Politics of *Miami Vice*," *The Journal of Communication Inquiry* 10, no. 3 (1986): 57.

48. David Bordwell, Janet Staiger, and Kristin Thompson, *The Classical Hollywood Cinema: Film Style and Mode of Production to 1960* (New York: Columbia University Press, 1986).

49. The series finale of the sitcom, *M*A*S*H* (1972–83), broadcast February 28, 1983, holds the top ratings spot—a record that will never be topped in this postnetwork era.

50. For an ethnographic consideration of the pleasures of *Dallas* experienced by viewers, see Ien Ang and Della Couling, *Watching* Dallas: *Soap Opera and the Melodramatic Imagination*, trans. Della Couling (New York: Routledge, 1985)—published the year after *Miami Vice* debuted.

51. Although a prime-time program, *Dallas* is still a soap opera and can be aligned with daytime soap operas, which may help explain its lack of stylization.

52. Geoffrey Nowell-Smith, "Minnelli and Melodrama," in *Movies and Methods, Vol. II*, ed. Bill Nichols (Berkeley: University of California Press, 1976), 193. See also Thomas Elsaesser, "Tales of Sound and Fury: Observations on the Family Melodrama," in *Home is Where the Heart Is: Studies in Melodrama and Woman's Film*, ed. Christine Gledhill (London: British Film Institute, 1987), 43–69; and Paul Willemen, "Distanciation and Douglas Sirk," in Imitation of Life: *Douglas Sirk, Director*, ed. Lucy Fischer (New Brunswick: Rutgers University Press), 3–28.

53. David Bordwell, *Figures Traced in Light: On Cinematic Staging* (Berkeley: University of California Press, 2005), 23.

54. David Bordwell, *The Way Hollywood Tells It: Story and Style in Modern Movies* (Berkeley: University of California Press, 2006), 121.

55. See footnotes to Bordwell's discussion of ASL in *The Way Hollywood Tells It*, 121–2.

56. Bordwell, *The Way Hollywood Tells It*, 122.

57. Barry Salt, *Moving Into Pictures: More on Film History, Style and Analysis* (London: Starword, 2006), 320.

58. See, for example, the Shot Logger data on the "The Silent Killer" episode (October 5, 1979), www.tcf.ua.edu/slgallery/shotlogger/TitleListDetailPage.php?recordID=158.

59. Bordwell, *The Way Hollywood Tells It*, 122.

60. Ibid., 134.

61. Ibid., 136.

62. Garrett Brown built a prototype of the Steadicam in 1973, but it was not regularly used in feature-film or television production until a decade later. According to Michael Allen, "The time-lag between first appearance and industry acceptance

was partly due to the difficulty in training competent operators." See "From *Bwana Devil* to *Batman Forever*: Technology in Contemporary Hollywood Cinema," in *Contemporary Hollywood Cinema*, eds. Steve Neale and Murray Smith (New York: Routledge, 1998), 121. See also, Serena Ferrara, *Steadicam: Techniques and Aesthetics* (Boston: Focal Press, 2001).

63. Bordwell, *The Way Hollywood Tells It*, 148–9.

64. Barry Salt, "The Stylistic Analysis of Television Drama Programs," in *Moving Into Pictures*, 259–76.

65. Ibid., 276.

66. Elizabeth C. Hirschman offers an analysis of television *mise-en-scène* during 1986–7 in "The Ideology of Consumption: A Structural-Syntactical Analysis of *Dallas* and *Dynasty*," *The Journal of Consumer Research* 15, no. 3 (December 1988): 344–59; but her interest is in locations and props as signifiers of the ideology of consumption. As is typical of structuralism, she does not analyze how those locations/props are represented through set/lighting design, cinematography and editing.

67. "Distant Relative," broadcast October 20, 1983.

68. "Day exteriors can be approached in three ways: filling with large [light] units such as a Brute Arc or 12K HMI, bouncing the existing light with reflectors or covering the scene with a large silk to control the contrast." Blain Brown, *Cinematography: Theory and Practice* (Burlington: Focal Press, 2002), 155.

69. The one possible exception is television's use of the zoom, which was not commonplace in 1935, even though the technology did exist by then.

70. Richard T. Jameson, "Men over Miami," *Film Comment*, April 1985, 66.

71. Kathleen Karlyn, "*L.A. Law, Miami Vice*: Power in Prime Time," *Jump Cut*, no. 33 (February 1988): 20–7, www.ejumpcut.org/archive/onlinessays/JC33folder/LAlaw-mVice.html (accessed July 24, 2008).

72. Schwichtenberg, "Sensual Surfaces," 53.

73. Caldwell, *Televisuality*, 66.

74. Bordwell, *The Way Hollywood Tells It*, 180.

75. Steven M. Sanders, "An Introduction to the Philosophy of TV Noir," in *The Philosophy of TV Noir*, eds. Steven M. Sanders and Aeon. J. Skoble (Lexington: The University Press of Kentucky, 2008), 12.

76. Steven M. Sanders, "Noir et Blanc in Color: Existentialism and *Miami Vice*," in *The Philosophy of TV Noir*, 97.

77. Welles, who was responsible for *Touch of Evil* (1958), one of the final films noir in the classic period, died a few days before the episode was broadcast.

78. According to an article in the *International Cinematographers Guild Magazine*,

> Deakins elected to shoot the film entirely on Kodak Vision 320T. "I find the 5277 to be quite fine-grained, and I wanted a bit of extra speed to avoid having to shoot interiors on a really slow stock. [Then] we had to go from Kodak color neg to a black-and-white release stock. After some searching, we came across something that typically is used for titles.... The folks at DeLuxe found that by manipulating the gamma on that title stock, the contrast could be altered a bit, and so we ended up with a really nice look, very sharp and grain free."
> (Kevin H. Martin, "Razor Burn: Roger Deakins, ASC Lights a Murder in Monochrome for *The Man Who Wasn't There*," *International Cinematographers Guild Magazine*, November 1, 2001, www.cameraguild. com/magazine/stoo1101b.htm [accessed October 9, 2008])

79. Emily Benedek, "Inside *Miami Vice*," *Rolling Stone*, March 28, 1985, 56.

80. Executive producer Michael Mann is presumed to have overseen the visual and sound style of the series, but he did not direct a single episode.

81. Haje Jan Kamps, "The Rule of Thirds," *Photocritic.org*, February 12, 2007, photocritic.org/the-rule-of-thirds (accessed October 13, 2008). See also, among

many others, Rob Sheppard, *Digital Photography: Top 100 Simplified Tips & Tricks* (Hoboken: Wiley, 2007), 80.

82. Steve Neale analyzes composition in widescreen films after 1960, when cinematographers grew concerned that visual designs might suffer when transferred to television's narrower aspect ratio. Writing in 1998, he concludes contemporary films seldom place significant, indispensable narrative elements at the edges of the frame. Steve Neale, "Widescreen Composition in the Age of Television," in *Contemporary Hollywood Cinema*, eds. Steve Neale and Murray Smith (New York: Routledge, 1998), 136.

83. R. Serge Denisoff, *Inside MTV* (New Brunswick: Transaction Publishers, 1991), 251.

84. It may be noted that Louis Althusser's primary example of ideology hailing or interpellating subjects is also an audio one: interpellation "can be imagined along the lines of the most commonplace everyday police (or other) hailing: 'Hey, you there!'" Louis Althusser, "Ideology and Ideological State Apparatuses (Notes Toward an Investigation)," in *Lenin and Philosophy and Other Essays*, trans. Ben Brewster (New York: Monthly Review Press, 1971), 174.

85. Ellis, *Visible Fictions*, 129.

86. Andrew Ross, "Masculinity and *Miami Vice*: Selling In," *The Oxford Literary Review* 8, nos. 1–2 (1986): 151.

87. These three episodes have been analyzed on Shot Logger, showing a mean ASL of 5.75.

88. Based on Shot Logger data on 13 episodes from 1979 and 1983.

89. "*Aleksandr Nevskiy*," *Cinemetrics*, November 3, 2007, October 10, 2008, www.cinemetrics.lv/movie.php?movie_ID=546 (accessed February 17, 2009).

90. John Fiske, "*Miami Vice*, Miami Pleasure," 113–15. Interestingly, when Fiske reworked this article into a chapter in *Television Culture* (New York: Methuen, 1987)—a section titled "The Pleasures of *Miami Vice*" (255–62)—he kept the table listing the individual shots, but deleted the calculation of average shot lengths.

91. This quickly cut montage is book-ended by shots that are each over 40 seconds long. Thus, the program is capable of both extremely long and extremely short shots.

92. "*Miami Vice* (movie)," *Shot Logger*, October 8, 2008, www.tcf.ua.edu/slgallery/shotlogger/TitleListDetailPage.php?recordID=163 (accessed October 13, 2008).

93. Fiske, *Television Culture*, 262.

94. Caldwell trenchantly critiques the application of the postmodernist label to any one specific television program, because postmodern properties are endemic to the medium:

> Any systematic look at the history of television soon shows that all of those formal and narrative traits once thought to be unique and defining properties of postmodernism—intertextuality, pastiche, multiple and collaged presentational forms—have also been defining properties of television from its inception.
>
> (*Televisuality*, 23)

95. Jason Mittell, "Policing Genres—*Dragnet*'s Texts and Generic Contexts," in *Genre and Television: From Cop Shows to Cartoons in American Culture* (New York: Routledge, 2004), 142–3.

96. "Doctored Will," *Shot Logger*, September 22, 2008, www.tcf.ua.edu/slgallery/shotlogger/TitleListDetailPage.php?recordID=157 (accessed October 10, 2008).

97. James Ursini, "Angst at Sixty Fields per Second," in *Film Noir Reader*, eds. Alain Silver and James Ursini (New York: Limelight, 1996), 276.

98. Ibid., 277.

99. Mittell, "Policing Genres," 124.

100. Ursini, "Angst at Sixty Fields," 284.
101. The first three seasons of *The Fugitive* were shot in black-and-white while the fourth was filmed in color.
102. Ursini, "Angst at Sixty Fields," 287.
103. Michel Mourlet, "Fritz Lang's Trajectory," in *Fritz Lang: The Image and the Look*, ed. Stephen Jenkins (London: British Film Institute, 1981), 13–14.
104. Schwichtenberg, "Sensual Surfaces," 54.
105. Robert Arnett, "Eighties Noir: the Dissenting Voice in Reagan's America," *Journal of Popular Film & Television* 34, no. 3 (fall 2006): 127.

3.

The Persuasive Power of Style

Most of this book analyzes the narrative power of style—its ability to signify, heighten, or occasionally undercut stories in television. But vast expanses of broadcast time in the United States are less concerned with storytelling than with product selling. Commercials might, and often do, rely on narrative to do that selling, but more often than not they employ other rhetorical strategies. Chief among these strategies are uses of television style to convince us to purchase products and services. But not all television advertising seeks to persuade us through verbal repetition and sledgehammer exhortations to buy. Many advertisers understand what Paul Messaris calls the "value of indirectness."[1] They use evocative imagery, enticing audio, and surprising editing to persuade viewers without attacking or numbing their sensibilities. And yet, commercials all still seek to persuade us in some fashion. Throughout this book, I have argued that style results from a mix of economics, aesthetics, technology, and standardized craft practices. While this is true for commercials as well, they are also the television texts that most baldly serve an economic function—to impel the consumer to take purchasing action.

This chapter views commercials as texts that have developed particular techniques of persuasion in order to serve the economic needs of the industry. We know that ads must sell us products in order to survive, but what the television analyst needs to understand is how that selling is accomplished. Most previous work on commercials focuses less on style and more on the ideologically determined meanings signified by commercials.[2] And since these meanings and the style that signifies them are so intertwined, it is worth outlining the socially defined meanings, values, and illusions—the polysemy—that are commonly employed in the service of selling products before analyzing their stylistic manifestation. Elsewhere, I group these meanings into broad categories: luxury, leisure, and conspicuous consumption; individualism; the natural; folk culture and tradition; novelty and progress; sexuality and romance; alleviation of pain, fear/anxiety, and guilt; and utopia and escape from dystopia.[3] Bearing these meanings in mind, I have identified eight stylistic techniques used to convince us that certain products contain them:

1. Metaphor
2. Utopian style
3. Product differentiation and superiority

4. Repetition and redundancy
5. Extraordinary and excessive style
6. Graphics and animation
7. Violating reality through visual effects
8. Reflexivity and intertextuality

Metaphor

Perhaps the most common way that advertisers assert the desirability of their products is to associate them with activities, objects, or people that are themselves desirable. Essentially, such association constructs a metaphor between the product and that desirable activity, object, or person. These metaphors often link products with unexpected or incongruous things or activities. One famous instance of metaphoric sex is a 1960s commercial for Noxzema shaving cream (available on TVStyleBook.com). In tight close-up, Gunilla Knutson, a former Miss Sweden, suggestively runs her lips across a string of pearls (Figure 3.1). With her distinctly Swedish accent, she breathlessly intones, "Men, nothing takes it off like Noxzema Medicated Shave." A brass band then begins to blare "The Stripper," which accompanies close-ups of a man shaving his face (Figure 3.2). "Take it off," Knutson commands, "Take it *all* off." Noxzema implies here that shaving is metaphorically equivalent to stripping. The metaphor in this case is created through the commercial's sound mix (the woman's dialogue and the music). By bringing together sound and image that are normally not connected, Noxzema creates a metaphoric meaning. That is, the commercial's meaning is not a literal one: "The man is stripping." But rather it is a metaphorical one: "Shaving is like stripping in that something is removed in both cases." It sounds bland when summarized so simply, but to suggest that removing shaving cream is similar to removing clothing fastens a sexually provocative connotation to a normally quotidian activity.

Another method for generating metaphors is through a sequence of images, much as advocated by Soviet montage theory in the 1920s. By bringing two or more images together in sequence, a film-maker can imply that

Figure 3.1 Noxzema Medicated Shave relies on metaphoric sex for its impact.

Figure 3.2 "Take it off. Take it all off."

one image should be compared with the other and that there are similarities between them. Sergei Eisenstein advocated the use of visual metaphor or, as he called it, intellectual montage, for political causes, not commercial ones.[4] In the instance of his film, *Strike*, he intercut heroic striking workers being beaten by police with shots of a bull being slaughtered (Figures 3.3–3.4; available on TVStyleBook.com). The metaphoric meaning is clear: strikers are cattle. And, further, it graphically argues that a gross injustice is being done to the workers.

Figure 3.3 Strike: Director Sergei Eisenstein intercuts a bull being slaughtered with…

Advertisers have usurped Eisenstein's principle to sell commodities. For instance, a commercial for a line of Hyundai cars begins with ten images of exhilarating activities: a mountain climber topping a peak, a surfer negotiating a wave, a girl twirling in a water sprinkler, children leaping into a swimming hole, and so on (Figure 3.5; available on TVStyleBook.com). These are followed by an equal number of shots of Hyundai cars on the road (Figure 3.6). The final image is a group of mountain climbers on a summit (Figure 3.7). The order of the images—cars

Figure 3.4 …workers being attacked by police—generating a visual metaphor of workers = cattle.

sandwiched between swimming children and mountaineers—suggests that driving a Hyundai is the same as the other actions.

Commercials are seldom satisfied only to hint at such meanings visually, however, and the significance of the images is often anchored by the sound. The Hyundai ad incorporates Cream's song, "I Feel Free," and thus makes clear what meaning ought to be generalized from this sequence of images.[5] Further, the commercial's narrator states,

> There are those moments in life when absolutely nothing weighs you down. When you feel totally, completely free. This fall, Hyundai is introducing a exciting new line of vehicles that are a joy to drive and virtually effortless to own, thanks to America's best warranty plan. Because we believe freedom should be more than a feeling. It should be something you can actually touch.

It should be noted, however, that the narration does *not* explicitly state, "Driving Hyundai cars is like flying a kite or jumping in a creek." The sequentiality of the images, aided by the music, carries this meaning *indirectly*.

Figure 3.5 The song, "I Feel Free," accompanies a girl twirling in a water sprinkler...

Figure 3.6 ...a Hyundai car driving down the road...

Figure 3.7 ...and mountain climbers on a summit.

As Messaris argues, indirectness is commonly used in advertising. He maintains that it has two advantages over direct approaches. First, an indirect, visual argument such as the Hyundai ad elicits a "greater degree of mental participation" from viewers.[6] It requires viewers themselves to make the semantic connection between the product and the other objects (e.g., between Hyundai cars and children swimming). Messaris contends that viewers are more likely to retain the commercial's message because they themselves have helped to generate it. Second, Messaris contends, "the [explicit] verbal claims made in advertisements tend to be held to much stricter standards of accountability than whatever claims are implicit in the ads' pictures."[7] His illustration of this is ads for cigarettes, which show happy, healthy-looking people smoking—thus making the indirect, implicit claim that smoking is a healthy activity when, of course, we know it is not. Commercials can metaphorically suggest many things in the visuals that they would be prohibited from stating explicitly in the dialogue.

Utopian Style

Commercials often promise admission to utopia through the purchase of commodities. In a Mercedes-Benz roadster ad, Peter Pan and Tinkerbell float into the bedroom of Michael, a middle-aged man. Michael is sleeping in respectable-looking pajamas next to a woman who is presumably his respectable spouse. Peter entices him, "Do you remember when we were eight and we went flying?" When Michael protests that he can't fly any more, Peter corrects him, "It's never too late to fly!" We then cut to Michael, still in his pajamas, driving a roadster and shouting, "Woooo-hooo!" Notably, his spouse is not beside him, but Peter and Tinkerbell are. The spot fades to black as Michael shifts into high gear. Then the only text in the ad fades in: "Exhilaration" (followed by the Mercedes-Benz logo). With its allusions to Neverland and the boy who won't grow up, this commercial associates its product with a utopian view of childhood pleasures and

passions. Richard Dyer contends that utopianism in mass entertainment is not just
evident in the worlds it portrays. He takes
the principle of utopianism a step further
and finds it in the style of presentation, in
aspects of *mise-en-scène*, cinematography,
and, crucially, music.[8] That is, he argues
that qualities of utopia (abundance,
energy, intensity, transparency, and community) may be found in a medium's
style. For Dyer, this is most evident in the
film musical. Since music is fundamental
to most, if not all, commercials, it seems
reasonable that we might look for this
utopian style in the television
commercial.

Figure 3.8 A rave in the woods to the
music of Basement Jaxx...

Soda commercials offer particularly
clear examples of utopianism's embodiment in style. To choose one instance
among many, consider a Coca-Cola spot
from 2000 that presents a rave party in
the woods. (The commercial is included
on TVStyleBook.com.) A mass of people
gyrate euphorically near a fire (Figure
3.8) to the music of Basement Jaxx's "Red
Alert." The handheld camera bumps and
jumps within the crowd, occasionally
craning above it. One stocky guy in a
T-shirt and shorts is featured dancing
quirkily by himself as three friends sit
nearby (Figure 3.9). There's no dialogue
and the lyrics of the music are virtually
indistinguishable. The only words in the
ad appear on the bottoms of Coke cans.
In total, they are: "Bliss ... comes from
... within. Enjoy" (Figure 3.10). With so
few words to anchor the meaning of this
commercial, it must rely on elements of
style (bass-heavy techno-styled music,
dancing technique, camera movements)
to signify its meaning. The utopian
"bliss" that we are to associate with

Figure 3.9 ...finds a young man caught up
in the music...

Figure 3.10 ...which we are meant to
associate with the blissful pleasure of
Coca-Cola products: "Bliss ... comes from
... within. Enjoy."

Coca-Cola imbues the image/sound style and encourages viewers to join the
dance, figuratively speaking. Energy and intensity—in Dyer's sense of these
terms—are embodied in the commercial's style.

Product Differentiation and Superiority

To survive in the marketplace, every product must distinguish itself from others in the same category. Coke must be perceived as different from Pepsi, Tide from Cheer, Ford from Toyota, Levi from Wrangler, and on and on. At the core of all advertising is the establishment and maintenance of a product's identity, its brand. The key to brand identity is a product's unique selling proposition (USP), as advertising standard-bearer Rosser Reeves termed that certain something that separates a product from the rest of the field.[9] Even when there is very little actual difference between commodities, the USP principle holds that the advertiser must find or even fabricate one. Reeves is often quoted as explaining the USP this way: "Our problem is—a client comes into my office and throws down two newly minted half-dollars onto my desk and says, 'Mine is the one on the left. You prove it's better.'"[10]

Reeves faced the challenge of brand parity, of the lack of difference between products, in 1952 while developing an advertising campaign for Anacin, a pain reliever whose active ingredients consisted solely of aspirin (acetylsalicylic acid [ASA]) and caffeine. How was he to differentiate Anacin from regular aspirin? His solution was a series of cleverly worded commercials that feature a fanciful animated representation of an ailment he dubbed the "tension headache" (Figure 3.11; available on TVStyleBook.com). A compressed spring and a jagged electrical spark metaphorically represent the overwrought human nervous system (several ads in the series include a small hammer pounding away, too). The ads' catchphrase of "fast, fast, fast relief" became part of the 1950s popular culture lexicon. But it wasn't enough for Reeves to explain how Anacin relieved pain. He also needed to prove that it lessened discomfort in a *different* manner from aspirin—even though aspirin was its main pain-relieving agent. He needed to find Anacin's USP. In one commercial from this long-running campaign, the announcer explains, "Aspirin has just one pain reliever. Add buffering, you still get just one. Only Anacin of the four leading headache remedies has special ingredients to relieve pain *fast*, help overcome depression *fast*, relax tension *fast*." Anacin's combination of ingredients comprises its unique selling proposition, according to Reeves, because only Anacin has that particular recipe. To emphasize this point, side-by-side animation shows Anacin relieving headache pain that aspirin cannot alleviate (Figure 3.12). Nowhere in this ad does the announcer reveal that the principal "special ingredient" in Anacin is aspirin itself. Instead, we're allowed to imagine that its ingredients are wholly different from aspirin. If we examine the text of the ad carefully, we find that the announcer does not deny that Anacin contains aspirin. He is just less than forthcoming about the nature of its ingredients. In fact, one premise of the commercial is that "Three out of four doctors recommend the ingredients in Anacin." He doesn't specify what those ingredients are, but we may well suppose that the primary one is aspirin. Note also that the copy does not say that the doctors specifically recommend Anacin, but rather just that they recommend the ingredients Anacin contains. To be fair to Reeves, we should note that in his book, *Reality in Advertising*, he contests the suggestion that Anacin's USP is a made-up one. He argues that the difference between Anacin and aspirin is not "minuscule." He claims that distinguishing Anacin from aspirin is not based on a "deceptive differential," but rather is "the stuff and substance of good advertising."[11]

Current craft practices disdain Reeves's hard-sell approach. It's said to be too simplistic for today's "sophisticated" consumers and yet television commercials continue to wage battles against brand parity. From the Apple Power Mac G4 commercials entreating computer users to "Think different" to the taste tests of the "Pepsi Challenge" to the Dodge ads beginning and ending with the word, "Different," we see the persistent influence of Reeves' unique selling proposition and the need for advertisers to differentiate their products from those of their competitors.

Repetition and Redundancy

In addition to the USP, Reeves was also known as an advocate of blunt force repetition in television commercials. The Anacin spot above exemplifies this in its use of the word "fast." It appears eight times in the 30-second spot and three times in the tagline alone: "Anacin—for fast, fast, incredibly fast relief."

Not only did Anacin's slogan contain repetition, but it was itself reiterated thousands of times in repeated airings of this commercial and in numerous different Anacin ads, which were themselves also frequently aired. All successful advertising campaigns use repetition within ads, in repeated airings of ads, and across numerous other ads in the same campaign.

Repetition in advertising serves one major, obvious function: reinforcement. The first time you hear a word or see an image, you may not remember it. Each repetition of it makes recall more likely. But what, in general terms, are television commercials reinforcing? They're doubtlessly reinforcing particular qualities of particular commodities, but in a more general sense they're reinforcing brand identity. If advertisers can get consumers to remember the names of their products when they visit a store, they feel they've achieved 75 percent of their goal. If they can get consumers to remember the superiority of their brands and subsequently purchase their products, they've achieved the remaining 25 percent.

Figure 3.11 Ad man Rosser Reeves invented the "tension headache"...

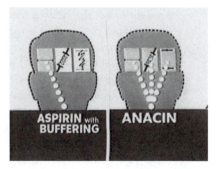

Figure 3.12 ...which his client, Anacin—and only Anacin—could remedy.

Another technique that is closely related to repetition is redundancy. Most of the information that we hear and see repeated in television commercials is redundant information. It exceeds what is necessary to make the point. Sound and image often redundantly convey identical information in commercials. For instance, in Apple's groundbreaking "1984" commercial the narrator speaks the same words that we see crawl up the screen at the end: "On January 24th, Apple Computer will introduce Macintosh. And you'll see why 1984 won't be like '1984.'" This is quite typical of the ends of commercials, where ads make their final bids to remain in the viewer's consciousness. Redundancy is common in much television—as when soap-opera characters redundantly rehash plot developments—but it exists at a much higher level in and is absolutely crucial to the commercial.

Extraordinary and Excessive Style: Televisuality and Counter Television

Viewers do not seek commercials. They do not tune into television for the commercials themselves (with the significant exceptions of shopping channels and the annual *Super Bowl* telecast). Indeed, they commonly use remote controls, time-shifted recordings on DVRs, and channel browsing to avoid watching commercial breaks. And so, advertisers are continuously challenged to develop mechanisms for snaring viewers' attention, for hailing them. Louis Althusser's notion of hailing pertains here as, for him, hailing has ideological implications:

> All ideology hails or interpellates concrete individuals as concrete subjects ... Ideology "acts" or "functions" in such a way that it "recruits" subjects among the individuals (it recruits them all), or "transforms" the individuals into subjects (it transforms them all) by that very precise operation which I have called interpellation or hailing, and which can be imagined along the lines of the most commonplace everyday police (or other) hailing: "Hey, you there!"[12]

According to Althusser, hailing is the process by which individuals are brought under the sway of ideology, are interpellated within it. Commercials are similarly designed to bring individuals under the sway of their ideas, of the polysemy of corporate capitalism. One way that hailing is achieved is through what Caldwell terms "televisuality"—"defined by excessive stylization and visual exhibitionism."[13] He believes that much 1980s narrative television, including *Miami Vice*, is marked by televisuality (see Chapter 2), but we will limit our application of it here to television commercials—returning to the concept in Chapter 5, on situation comedies.

In order to understand excessive or exhibitionistic television, we must recall its stylistic norm, its standardized craft practices and stylistic schema. By the 1970s, narrative television had found its own classical, and mostly attenuated, style. This conventional television style may be observed in sitcoms, soap operas, prime-time dramas, and other narrative programs (see Chapter 2 for a detailed consideration of attenuated classical style in *Dallas*). Central to this approach is that style should not draw attention to itself, that it should in a sense be invisible—that style should support the narrative so effectively that the viewer may submerge into the story without being "distracted" by the style. One of the quintessential principles of commercials is that television's classical conventions may be intensified, exceeded, or even violated in order to attract the viewer's attention. Stylistic excesses and violations are used by commercials to snap viewers out of their dreamlike connection with television narrative, to shock them out of their television lethargy and make them sit up and take notice of the advertised products. Theatrical-film style since the 1970s can also be excessive, or as we saw in the Pillsbury commercial (Chapter 1) they may exemplify Bordwell's intensified continuity.[14] Television commercials borrow liberally from contemporary, intensified continuity in theatrical film and some critics, such as Pauline Kael, even say that they are to blame for that intensification.[15] However, commercials go well beyond intensified continuity or perhaps one could say they are of a different order of continuity. The commercial needs to stand apart from the television material that surrounds it—including programs that themselves are influenced by intensified continuity (e.g., *Miami Vice* and *CSI*). Thus, the commercial does not merely "amp up" classical continuity. It also breaks the rules of continuity in order to more effectively hail the viewer, or, to put it in pejorative terms, as Kael does, "the 'visuals' of TV commercials" are little more than "a disguise for static material, expressive of nothing so much as the need to keep you from getting bored and leaving."[16] Still, her point coexists with mine as we both are arguing that aggressive style serves a hailing function. Following Bertolt Brecht's "epic theater" and Peter Wollen's claims for a Brechtian "counter cinema" in the 1960s and 1970s, we might think of the commercial's disruptive stylistic approach as "counter television."[17] Although epic theater and counter cinema are both Marxist attempts to combat capitalism and consumerism and although the notion of Brechtian commercials may make Brecht spin like a top in his grave, it is impossible to deny that techniques once associated with experimental theater and film are now routinely used in television commercials. These counter-television techniques may be sorted into aspects of *mise-en-scène*, videography, editing, and sound.

Mise-en-scène

There are several unusual aspects of performance, of figure expression and movement, in television commercials. The most significant aspect in terms of the commercial's hailing function is the manner in which the camera is directly addressed, whereby persons on television look "back" at the television viewer and speak directly to him or her. The issue of the look or the gaze has been a contentious one in film studies ever since Laura Mulvey's revolutionary article, "Visual Pleasure and Narrative Cinema," was published in 1975.[18] For her, and the many who followed in her wake, looking is fundamentally a psychoanalytic question of power and sexuality, rooted in Freudian notions of voyeurism. And in a related area of film studies from the 1970s, looks of the characters are central to the "system of the suture," in which shot-counter shot and POV editing pull the viewer into the realm of the film.[19] Central to these approaches is the taboo against looks at the camera—what Wheeler Winston Dixon calls the "returned gaze"—in classical cinema.[20] The breaking of that taboo through the direct address of the camera attracted considerable discussion in this context. Marc Vernet begins his article, "The Look at the Camera" (1989), by outlining this discussion:

> According to traditional approaches, the look at the camera has a double effect: it foregrounds the enunciative instance of the filmic text and attacks the spectator's voyeurism by putting the space of the film and the space of the movie theater briefly in direct contact. In such a situation, it is supposed traditionally that the discursive form "I/you" comes to accentuate the relation of the two interlocutors in contrast to the narrative cinema that would seem to have opted in general for the form "he," which, according to Émile Benveniste, characterizes a narrated story [*histoire racontée*].[21]

Figure 3.13 Actor Anna Karina gazes at the camera in *Vivre sa vie*, shattering the fourth wall.

Figure 3.14 Vivre sa vie: Voyeurism denied? Director Jean-Luc Godard shoots a nude figure through a doorway.

To transpose Vernet's "double effect" to television we might say, first, that a look at the camera in narrative television makes viewers aware of television as television, as a signifying apparatus. Enunciation (the linguist, Benveniste's *énonciation*) is the *act* of enunciating or uttering—in cinema/television, the process of signifying a meaning to a viewer. It is argued, for example, that when Anna Karina, an actor in Jean-Luc Godard's *Vivre sa vie*, looks directly at the viewer (Figure 3.13) she causes a Brechtian break in the fourth wall and thereby makes the viewer aware of that fourth wall, of the conventional signification processes of the cinema. Vernet's second effect, the disruption of voyeurism, may also be seen in the *Vivre sa vie* example. A film about prostitution, *Vivre sa vie* explicitly interrogates the economic and sexual exploitation of women and includes scenes, within the narrative, of voyeurism. It also contains some nudity, but Godard frustrates the potential voyeur by shooting the nude scenes through doorways and in a non-erotic manner (Figure 3.14). The voyeur's pleasure is then specifically confronted when Karina looks at the lens and, by extension, at the spectator. At that point, the spectator and the "spectacle" (Karina and her character, Anna), enter into an "I/you" relationship where previously the spectator experienced her in third person ("she"). The essential component of a voyeur's pleasure and power is that he not be acknowledged by the woman upon whom he gazes and that is exactly what Karina/Anna appears to do. By returning his (our) gaze, she challenges the power of his gaze to use her as an object; in psychoanalytic terms, she asserts herself as a subject.

Vernet takes exception with several assumptions of prior theorists and contests them by, among other things, placing these looks at the camera in the context of popular-culture traditions such as the music hall—in which a look at the spectator is definitely not taboo. Similarly, the television commercial provides particularly complicated instances in which the look at the camera is not only not taboo, it is essential to the enunciation. In non-narrative television, direct address cedes power to the text over the spectator, disturbing his or her position as voyeur. News anchors typically address viewers directly by looking straight into the camera lens, engaging the viewer in an I/you exchange: "*I* am telling *you* that this is all the important news happening today. *You* must believe it." Diegetic television, on the other hand, follows the conventions of the narrated story, with characters (*he, she*) addressing one another and not the spectator.[22] Commercials, however, incorporate direct address in both non-narrative and narrative instances.[23] These direct-camera looks are a common incarnation of the persuasive hailing of the viewer. Remembering Althusser's hailing example—"Hey, *you* there!"—we can see that hailing invokes Benveniste's pair of interlocutors, positioning viewers so that they will respond with their attention to the product being pitched and awake from their narrative-induced sleep-walking.

In a non-narrative commercial for the Hair Club a client looks straight at the camera and details the benefits of its product (Figure 3.15). He clearly addresses viewers directly—specifically hailing men who feel anxious about hair loss and implying, "*You* must buy our product to solve *your* problem." One might think that it is only non-narrative commercials that so brazenly address/implore/hail the viewer but this distinction crumbles because commercials are remarkably cavalier about the division between narrative and non-narrative. Television commercials casually and inconsistently blur the line between narrative characters and the non-narrative actors that portray them—as illustrated in the 1980s series of Vicks cough medicine commercials where actors proclaimed, "I'm not a doctor, but I play one on TV."[24] The function of that disclaimer is clearly to encourage the viewer to think of the actor in his character's role, overlapping the two. In reverse fashion, commercials for Bartles & Jaymes wine coolers encourage the viewer to think of characters as actors. In this case we have fictional characters looking into the camera and speaking their lines (Figure 3.16) as if they were authentic producers of wine and pitchmen for it. In both cases— the actor as doctor and the characters as wine merchants—the figures before us violate the taboo against direct-camera gazes and they do so in a fashion that implores the viewer's return gaze.

Figure 3.15 A client of the Hair Club looks directly at the camera as he presents his testimonial.

Figure 3.16 Actors speak to the camera as if they were the actual creators of Bartles & Jaymes wine coolers.

Despite the lack of consistency or clarity in the commercial's mixture of narrative and non-narrative materials, it is indisputable that the clusters of commercials that interrupt narrative broadcasting demand viewers radically shift their spectatorial position. These commercials hail the viewer in a manner quite different from the address of both narrative television programs and theatrical film. It is important to recognize the slippery nature of address in commercials, because it may well call into question presumptions about the look, the gaze and the returned gaze, and the system of the suture that are based on theatrical film models.

Commercials' performance style is commonly pitched a notch or two higher than the acting in narrative programs and the behavior of individuals in nonnarrative programs. The goal of performers in many commercials is not so much plausibility or realism as it is noticeability. An excessive performance style can get commercials noticed during their 30-second bid for our attention. In the 1980s, Federal Express featured fast-talker John Moschitta, Jr. in a series of successful ads (an example is available on TVStyleBook.com). Moschitta's ability to speak at the rate of 530 words per minute served a dual purpose for FedEx: to capture viewers' attention and to make a metaphoric connection between their delivery service's rapidity and Moschitta's speech. Excessive speed is also used in the selling of automobiles—where vehicles frequently careen recklessly around racetracks, desert trails, and mountain passes. A notice on such ads tells us that these are "professional drivers on a closed course" and that we shouldn't attempt such stunts ourselves, but if risky driving draws viewers' attention then its persuasive function has been served (see the Mercedes-Benz C63 commercial on TVStyleBook.com).

Non-human figures also perform in unconventional ways in commercials. Animals frequently talk, sing, and dance. And objects which usually cannot move on their own commonly violate the laws of physics in commercial performances. We've seen singing raisins and talkative M&M candies and we've been introduced to Speedy Alka-Seltzer and the Pillsbury Doughboy (Figures 3.17, 1.56). By giving animals the human property of speech and by animating normally inanimate objects, commercials violate the behavioral rules of the real world.

Direct gazes at the camera, the excessive performance of actors, and the unconventional behavior of non-human "actors"
all hail viewers—entreating them to pay
attention and to be persuaded by commercials, or, in Althusserian terms, for the
viewing subject to be interpellated into the
polysemy of commercials.

Figure 3.17 Non-human figures such as the
Speedy Alka-Seltzer often pitch products.

Videography

Despite the televisual exhibitionism Caldwell has found in several 1980s and 1990s
programs and the intensified continuity Bordwell has identified in theatrical
film, most television since the 1970s has adhered to television's rather attenuated classical schema in terms of videography. Music television, however, is a
significant exception.[25] When it arrived in the early 1980s, its stylistic flourishes and visualization of music had a major impact upon the videography/
cinematography of programs such as *Miami Vice* (1984–9) and the short-
lived *Cop Rock* (1990). More importantly, it inspired a small revolution in the
videography of commercials, which use music-video style to distinguish
themselves from the program material they are interrupting. For commercial
directors, the counter-television videographic schema is yet another way to
draw the viewer's attention.

Table 3.1 counterposes the principal videographic elements of the narrative-television classical schema with a counter-television schema that commercials use to catch our eye. Letterboxing, out-of-focus shooting, and
imbalanced composition are all illustrated in a single commercial for Micro-
Strategy, an online company specializing in business consulting (Figure 3.18;
video clip available on TVStyleBook.com). In letterboxing, the black bars at
the top and bottom effectively reshape the aspect ratio of the frame—making
it wider than normal television. This width is emphasized in a later shot where
the same woman is placed on the extreme left of the frame while a frazzled

Table 3.1 Conflicting schemas: classicism vs. counter-television

Classical Videography	Counter-television Videography
Image fills the frame	Letterboxing
Balanced composition (Objects centered)	Imbalanced composition (Objects at the frame's edges)
In-focus main figure	Out-of-focus main figure
Regular speed action	Slow motion and fast motion
Color	Black-and-white
Limited camera movement	Extremely active camera movement
Eye-level camera angle	Extreme low and high angles
"Normal" focal length	Extreme wide angle and telephoto

Figure 3.18 Letterboxing reshapes the frame of a MicroStrategy commercial...

Figure 3.19 ...and allows it to create an imbalanced composition with a woman in focus on the edge of the frame and a man, in the center of the image, out of focus.

man appears in the background (Figure 3.19). This image would be more conventional if she were moving towards the man and into the center of the frame, but she is not. Instead, she's walking to the left and out of frame. The result is a strikingly imbalanced composition. Also notable is the fact that two-thirds of this shot is markedly out-of-focus and remains that way for the duration of the shot. That is, we do not pull focus to the man in the background.

Although variable speed action in commercials was partially inspired by music videos, television sports was more significant to its popularization. Ever since the 1960s—when advances in videotape technology enabled television to replay action at variable speeds—slow motion has been an integral part of televised sports. As we have seen with *mise-en-scène* and videography, variable speed action can be a hailing technique. Because narrative programs don't normally use variable speeds, slow motion and fast action make us attentive. They may also be used, as they are in sports programs, to emphasize strength and majesty and to show viewers actions that normally occur too quickly for the human eye to comprehend. Consider the Mountain Dew commercial in which a cyclist chases a cheetah and pulls a can of soda from its throat—initially aired during the 2000 *Super Bowl* (available on TVStyleBook.com). Both fast and slow motion are used in this spot. The cyclist's pedaling as he gains on the cheetah is shown in speeded up action—making it seem faster than is humanly possible. Slow motion is used in several shots: the cheetah running, the bicyclist leaping on it, and the bicyclist's friends pouring Mountain Dew down their throats. By using slow motion, we are able to see details in the cheetah's running and the bicyclist's leap that we wouldn't discern at regular speed. And the slow-motion pouring enhances the appearance of the Mountain Dew—in theory making it more appealing.

Color was the last major videographic component of television classicism to evolve—coming to television through a complicated and circuitous route during the 1950s and 1960s. Once it was established, however, narrative programs discontinued use of black-and-white, with only very rare exceptions. Color's arrival thus signaled the beginning of black-and-white as a counter-television component. Before color became the norm, it was itself capable of hailing viewers. Imagine how striking a color commercial must have seemed to viewers who were accustomed to black-and-white imagery. Today, commercials commonly use black-and-white or sepia-toned images to allude to the past, but, as in many music videos, the significance of black-and-white imagery is not always so clear. Take for example a spot about estrogen loss during menopause, sponsored by the pharmaceutical company American Home Products and broadcast, among other places, during the sitcom *Everybody Loves Raymond* (1996–2005), which, not surprisingly, is in color (available on TVStyleBook.com). Actress Lauren Hutton is shown cooking vegetables, running along the beach, and talking about menopause. Half of the shots are in color and half are in black-and-white. The black-and-white images are not supposed to be from the past and, indeed, there is no obvious meaning one can glean from the black-and-white cinematography—aside from the counter-television function of differentiating this commercial from the color programs during which it appears.

Extreme camera movement, angle, and focal length—the final three videographic elements in Table 3.1—are not as distinct as the other videographic techniques. Instead of being unambiguous violations of classical television style, they are more intensifications of techniques ordinarily used in conventional narrative programs. Where classical programs often include some camera movement (to follow action), slightly low/high angles and various focal lengths (wide angle to telephoto), commercials incorporate camera gyrations, odd low/high angles and focal lengths that are so extreme the optical distortion is evident. Unusually active camera movements are apparent in the Coca-Cola rave commercial discussed above. And strange angles and focal lengths may be observed in the off-balance, low-angle shot of a scooter-rider in a WorldCom commercial (Figure 3.20) and the wide-angle shot of an Infiniti car (Figure 3.21). When distortion is this exaggerated it draws attention to itself and violates the principal classical tenet of invisible, unobtrusive style. This, then, is the definition of Caldwell's televisual exhibitionism.

Figure 3.20 WorldCom: an excessively low and wide-angle shot of a man on a scooter.

Editing

The first thing one notices about the editing of many commercials is its speed—as is discussed in the Pillsbury Crescent roll commercial in Chapter 1 (Figures 1.43–1.57). The editing in commercials is typically paced faster than that in soap operas, sitcoms, and prime-time dramas.

Figure 3.21 A wide-angle lens distorts the hood of an Infiniti car.

The sample episodes from *As the World Turns* analyzed above, for example, have an average shot length (ASL) of 4.84 seconds, while the Pillsbury commercial's ASL barely tops one second, which is still considerably quicker than the ASLs of two and three seconds which are common in intensified-continuity programs and theatrical films.[26] Rapid editing serves as a hailing device because each shot quickly presents new information for viewers to absorb. Additionally, viewers are constantly adjusting to different framing, composition, and camera angle. Each cut is a potential disruption as we instantaneously move from one camera position to another and new visuals are thrown before our eyes. This visual disorientation is used by commercials to jolt us into gazing at the advertised product.

Commercials, even narrative-based ones, are also not bound by the rules of classical, continuity editing and its pursuit of an invisible, seamless style. Jump cuts and breaches of the 180-degree rule abound in television ads. A 2008 commercial for Taco Bell illustrates the commercial's flexible use of continuity editing (see TVStyleBook.com). Broadcast on cable-television network, Comedy Central, on June 14, 2008, during *Reno 911!* (2003–), it tells the story of a group of individuals buying inexpensive food and ecstatically consuming it. In 15 seconds, the commercial presents 24 shots—most less than one second long and three only ten *frames* long (one-third of a second). Its average shot length is a mere 0.6 seconds (18 frames) and its median shot length is only 0.52 seconds (15.5 frames). Table 3.2 presents its first five shots and two later shots.

The commercial begins with a fairly conventional handheld establishing long shot of a Taco Bell restaurant taken from a moving car, a portion of which is barely visible in the frame (Figure 3.22). The camera cuts to a close-up of the driver of a convertible—a conventional cut from long shot to close-up (Figure 3.23). But then the classical editing goes haywire. The driver begins to point with her left hand, but we cut to another passenger, from an indeterminate position, pointing with her (presumably a woman's) right hand in shot three (Figure 3.24). This violates the classical stylistic schema because it does not match the action of the first shot and does not clearly establish the space of the scene; in fact, it confounds it. This third shot rapidly pulls focus to an illuminated menu (Figure 3.25), showcasing Taco Bell's inexpensive offerings. "Why pay more!"—which is the main point of the commercial—is visible at the top of the menu. A grammatically correct question mark has been replaced by the more emphatic exclamation point. The commercial's on-screen text later reinforces this thrifty message (again without a question mark): "More stuff. Less cash. Why pay more." The fourth, following shot is an overhead medium close-up of the driver picking through change (Figure 3.26), an acceptable classical cut showing us a detail from the scene. Close examination of Figure 3.26 reveals that the driver's seat is mostly empty, as if the driver is now out of the car; but this would probably not be perceived by the television viewer since the shot is only 19 frames long (about two-thirds of a second). The next cut, however, violates classical principles as we jump cut from the driver's hands to a man who has not previously appeared, giving

Table 3.2 Taco Bell Commercial *découpage*

Shot Number, Scale, and Length	Figure	Sound	Action/Camera Movement
1 long shot 11 frames (*Figure 3.22*)		No dialogue. Music, with lyrics, throughout.	All shots are handheld.
2 close-up 20 frames (*Figure 3.23*)			
3 close-up 33 frames (*Figures 3.24–3.25*)			Pull focus to...

continued

Table 3.2 continued

Shot Number, Scale, and Length	Figure	Sound	Action/Camera Movement
4 medium close-up 19 frames (*Figure 3.26*)			
5 medium shot 24 frames (*Figure 3.27*)			
Additional shots 15 close-up 13 frames (*Figure 3.28*)			
20 long shot 29 frames (*Figure 3.29*)			

the change to a mostly off-screen Taco Bell employee (Figure 3.27). The rest of the commercial contains seemingly random images of people eating—including the driver (Figure 3.28)—interspersed with shots of menu prices. One individual is so overcome with Taco Bell *jouissance* that he leaps on to the top of a car and throws his arms in the air (Figure 3.29). The camera hops from one person to the next, with little regard for continuity conventions. If this editing were used in a conventional segment from a narrative program, it would violate contemporary stylistic schemas, but it works effectively in this commercial because it:

1   uses utopian style to strongly convey the celebratory response provoked by Taco Bell's menu choices (as imagined by Taco Bell's advertising team); and
2   its editing style differentiates it from the narrative program it interrupted, the mockumentary, *Reno 911!*

Jerky, discontinuous editing is not unheard of in narrative programs, but series of shots such as those in Table 3.2 would commonly be relegated to Eisensteinian montage sequences where time and information are compressed. Such montages are relatively rare in narrative programs and so their frequent use in commercials helps distinguish them from the program they're interrupting.

Sound

Sound in commercials may be broken down into terms of speech and music. The style of speech in commercials has been addressed at numerous points above—including its importance to hailing and direct address. Unlike dialogue in narrative programs, commercial speech must be persuasive in some fashion and it must be succinct because it doesn't have much time to persuade us. Also, the presence of an announcer's voice distinguishes commercial speech from narrative programs and aligns it with news and sports programs. As in news and sports, a voice that is not part of the commercial's diegetic world talks over it. It is a voice of authority—speaking directly to viewers and urging them to be convinced by the commercial's rhetoric. In both the Apple "1984" and Pillsbury Crescent rolls commercials discussed previously, non-diegetic narrators conclude the spots with final attempts at persuasion.

The music of commercials is yet another rhetorical device that has less in common with narrative programs than with another television genre—specifically, the music video. This is not surprising since music videos are essentially commercials for music and musicians. The principal similarity between commercial music and music videos and the crucial difference between it and non-diegetic music in narrative programs is a seemingly simple one: both commercials and music videos use songs with lyrics while non-diegetic music normally does not (excepting non-diegetic music where it is clearly commenting on the action—as when a popular love song plays while lovers walk beside a river). Why is this apparently modest distinction so important? Because the use of lyrics—jingles in the case of commercials—draws one's attention to the music itself and classical, non-diegetic music isn't devised for that. Non-diegetic music strives for invisibility, hoping to shape the emotions of viewers without being noticed. Jingles, in contrast, are designed to be noticed and, of course, to be remembered.

Graphics and Animation

Almost every commercial on television contains some graphics (letters, numbers, cartoon characters, and corporate logos) on the screen. As we have seen exemplified in Apple's "1984" spot, the most common use of text is a redundant reinforcement of speech. Announcers speak their scripts and the same or similar words crawl up the screen—frequently at the conclusion of the spot and usually accompanied by the product's visual emblem, its brand identity further reinforced by its logo. In the case of "1984," the distinctive Apple logo (an apple with a bite taken out) follows the concluding text. Text is not limited to this redundant function, however. It may also supplement, clarify, and disclaim the explicit meanings of the dialogue and the implicit meanings of the images. The supplementing role of text is best exemplified in the nearly illegible legal qualifications included at the end of commercials for contests, car dealerships, and the like. Tiny on-screen text provides disclaimers and clarifications that the advertisers wish to downplay. Since the 1960s, the U.S. Federal Trade Commission has cracked down on misleading claims in medicinal and food advertising—leading to more and more disclaimers. Consequently, many ads now contain seemingly unnecessary warnings such as, "Use only as directed," in order to avoid legal liability. A Crest toothpaste commercial's spoken dialogue entreats us to "Get ready for a whole new level of clean. Introducing advanced cleaning from Crest Multi-Care." The dialogue implies that Multi-Care is measurably superior to other brands. However, in small text the ad clarifies that Multi-Care is only advanced "VS. CREST CAVITY PROTECTION"—that is, in comparison to other Crest products. It might well lag behind other brands in terms of toothpaste technology. The ad only certifies that the product has advanced beyond Crest's previous level of cavity protection, just in case the FTC or the lawyers for Colgate were preparing litigation.

One final example of textual disclaimers is found in the case of dramatizations. For instance, a Saran Wrap ad visually presents what appears to be a documentary—an unmanipulated record—of a test of its plastic wrap and that of its competitor, Reynolds Aluminum. A blind-folded woman sniffs an onion in both wraps and is repelled when the smelly odor escapes from Reynolds Wrap. But it's all a fiction, a dramatization. However, we must read the fine print to realize this. Only there does text disclaim what the images proclaim—that, despite appearances, this is an actor pretending to be repulsed (Figure 3.30). Once again, television blithely blurs the distinction between character and "real person"—as previously discussed in Vicks cough medicine and Bartles & James commercials.

Redundant, reinforcing text and small-print disclaimers are important functions of television graphics, but equally significant is the ability of graphics to catch viewers' eyes, to hail or entreat them to look at the screen. In this regard, they may be added to our list of counter-television techniques. Classical narrative television and film do not overlay the image with graphics. Counter cinema, as can be seen in the work of Jean-Luc Godard, often counterpointed images with graphics, providing the film-maker with a way of breaking classical illusionism and making pointed commentary about contemporary consumer culture. Commercials also break narrative illusionism as they interrupt the diegetic flow in order to pointedly sell products to consumers. As noted before, Marxist counter-cinema techniques may be co-opted for rather anti-Marxist purposes. Of course, text-over-image is less distinctive in the television context because it is a common feature of sports and news programs. Still, the argument may be made that graphics-heavy commercials, inserted into the midst of a soap opera, sitcom, or police drama may use text-over-image to jar viewers out of their narrative cocoon. Certainly, hailing viewers is the function of promotional text displayed in the lower-third of images during narrative programs (as in *As The World Turns*, Figures 1.8–1.11).

Figure 3.30 Saran Wrap: the fine print disclaims what the image proclaims. What appears to be a "real person" is actually an actor.

One feature of television graphics that makes them particularly compelling is the ability of text and cartoon elements to be animated, for moving graphics are enormously more attention-grabbing than static ones. The promotional text in Figures 1.8–1.11 does not just blink on and off the screen. Rather, it slides on and off the screen and includes an animated accent in the background. Animation in commercials arrived with television's growth in the 1940s and early 1950s, but it was initially limited to techniques borrowed from the cinema. For example, a 1950s commercial for Philco refrigerators has a cartoon pixie flitting about the crisper and ends with text fading in over a seal of quality: "Philco famous for quality the world over" (Figures 3.31, 3.32; available on TVStyleBook.com). The animated pixie and the simple fading in of the characters were created on film, using an optical printer. On most commercials, the graphical elements are sliding or floating or otherwise moving. Further, commercial graphics use an illusion of three-dimensionality to make letters and numbers appear to rise toward the viewer. Even in this 40-year-old spot, the 3-D shading on the "Philco quality" letters gives them a more dynamic aspect.

As Margaret Morse explains in her history of television graphics, the movement and three-dimensionality of graphic elements accelerated phenomenally with the development of computer technology in the late 1970s and 1980s. Today, hyperactive letters and logos often seem to be flying past us

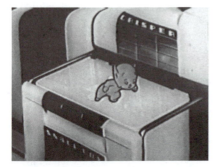

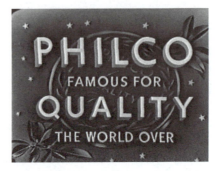

Figure 3.31 An animated pixie appears on top of a photograph of a Philco refrigerator.

Figure 3.32 Shading creates a primitive three-dimensional effect...

or us toward them. In the opening credits for *As the World Turns*—a program not known for its visual flourishes—the title comes from a virtual space *behind* us (Figure 3.33), rotating and swooping towards a globe constructed out of images from the program (Figure 3.34; available on TVStyleBook.com).[27] The title then comes back toward us and we ostensibly pass *through* the "o" of "World" (Figure 3.35). "The viewer ... seems to be freed from gravity in a virtual experience of giddy speed through a symbolic universe of abc's,"[28] notes Morse regarding similar sequences. In such a universe, the letters are far from flat or two-dimensional. The movement of the *As the World Turns* letters and their design makes them look like thick pieces of glass, with a sense of density and smooth texture.

Graphics flying toward the viewer are the visual equivalent of verbal direct address. Consider that, in narrative programs, the visuals are designed much like the theater—as if a fourth wall has been removed and you are peering into a room. This is particularly true in sitcoms and soap operas because their sets are constructed with a missing fourth wall, but it also holds true for prime-time dramas shot on location. Consequently, there is limited actor movement in

Figure 3.33 ...which became much more elaborate in the era of computer-generated graphics. Even *As the World Turns*, a soap opera, features text virtually flying through space...

Figure 3.34 ...nearly colliding with this world of images...

depth—toward or away from the camera. The action mostly occurs on a plane perpendicular to the camera's and thus more left-and-right and less back-and-forth. Actors do not enter sitcom/soap opera sets from behind the camera the way the letters in the *As the World Turns* title sequence do. And actors do not exit by walking toward and past the camera the way the *As the World Turns* title does. When graphic elements behave this way, they, in a sense, say to viewers, "Pay attention! Here we come— right towards you." In commercials, animated graphics serve a similar purpose to

Figure 3.35 …and seeming to careen toward the viewer, as if the camera could move into the letters.

announcers speaking directly to the viewers. Both hail viewers—one through visually moving words and the other through verbally spoken ones. As Morse argues, these graphics are predecessors of increasingly interactive computer environments, from first-person games (popularized by *Doom* and *Quake*) to virtual reality worlds (e.g., *Second Life*).

A final and obvious form of animation in television commercials is the use of cartoon characters. The Pillsbury Doughboy and Speedy Alka-Seltzer, discussed above (see Figures 3.17 and 1.57, respectively), are just two of the non-human entities called upon to pitch products on television. The function of these characters (differentiating products) has not changed much over the past 60-odd years of television commercials. However, it should be mentioned that computer animation has had a major impact upon the technology used to create these characters. Up until the 1990s, animated characters were either drawn or were created through stop-action animation (the frame-by-frame movement of dolls), as in the case with Speedy Alka-Seltzer. Now, however, animated characters are usually computer generated—as in the current incarnations of Speedy and the Pillsbury Doughboy.

Violating Reality Through Visual Effects

"In a medium whose very essence is the ability to reproduce the look of everyday reality, one of the surest ways of attracting the viewer's attention is to violate that reality,"[29] contends Messaris. What intrigues him is advertising's use of distorted imagery to make a viewer notice a product. Studies in cognitive psychology show that this distortion is most effective when it varies only slightly from a familiar object. As Messaris explains,

> if the discrepancy between the unfamiliar shape and some preexisting one is only partial, the mental task of fitting in the new shape becomes more complicated. As a result, such partially strange shapes can cause us to pay closer attention.[30]

If an object is wholly different from what you are familiar with, you may ignore it completely or place it in a new visual category; but if it is partially similar then your cognitive processes work overtime to figure out whether or not it is a familiar object.

Messaris cites computer morphing as a prime example of this principle. Michael Allen takes Messaris' perspective one step further, contending, "One particular type of digital effect—morphing—has almost become an emblem for the entire field [of digital visual effects] in the public imagination."[31] A morph takes two dissimilar objects and creates a seamless transition from one to the other. In so doing, it creates a strange, reality-violating hybrid of two familiar objects. Morphing first came to viewers' attention in the films *Willow* (1988) and *Terminator 2: Judgment Day* (1991) where humans morph into various animal and robotic shapes, but it found its widest exposure in Michael Jackson's *Black or White* music video (with digital effects created by Pacific Data Images) and television commercials in the 1990s (see examples on TVStyleBook.com). Notably, *Black or White* and a Schick Tracer razor commercial both morph between a variety of faces. In the former, individuals of

Figure 3.36 In Michael Jackson's music video for the song "Black or White," an image of a Caucasian woman...

Figure 3.37 ...morphs into...

Figure 3.38 ...an African-American woman.

Figure 3.39 Cinnamon Toast Crunch cereal: a commonplace office is disrupted by a giant hand—fabricated through digital special effects.

various races blend together—a young Caucasian woman turning into an African-American one, for example (Figures 3.36–3.38). And in the latter, the shifting faces effectively communicate the idea that the Tracer will fit any shaped face and, simultaneously, they entice viewers to concentrate on the ad by violating the reality of human physiognomy—when one man transforms into another. Morphing is just one example of violating reality through visual effects (VFX).[32] By the 2000s it was already being surpassed by new advances in computer-generated imagery (CGI)—leading to widespread incorporation of visual effects in commercials. What makes digital effects particularly successful is their uncanny resemblance to the real world. To choose one example from many, consider a Cinnamon Toast Crunch cereal ad where a man is slaving away in his office cubicle. Suddenly, a giant, VFX hand reaches down and starts pushing him around, giving him tasty cereal to eat and a video game to play with (Figure 3.39). Initially, it looks like the familiar office scene, but then an incongruous and fantastic element intrudes into that reality. As Messaris might say, "It gives us a jolt, and it gets us to look."[33]

Reflexivity and Intertextuality

Commercials thrive on the television cannibalism that is reflexivity. Television commercials frequently parody films, television programs, other commercials, and even themselves in their efforts to market a product. Energizer batteries were featured in a series of advertisements where a plausible but sham commercial (usually a sly spoof of a familiar one) is interrupted by a battery-powered toy rabbit intruding into the frame. In one, a commercial for the non-existent Nasatine sinus medicine is suspended when the drum-beating bunny comes through (Figure 3.40). In essence, the Energizer rabbit spots are commercials consuming other commercials. The Energizer spots were particularly remarkable for the accuracy of their parodies. The Nasatine spot includes Anacin-style animation and a copyright notice for a fake pharmaceutical company, Clow Laboratories. Reflexive commercials refer first of all to other television material, rather than referring directly to reality where their products actually reside. In essence, an extra layer of television has been added. A close relation to parody is pastiche, the use of fragments of previous texts that is presumed to be one of the foundations of the postmodern condition.[34] Popular songs, for example, are regularly put to new uses by advertisers. The Knack's "My Sharona" was turned into "My Chalupa" by Taco Bell and Cream's "I Feel Free" sells Hyundai cars (discussed above). Even the Beatles' "Revolution" has been used in a Nike shoe commercial (though it did result in a lawsuit against Nike). Pastiche

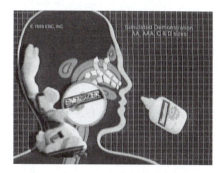

Figure 3.40 In reflexive fashion, the Energizer Bunny spoofs a commercial for a non-existent nose-spray product.

Figure 3.41 A Diet Coke ad creates a digital pastiche of singer Paula Abdul and long-dead comedian Groucho Marx.

in television commercials has reached new heights of technological sophistication since the advent of digital visual effects. One Diet Coke ad, for instance, has Paula Abdul dancing with and talking to film actors/characters Gene Kelly, Cary Grant, and Groucho Marx (Figure 3.41).

Parody and pastiche are two examples of television's high degree of intertextuality, drawing it away from the world outside television and reflecting it back on itself. One television text (a commercial) refers to another (a program or previous commercial), which may well refer to another and another. Commercials are an integral part of this network of meanings and allusions. Familiar songs and images provide a shorthand for developing the persuasive argument for a product. Why write a new jingle when an old tune is already inscribed on our minds? Why refer to real events when we are more comfortable with television reality? Commercials nourish and are nourished by intertextuality and reflexivity. One irony here, however, is that commercials must always contain a call to action that will occur outside the television world and at a later time. They can never wholly submerge into a postmodern miasma of sliding, shifting simulacra with no anchors in "reality."[35] For it is only in that reality that products are purchased and money exchanged.

"Capitalism in Action"

Narrative television may exist in a hermetically sealed universe where the characters only see each other (and not the viewer) and reality is highly mediated through genre conventions and stylistic schemas. The commercial, however, is not allowed those luxuries. It must hail viewers and it must provoke them to take action in the real world and it need not be subtle about it. Commercials' style may be rude and obvious or entertaining and obscure, but in some fashion it must always attempt to convince the viewer. Style in commercials, unlike that in classical narrative television and film, doesn't need to be invisible. Indeed, its forthright visibility may well help draw viewers' interest to the product and impel them to make a purchase. At the start of a commercial break on ABC one evening in fall 2000, a graphic appeared that mocked itself: "And now capitalism in action." On U.S. television, commercials are the most visible effect of the medium's underlying economic system. Multinational corporations strike deals with wholesalers (networks, syndicators, and national spot representatives) when they wish to buy television time for national exposure. And local merchants buy television time from individual stations and cable systems when they are shopping for exposure in a specific designated market areas (DMAs). These purchases of time are essentially purchases of viewers' attention as it has been calculated by

Nielsen Media Research. TV's wholesalers and retailers use the money they have exchanged for their viewers' time to rent programming materials from production companies, with the goal of attracting more viewers and/or viewers of a more desirable demographic. And that is U.S. television capitalism in action.

The television commercial is currently under siege from DVRs, remote controls, online video, and other devices, services, and distractions that undercut the commercial's ability to hail the viewer. Advertisers are understandably panicked and are desperately seeking new ways to reach the consumer. At the time of this writing (spring 2009), the future of the television commercial is murky; but it seems likely that it will reinvent itself, as the past 60 years of broadcasting have shown how resilient the television commercial is. Too much of broadcast television's infrastructure relies upon the commercial for it to disappear. It also seems like that the commercial's reinvention will feature new articulations of television style.

Notes

1. Paul Messaris, *Visual Persuasion: The Role of Images in Advertising* (Thousand Oaks: Sage, 1997), 164.
2. See Mike Budd, Steve Craig, and Clay Steinman, *Consuming Environments: Television and Commercial Culture* (New Brunswick: Rutgers University Press, 1999); Sut Jhally, *The Codes of Advertising: Fetishism and the Political Economy of Meaning in the Consumer Society* (New York: Routledge, 1987); Jean Kilbourne, *Deadly Persuasion: Why Women and Girls Must Fight the Addictive Power of Advertising* (New York: The Free Press, 1999); Messaris, *Visual Persuasion*; and Ellen Seiter, *Sold Separately: Children and Parents in Consumer Culture* (New Brunswick: Rutgers University Press, 1993).
3. Jeremy G. Butler, *Television: Critical Methods and Applications*, 3rd edn (Mahwah: Lawrence Erlbaum Associates, 2007), 363–88.
4. Sergei Eisenstein, "Methods of Montage," in *Film Form*, trans. Jay Leyda (New York: Harcourt, Brace & World, 1949), 72–83. Further elaborated in Jacques Aumont, *Montage Eisenstein*, trans. Lee Hildreth, Constance Penley, and Andrew Ross (Bloomington: Indiana University Press, 1987), 156–70.
5. See Messaris, *Visual Persuasion*, 196–203, for further discussion of generalization in ads.
6. Ibid., xviii.
7. Ibid., xix.
8. Richard Dyer, "Entertainment and Utopia," in *Movies and Methods: An Anthology*, vol. 2, ed. Bill Nichols (Berkeley: University of California Press, 1985), 222–6.
9. Rosser Reeves, *Reality in Advertising* (New York: Alfred A. Knopf, 1961), 46–9. Moreover, he defined advertising as "the art of getting a unique selling proposition into the heads of the most people at the lowest possible cost" (121).
10. Sut Jhally, *The Codes of Advertising*, 127; quoting D. Pope, *The Making of Modern Advertising* (New York: Basic Books, 1982), 287.
11. Reeves, *Reality in Advertising*, 62.
12. Louis Althusser, "Ideology and Ideological State Apparatuses," in *Lenin and Philosophy and Other Essays*, trans. Ben Brewster (New York: Monthly Review Press, 1970), www.marxists.org/reference/archive/althusser/1970/ideology.htm, *Louis Althusser Archive* (accessed June 12, 2008).
13. John Thornton Caldwell, *Televisuality: Style, Crisis, and Authority in American Television* (New Brunswick: Rutgers University Press, 1995), 352.

14. David Bordwell, *The Way Hollywood Tells It: Story and Style in Modern Movies* (Berkeley: University of California Press, 2006), 120.

15. She writes,

> Technique is hardly worth talking about unless it's used for something worth doing: that's why most of the theorizing about the new art of television commercials is such nonsense. The effects are impersonal—dexterous, sometimes clever, but empty of art. It's because of their emptiness that commercials call so much attention to their camera angles and quick cutting—which is why people get impressed by "the art" of it. Movies are now often made in terms of what television viewers have learned to settle for.
>
> (Pauline Kael, "Trash, Art and the Movies," in *Going Steady* [New York: Bantam, 1970], 116, www.paulrossen.com/paulinekael/trashartandthemovies. html [accessed June 17, 2008])

16. Ibid. Quoted in David Bordwell, *Figures Traced in Light: On Cinematic Stage* (Berkeley: University of California Press, 2005), 32.

17. Bertolt Brecht, "The Modern Theatre is the Epic Theatre," in *Brecht on Theatre*, ed. John Willett (New York: Hill and Wang, 1964), 33–42; Peter Wollen, "Godard and Counter Cinema: *Vent D'est*," in *Readings and Writings: Semiotic Counter-Strategies* (London: Verso, 1982), 79–91.

18. Laura Mulvey, "Visual Pleasure and Narrative Cinema," *Screen* 16, no. 3 (autumn 1975): 6–18, wiki.brown.edu/confluence/display/MarkTribe/Visual+Pleasure+and +Narrative+Cinema (accessed June 13, 2008).

19. Summarized toward the end of the decade in Stephen Heath, "Notes on Suture," *Screen* 18 no. 4 (winter 1977/8): 48–76, www.lacan.com/symptom8_articles/ heath8.html (accessed June 13, 2008). A recent overview is provided by Edward Branigan, *Projecting a Camera* (New York: Routlege, 2006), 133–45.

20. Wheeler Winston Dixon, *It Looks at You: The Returned Gaze of the Cinema* (Albany: State University of New York Press, 1995).

21. Marc Vernet, "The Look of the Camera," trans. Dana Polan, *Cinema Journal* 28, no. 2 (winter 1989): 48.

22. Of course, there are many exceptions, especially in the realm of comedy. Among the earliest is George Burns directly addressing both the television viewer and the in-studio audience during *The George Burns and Gracie Allen Show* (1950–8).

23. John Ellis explores the power of direct address in television: John Ellis, *Visible Fictions: Cinema Television Video* (New York: Routledge, 1992), 134.

24. Jeremy G. Butler, "'I'm Not a Doctor, But I Play One on TV': Characters, Actors, and Acting in Television Soap Opera," *Cinema Journal* 30, no. 4 (summer 1991): 75–91. Reprinted in *To Be Continued ... Soap Operas Around the World*, ed. Robert C. Allen (New York: Routledge, 1995), 145–63.

25. For more on music videos, see Blaine Allan, "Musical Cinema, Music Video, Music Television," *Film Quarterly* 43, no. 3 (spring 1990): 2–14; Gary Burns and Robert Thompson, "Music, Television, and Video: Historical and Aesthetic Considerations," *Popular Music and Society* 11, no. 3 (1987): 11–25; Andrew Goodwin, *Dancing in the Distraction Factory: Music Television and Popular Culture* (Minneapolis: University of Minnesota Press, 1992); Andrew Goodwin, Simon Frith, and Lawrence Grossberg, eds., *Sound and Vision: The Music Video Reader* (London: Routledge, 1993); E. Ann Kaplan, *Rocking Around the Clock: Music Television, Postmodernism, and Consumer Culture* (New York: Methuen, 1987); Margaret Morse, "Post Synchronizing Rock Music and Television," *Journal of Communication Inquiry* 10, no. 1 (winter 1986): 15–28, reprinted in *Television Criticism: Approaches and Applications*, eds. Leah R. Vande Berg and Lawrence A. Wenner (New York: Longman, 1991). I am indebted to Blaine Allan for these suggestions.

26. Bordwell, *The Way Hollywood Tells It*, 121–4.

27. From November 1, 1999 to July 5, 2002, according to David R. Jackson, "ATWT

Opening/Closing Sequence," *Classic As the World Turns*, www.geocities.com/Tele-visionCity/Studio/5185/titles.html (accessed June 12, 2008).

28. Margaret Morse, *Virtualities: Television, Media Art, and Cyberculture* (Blooming-ton: Indiana University Press, 1998), 72.
29. Messaris, *Visual Persuasion*, 5.
30. Ibid., 7.
31. Michael Allen, "From *Bwana Devil* to *Batman Forever*: Technology in Contempor-ary Hollywood Cinema," in *Contemporary Hollywood Cinema*, eds. Steve Neale and Murray Smith (New York: Routledge, 1998), 125.
32. In contemporary usage, "visual effects" (VFX) most commonly refers to image manipulation in post-production. In contrast, "special effects" typically designates physical or mechanical effects created on the set, such as pyrotechnics or model work.
33. Messaris, *Visual Persuasion*, 7.
34. Fredric Jameson, *Postmodernism, Or, The Cultural Logic of Late Capitalism* (Raleigh: Duke University Press, 1991). A summary, although a bit dated, of the connection between television and postmodernism is Jim Collins, "Television and Postmodernism," in *Channels of Discourse, Reassembled* (Chapel Hill: University of North Carolina Press, 1992), 327–53. For a broader consideration of "pastiche," see Richard Dyer, *Pastiche* (London: Routledge, 2007).
35. For a discussion of simulacra, see Jean-Louis Baudrillard, *Simulations* (New York: Semiotexte, 1983).

4.

Style in an Age of Media Convergence

> We are in an age of media transition, one marked by tactical decisions and unintended consequences, mixed signals and competing interest, and most of all, unclear directions and unpredictable outcomes.[1]
>
> (Henry Jenkins)

A printed book may well be the worst medium in which to discuss the quickly accelerating and recondite changes going on in television today. A book's lead time of a year or more virtually guarantees it will be out of date the moment it appears.[2] The only future-proof aspect of media convergence is what was already evident in 1983 to the "prophet of convergence," Ithiel de Sola Pool, who wrote, "There is no immutable law of growing convergence; the process of change is more complicated than that."[3] Today, Old Media are flailing about, keening about their precipitously declining revenues while New Media make grand claims about the digital revolution, but cannot seem to make that revolution profitable, to "monetize" it, in their parlance.[4] Thus, although it is clear that the broadcast and print media are changing in ways as significant as the impact television had on radio after World War II, there is little consensus on how the process will evolve or what the end result will be. When Jenkins assayed the state of television's convergence with other media in 2006's *Convergence Culture* he encountered a profoundly unclear situation and bemoaned, "Writing this book has been challenging because everything seems to be changing at once and there is no vantage point that takes me above the fray."[5] Yet even though the endpoint of the process remains unclear, there are important lessons to be learned from examining how the current process of convergence has historically developed. The clumsy online efforts of NBC's long-running, old-media program, *ER* (1994–2009), in the late 1990s can elucidate how convergence can both fail and succeed, semiotically and aesthetically. Most importantly in the context of this book's overarching project, an examination of the show can help us begin to understand how convergence will affect television style. Technological changes frequently have their greatest impact in the realm of style, as, for example, the move to color television did in the 1960s. The current evolution/revolution is no exception. We can already see how the YouTube generation has different expectations for the look and sound of visual stories than do previous generations raised on television and the cinema, *sans* Internet. *ER* taps into much of that stylistic change, making for an illuminating case study of the impact of technological and cultural change upon stylistic schemas.

The State of Convergence in the 1990s

In an attempt to generate media and public interest in *ER*'s fourth season, the debut was broadcast live and several online events accompanied it. NBC touted it as more than just a television broadcast. It was to be a "cyber-event"—the first joint effort of NBC and Warner Bros. Online.[6] "Anything Can Happen On-Air or Online!," warned one breathless press release about this "unprecedented" season premiere.[7] We were told to expect spontaneous, perhaps obscene, improvisation and daring, without-a-net performances. The tight hegemonic control that broadcast networks exercise over their programming was going to be rent asunder, we were led to believe. Clearly, NBC succeeded in its attempts to create a media event with this broadcast. The episode scored a 31.2 Nielsen rating and a massive 46 share—making it the third most watched episode in the history of U.S. television dramas, trailing only *Dallas*' "Who Shot J.R.?" episode and the series finale of *Magnum, P.I.* (from 1980 and 1988, respectively).[8] However, the "liveness" of this live event was actually quite limited. The actors improvised very little—staying remarkably close to the script, according to the person who did the closed captioning—and there were few disruptions of the staging.[9] Moreover, the success of its simultaneous cyber-event was debatable. Its website offered little more than text-based, behind-the-scenes chats with the cast and crew, a "virtual tour" of its sets, and a few meager RealVideo clips. This was hardly state-of-the-art digital technology for 1997.

What intrigues me about *ER* (the program), "Ambush" (the live episode), and *ERLive* (the website) is what they can tell us about the convergence of film, television, and the digital realm. As the millennium ended we began to see useful, interdisciplinary investigations into these converging media. Much as John Ellis' *Visible Fictions* mapped the media terrain of the 1980s, so did Margaret Morse's *Virtualities* and Janet H. Murray's *Hamlet on the Holodeck* provide insights into film, television, and digital media of the 1990s and beyond.[10] What I propose to do here is offer some thoughts on *ER*'s use of the conventions of the cinema, television, and digital, online media in the 1990s. I am most interested in identifying the stylistic conventions in the program and its Web presence and interrogating their signifying functions. How does *ER* use apparatuses of the cinema, television, and the digital realm to construct an immensely popular, meaning-bearing cultural artifact?

Jean Renoir's Legacy: *The Crime of M. Lange* Comes to Prime-Time Television

Although many of its fans would bristle at the suggestion, *ER*'s thematic and narrative structures are virtually indistinguishable from the less prestigious daytime soap operas examined in Chapter 1. In both *ER* and soap opera, a large set of characters interacts with one another in continuing stories, some of which take months to resolve. A quick examination of its narrative threads leads one to issues of birth, death, disease, guilt, innocence, gossip, and romance—all of which have previously been identified in soap operas.[11] And yet, *ER* is not perceived as a soap opera or "normal" television. A large part of this perception is due to its "cinematic" stylistic schema. As we have seen in *Miami Vice* (Chapter 2), *ER*'s *mise-en-scène* and cinematography resemble those of a theatrically released film. This style serves several functions, but the most important of these is product differentiation. *ER*'s cinematic single-camera schema differentiates it from multiple-camera daytime soap opera (compare with the contrast between single-camera and multiple-camera television comedies, as arrayed in Table 5.3). Its *particular use* of cinematic style helps set it apart from similarly themed prime-time shows such as *Chicago Hope*, which premiered just one day before *ER* (September 18 and 19, 1994).[12] Aside from product differentiation, however, *ER*'s visual/audial style is significant as an emblem of media convergence. Examining *ER*'s articulation of a cinematic schema will thus help us understand how film and television are approaching one another, and, also, as I will discuss later, it can help us understand how these two media are blending with digital media.

As one might expect from a program named for a particular space (the emergency room), the design of *ER*'s space, of its set, is a critical part of its cinematic style. *ER* director Chris Misiano has said, "The space is the through-line for the story."[13] The admitting desk and trauma and operating rooms are fundamental to the program. They serve clear metaphoric functions as the physical incarnation and objective correlatives of birth, disease, violence, and death. In this respect, they are not that different from daytime soap operas. What is remarkable about *ER*'s set design is its three-dimensional articulation of space. To understand its significance, consider first the schematic norm in set design for multiple-camera fictional programs. Daytime soap operas are shot on standing sets on a sound stage (Figure 2.34). Their three-walled sets are typically placed in a row—next to one another, but not connected by doorways or halls. The space of these sets is notably shallow—resembling sets done for live theater with a conventional proscenium. Multiple-camera sitcoms shot before live audiences have developed similar conventions of set design—placing the raisers for the audience behind the cameras (see Chapter 5 for more on sitcom schemas). On such shallow sets, the options for actor movement are rather limited. Directors must "spread performers out like a clothes line," as Bordwell has noted in some early films.[14] In such "planimetric" staging, the actors seldom move toward or away from the camera (the term is art critic Heinrich Wölfflin's, borrowed by Bordwell).[15] Rather, they shuffle back and forth on a plane perpendicular to the dominant camera angle. Or, in geometric terms, one could say they principally move along the x-axis (side-to-side) and seldom move along the z-axis (back-and-forth)—as is discussed by Herbert Zettl.[16]

In striking contrast, *ER*'s principal sets are constructed with four full walls. Some of these walls are "wild," meaning they may be removed for additional shooting space, but reportedly the directors/producers prefer not to "wild out" a wall.[17] Instead, the sets incorporate enough room to allow the presence of cast, crew, and cameras within their four walls. Due to the capacious nature of the sets, *ER* sprawls over *four* sound stages on the Warners lot in Los Angeles—occupying an enormous amount of studio real estate. One sound stage contains the admitting and trauma rooms. Two are devoted to the operating rooms, the "clean" space, and the connecting hallways. The fourth is given over to "swing sets"—sets which change based on the weekly needs of the story and include locations such as the apartments of the characters. These production decisions have evident aesthetic results. With four walls and connecting hallways, the blocking does not have to adhere to proscenium-based aesthetics. The actors may roam the sets at will (or, rather, at the will of the directors) and action may take place in depth.

This freedom of staging has an impact upon *ER*'s lighting design, a design that harkens back to *ER*'s daytime brethren. Because the staging moves fluidly and quickly through several rooms, the cinematographer must light all the rooms relatively evenly. Lighting a stage is a complicated and time-consuming task—made even more difficult in the case of *ER* by the inclusion of *ceilings* on many of the sets. In soap operas/sitcoms, the ceilings are left off so that the lighting grid can illumine the sets. In *ER* the grid is partially blocked and lighting must be done from "natural" sources within the frame; these sources are called "practicals." Although *ER* is one of the most expensive shows on television, it would be prohibitively expensive to light each shot separately, as would be the case in a feature film. Consequently, the lighting in *ER* is usually high key and flat—as was established very early in the program's run. In fact, this shooting style was evident in the title sequence of the series premiere (Figures 4.1–4.3); featuring a series of shots that even includes diegetic maintenance men changing a fluorescent tube in one of the ceiling lights, getting in Mark's way (Figure 4.2).

Zettl maintains that flat lighting carries thematic connotations that contrast with low-key chiaroscuro lighting. Usefully for my purposes, in *Sight Sound Motion* he refers to a hospital corridor as an example of flat lighting:

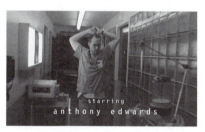

Figure 4.1 The pilot of *ER* begins with Mark making his way down a cluttered hallway with a visible ceiling …

Figure 4.2 … where his path is obstructed by diegetic maintenance men, replacing "practicals."

Figure 4.3 The space of the emergency room, with its four-walled sets, is established as the pilot begins.

Due to the profuse amount of shadowless illumination and increased visibility, we are now inclined to feel that the corridor and so the entire hospital is clean and germ-free; nothing is hidden in dark corners ... it is a
place where we can easily find our way around; and its staff and doctors
must be equally bright and efficient.[18]

Zettl's point is partly borne out by the lighting style employed on *ER*. Cook
County General Hospital (the program's fictional setting) is indeed clean,
sanitary, and remarkably well equipped for an indigent care facility, even if its
staff and doctors are not always so "bright and efficient." As often as not, *ER*'s
literally bright illumination stands in counterpoint to the metaphoric darkness of emergency medicine and the doctors' flawed personal lives.

ER's Kino-Eye

I am kino-eye, I am a mechanical eye.... Now and forever, I free myself
from human immobility, I am in constant motion, I draw near, then away
from objects, I crawl under, I climb onto them.... I plunge and soar with
plunging and soaring bodies. Now I, a camera, fling myself along their
resultant, maneuvering in the chaos of the moment, recording movement,
starting with movements composed of the most complex combinations.[19]

(Dziga Vertov)

ER's distinctive sets would be useless if it weren't for the program's cinematography and overall mode of production, which governs its stylistic schema. It is here
that the program firmly establishes its "cinematic" character. While the majority
of fictional programs on 1990s television were shot using multiple-camera mode
of production—as one can see in the decade's daytime soap operas and prime-
time sitcoms—*ER* was shot on 35 mm film using single-camera mode of production. Of course, single-camera film shooting is also the standard on all 1980s and
1990s prime-time dramas—from the previously discussed *Miami Vice* and
Chicago Hope to the critically acclaimed *NYPD Blue* (1993–2005) to the era's
highest rated single-camera program, *Murder, She Wrote* (1984–96).[20] One could
therefore argue that those programs also embody a cinematic schema. Yet *ER*
employs techniques that differentiate itself from both its narrative cousin, the
soap opera, as well as from other single-camera, prime-time productions.

In multiple-camera shooting, two or three cameras peer into a set from outside
its (absent) fourth wall—seldom entering the space of the set. It is as if they are
covering a basketball game without setting foot on the court. *ER* breaks the virtual
proscenium and positions cameras *within* the set. This has a significant impact on
the way that stories are told. Cutting into the set permits the director to subtly shift
the point-of-view of a scene. As the visual POV shifts, the viewers' attention and,
perhaps, their emotions shift as well. Ken Kwapis, the director of "Be Patient,"
stretched the 180-degree rule to the limit in a "Trauma One" room scene in which
Luka (Goran Visnjic) works on a young girl while her mother watches and Mark
(Anthony Edwards) barks directions (Figures 4.4–4.9). Kwapis cuts among the

various participants—modulating the viewer's center of attention and emotional allegiances. A sequence of shots like this could never have been achieved in a multiple-camera soap opera. The first cut within the "proscenium" would reveal the other cameras looking on from the missing fourth wall of the room. In this instance, the conventional fourth wall, if there were one, would be located at the doors to the Trauma One, from which the camera observes the doctors in action— the point of view shown in Figure 4.4. However, Kwapis reveals those doors and the mother waiting behind them (Figure 4.6) and, more significantly, cuts to a camera positioned from Kovac's POV at the head of the gurney (Figure 4.9), which shows the entire room from across the 180-degree line.

Figure 4.4 Director Ken Kwapis manipulates the 180-degree rule in a complicated *ER* scene where Luka works on an injured girl. This shot initially establishes the orientation of the axis of action.

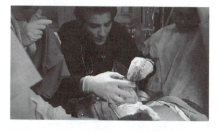

Figure 4.5 Kwapis cuts to a shot on the left side of the gurney, but then cuts back...

Figure 4.6 ...to the girl's mother at the door to the room, where, in a multiple-camera set-up there would be no wall (and, in a sitcom, there would be an audience).

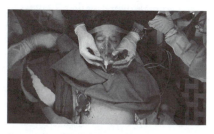

Figure 4.7 An overhead shot is also atypical for multiple-camera productions.

Figure 4.8 Kwapis returns to a tight shot of Luka at the head of the gurney, but then cuts to...

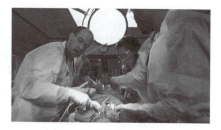

Figure 4.9 ...a reverse angle that breaks the axis of action and reveals three walls of the set.

ER's principal visual strategy to avoid problems with the 180-degree rule and screen direction is to move the camera. When the camera arcs around a character, it quickly establishes new axes of action and reorients the viewer's sense of screen direction. Kwapis's shot list for the scene above illustrates the program's reliance on camera movement:

> STEADICAM/CLOSE on Judy/OTS Wright. PAN w/Wright to find Cleo who leads us to Benton. ARC to find Greene & Kovac. They switch places (Greene moves to palpate belly/Kovac moves to the head of the bed). PUSH-IN and hold as CLOSE TWO-SHOT Kovac & Laura.[21]

Another example from a commonplace, simple scene from "Truth and Consequences" (directed by Steve de Jarnatt) incorporates relatively sophisticated camera movement arcing 360 degrees around Kerry (Laura Innes) and a patient, and showing all four walls of the set (Figures 4.10–4.16), after which the Steadicam backs up into a separate room and travels through it. These arcing, spinning camera movements are fundamental to *ER*'s signature style. Not only did these kinds of movement separate *ER* from soap operas, they also distinguished it from other prime-time dramas, few of which, in 1994, employed much camera movement at all. Even the few earlier programs that were known for their camera movement—particularly Steven Bochco's *Hill Street Blues* (1981–7) and *NYPD Blue* (1993–2005)—do not resemble *ER* in their implementation of it. Bochco's shows utilize overwrought handheld camera work while *ER* favors Steadicam shots. Indeed, *ER* was among the first television programs to employ a Steadicam everyday, a technique later employed by shows such as *Sports Night* (1998–2000) and, more prominently, *The West Wing* (1999–2006).[22] A side effect of the aggressive use of camera movement is that the average length of shots in *ER* is considerably greater than that of contemporary television. The camera moves to reframe actors instead of cutting to a new angle. At a time when, even on sitcoms, the average shot length (ASL) hovered around four seconds, shots on *ER* averaged six or seven seconds, with precredit sequences' ASLs often running around ten seconds. "Ambush" may have set an ASL record for longevity with its long, moving-camera shots and surveillance-camera simulations clocking in at an ASL of over 80 seconds![23] One shot, in particular, lasts almost three and a half minutes. The live telecast of "Ambush" was an aberration, but in some respects it was just the logical conclusion of *ER*'s visual style.

Steadicam movements are quite different from handheld movements—in both their appearance and what they connote. In fictional contexts such as *NYPD Blue* and *The Blair Witch Project* (1999), the stylistic cliché of handheld camera has come to signify a particular sense of realism rooted in the *cinéma vérité* schema (or, at least, in the common perception of *cinéma vérité*). The live episode of *ER* repeatedly takes pains to draw attention to this documentary signification. In the very first shot of "Ambush," a production assistant adjusts a fixed, wide-angle, surveillance-style camera in the lounge (Figures 4.17–4.18). He dusts the lens as he looks directly into it—signaling to the

Figures 4.10–4.15 ER's signature style is built on swirling Steadicam shots. In this one, the camera arcs 360 degrees around Kerry and a patient showing all four walls of the set.

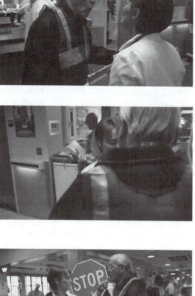

Figure 4.16 The Steadicam shot ends close to where it began its journey.

viewer that this is not a normal broadcast of *ER*, that the camera will be acknowledged. But we should be clear about this. The camera that is acknowledged is still folded within the fiction. This is not counter cinema where the television/cinematic apparatus itself is foregrounded.[24] Just as the production assistant is a character within the diegesis, so is the camera that is acknowledged part of the diegetic world. In this instance, however, a diegetic camera and the non-diegetic camera (the one positioned by *ER* director Thomas Schlamme) record the same images. The signification process of the non-diegetic camera is repressed (*histoire*) while the diegetic camera is marked as a signifier of documentariness. Moreover, the focal length and high camera angle of the episode's first shot signify a new type of documentariness that is currently evolving—nurtured by the surveillance camera footage of

Figure 4.17 An actor portrays a production assistant on the fictional film crew shooting a documentary in the ER. He checks a surveillance camera and…

Figure 4.18 …wipes it clean.

robberies and employee misbehavior shown on nightly news broadcasts and so-called "reality" specials on Fox.[25] The diegetic production assistant explains the function of the break-room camera to Carol (Julianna Margulies): "Get some wide-angles to cut with what the handheld guys shoot. For pace, variety." From this wide-angle shot we cut to one of the "handheld guys'" cameras and the episode is off and running—sometimes literally as when we see the camera operator's feet as he struggles to follow the action. Here, as in "X-Cops," the *X-Files* episode (February 20, 2000) presented as if it were *Cops* (1989–), handheld camera work has obvious documentary connotations.[26] To be precise, however, "Ambush" uses Steadicam shots posing as handheld ones—with significantly steadier results.

"Ambush" aside, *ER*'s numerous Steadicam shots do not normally share these connotations of documentariness with the handheld camera. As Jean-Pierre Geuens has noted, Steadicam movements more closely resemble cinematic tracking shots—effortlessly gliding around the actors—than they do jittery handheld work. He then takes this argument a step further and separates Steadicam movement from dollying or tracking. The Steadicam, he avers, "disembodies vision:" "As a made-to-order companion, the floating, impersonal, inhuman presence penetrates space, appropriating it for the decentered, transnational, postindustrial corporate state of the late twentieth century."[27] Although I am not prepared to argue that Steadicam shots are some sort of panoptic confirmation of the postindustrial corporate state, it seems to me undeniable that Steadicams do not move in the same way that humans do. Rather, they move the way tracking cameras associated with the cinema do—as is exemplified in the opening of Orson Welles's *Touch of Evil* (1958) and the murder scene in Jean Renoir's *The Crime of M. Lange* (1936). The *Lange* scene consists principally of two 180-degree movements cut together into a 360-degree pan/track/crane around a courtyard. André Bazin calls it the "pure spatial expression of the entire *mise en scène*."[28] *ER*'s Steadicam movements function similarly. With camera movements rooted in the cinematic, single-camera mode of production—and nearly impossible in multiple-camera mode—the all-important space of the emergency room, the program's *raison d'être*, is constantly re-articulated. The Steadicam is a marker of a cinematic aesthetic, of prestige, suggesting the presence of a text that might have been directed by a Welles or a Renoir. It thus helps differentiate *ER* as a television product while also solving the problem of maintaining/modifying screen direction on sets that encourage staging along *x*-, *y*-, and *z*-axes.

One final, subtle signifier of cinematic stylistic schema is the control over framing that is permitted by a single-camera mode of production. This is true of stationary shots, but is even more evident in moving camera shots. Consider a simple "walk-and-talk" scene from "Be Patient" (directed by Ken Kwapis; Figures 4.19–4.20). Elisabeth (Alex Kingston) is talking to Mark about a night out his father has planned. Mark has just learned his father has lung cancer and is concerned about him. Note that Kwapis has selected a slightly high-angle shot, one that makes Mark more prominent in the frame even though Elisabeth has

most of the lines. In this fashion, the viewer's attention is subtly directed toward him, despite his almost total silence. The scene begins with a low-angle shot showing the entire hallway and its ceiling (Figure 4.21; cf. Figures 4.1–4.3). Obviously, a multiple-camera shoot wouldn't normally position the camera that low as it would show the lighting grid. Although a multiple-camera production could conceivably dolly next to a pair of conversing actors with an elevated camera, as a practical matter there would not be time to set up such a shot. The point is not that multiple-camera productions are slipshod, but that they have developed a different method for dealing with production issues. Soap operas are taped much like the filming of a stage play, in which the director has worked out an intricate choreography of actors and cameras. The camera operators know where the actors will be moving and where they should be at a particular point in the script, but despite those general indications, the operators must struggle to keep up with the actors. This results in framing that is more approximate, and sometimes even misses action that would be included in a single-camera production.[29]

What is the significance of this approximate framing? One important result is that soap operas *appear* as if they are being broadcast live. In this respect, they resemble television coverage of sports and other live events, in which important action is sometimes missed. Building on Barthes'

Figure 4.19 In one of *ER*'s numerous "walk-and-talk" scenes, the camera is on a slight high angle, favoring Mark…

Figure 4.20 …but it is Elisabeth who does most of the talking as they move down the hall.

Figure 4.21 The *ER* walk-and-talk scene above starts with a low-angle establishing shot, showing, once again, the ceiling.

notion of a photo effect, Ellis emphasizes television's immediate presence, as I explored in regard to the soap opera in Chapter 1.[30] He argues that photographs and theatrical films carry a signifier of "this is was," a "presence-absence."[31] A photograph of a birthday party or soldiers raising the U.S. flag on Iwo Jima signifies: "this event happened *in the past* and it happened *elsewhere.*" In Barthes' words:

> The type of consciousness the photograph involves is indeed truly unprecedented, since it establishes not a consciousness of the *being-there* of the thing ... but an awareness of its *having-been-there*. What we have is a new space-time category: spatial immediacy and temporal anteriority, the photograph being an illogical conjunction between the *here-now* and the *there-then*.[32]

For Barthes, the cinema began to break down the photo effect. For Ellis, television goes even further in this direction. As Stephen Heath and Gillian Skirrow have similarly argued,

> The immediate time of the [television] image is pulled into a confusion with the time of the events shown, tending to diminish the impression of the mode of presence in absence characteristic of film, suggesting a permanently alive view of the world; the generalized fantasy of the television institution of the image is exactly that it is *direct*, and direct for *me*.[33]

This holds true for television soap opera, but what of *ER* and its apparently *cinematic* presence in absence? And what are we to make of *ER*'s choice to promote *presence*-presence by broadcasting live, directly to the U.S. viewer?

On September 25, 1997, *ER*'s producers resurrected broadcasting practices from the 1950s with the live telecast of "Ambush." It was hardly the "unprecedented" event that NBC publicists trumpeted.[34] During the 1950s and early 1960s, live telecasts were the everyday mode of production for *ER*'s close relation, the soap opera. And even before *ER*'s live broadcast there have been instances of conventional, scripted programs shifting to a live format for an episode (e.g., *Gimme a Break!* [February 23, 1985]) or even an entire season (*Roc* [1992–3 season]). Moreover, as Ellis and Heath and Skirrow contend, liveness and simultaneity persist as television's dominant mode.[35] *ER*'s use of liveness, however, was not a simple return to the days of live telecasts of *Guiding Light* (1952–) and *Playhouse 90* (1956–61). In its own way, it pulled the viewer into new forms of confusion. Unlike previous live drama on television, "Ambush" did not use multiple cameras in individual scenes. Even though it was shot with 11 different cameras, they were not used in a conventional three-camera configuration on individual sets. Instead, single video (not film) cameras shot individual scenes with handheld cameras and Steadicams that evoked *cinéma vérité*-style videotaping and drew attention to the television apparatus itself—as when the production assistant adjusts the surveillance camera (Figures 4.17–4.18). "Ambush" also provides a unique instance for the analysis of approximate framing in live or live-on-tape tele-casts. Because the show was broadcast live twice—once for the Eastern and Central time zones and once for the Pacific—one can see the small adjust-ments camera operators made during the telecasts.[36] For instance, Anna (Maria Bello) assists Doug (George Clooney) as he treats a baby who has been bitten. In both versions, similar framing is used for a line of dialogue in which Doug asks Anna for more light—although the East Coast version is framed more tightly than the West Coast and the baby is crying in the former, but not in the latter (Figures 4.22, 4.23, respectively). When Anna swings a light over the bed in the East Coast version we do not see her do it, although we do see the additional illumination (Figure 4.24). In the West Coast version, we see her arm in the frame (Figure 4.25, contrast with the East Coast version in figure 4.24 where there is also less headroom above the father). Although these are obviously minor differences, they do illustrate the approximate nature of framing in live and live-on-tape modes of production.[37]

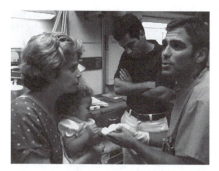

Figure 4.22 In the East Coast version of the live *ER* episode, Doug tends to a crying baby's bite wound.

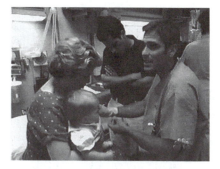

Figure 4.23 In the West Coast version of the same scene, the action is not framed as tightly (and the baby is not crying).

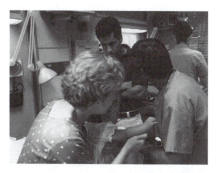

Figure 4.24 Another slight difference bet-ween East Coast and West Coast versions of this scene can be observed after Doug asks for more light. In the East Coast version we see the light on the mother's shoulder, and...

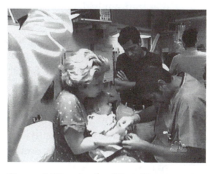

Figure 4.25 ...in the West Coast version we also see Anna's arm as she adjusts the light.

The irony here is that the live broadcast was presented as if it were *not* live, as if we were viewing videotape that had been shot previously for a documentary about the emergency room—much like the "found" film/tape in *The Blair Witch Project* and imitators such as *Cloverfield* (2008). In this respect, the broadcast also resembles *Cops*, a show whose viewers recognize that what they are seeing, despite television's strong evocation of simultaneity, is a tape of past events. *The X-Files*'s mock documentary, "X-Cops," illustrates this confusion well. Mulder (David Duchovny) and Scully (Gillian Anderson) track a monster in Los Angeles while a *Cops* camera crew tapes the incident. Scully resents the intrusion and complains to Mulder about being on "live TV." Mulder responds, "It's not live. She just said [bleep]"—referring to an expletive ostensibly censored by the *Cops* producers. Or rather, he refers to an expletive censored by the fictive *Cops* producers within the *X-Files* diegesis. Obviously, documentary telecasts can be live and, perhaps less obviously, most television programs carry connotations of liveness, but "Ambush," "X-Cops," and *The Blair Witch Project* all suggest that their presents are past. Only in the case of "Ambush" does that paradoxically double back onto itself where actors in the present—performing at the same time that we are watching—pretend to be characters in a videotape of the past.

Re-Presenting *ER* on the Web: *ERTV* and *ERLive*

I have established that *ER* is a television program grounded in its fluid visual style—a style that cuts across media boundaries, linking it specifically with the cinematic medium. *ER*, as with all television programs since the late 1990s, also has a substantial Web presence—starting with Warner Brother's official website (*ERTV*) and the site created by Warners and NBC specifically for the "cyber-event" of the live broadcast (*ERLive*). The questions I would like to raise about these sites are stylistic ones: can a program that places so much emphasis on visual movement translate that kinetic energy to the Web? Is there an equivalent to the Steadicam on the Web or in other digital media such as video games?

Mark J.P. Wolf has created a taxonomy of on- and off-screen space in video games.[38] His article provides a starting point for an understanding of the articulation of space in webpages, which, in many respects, closely resemble video games. Both webpages and video games appear on computer monitors. Both contain many images that have been wholly generated digitally, possessing no "real world" referent. Both contain illusions of movement. And, perhaps most significantly, the movement in both can be interactive, it can depend upon the input of users. Let us consider more closely this matter of spatial articulation on the Web as it appears in *ERTV* and *ERLive*, within the larger context of a taxonomy of online space and movement. The first and least revolutionary form of movement on webpages is that which it inherited from the cinema and television: video clips and conventional animation. Just as spectators cannot control the editing or the Steadicam moves they witness while watching *ER*, so they cannot control the website's video clips or influence the GIF animation dancing through the banner ads (for exceptions, see the discussion of online video editing experiments later in this chapter). *ER*'s website's banner ads and pedestrian video clips of the cast and crew—as with the photographs and *ER* theme music—are positioned on the webpages as if they were photographs and scraps of memorabilia placed into a photo album. As Janet Murray argues, "The equivalent of the filmed play of the early 1900s is the multimedia scrapbook ... which takes advantage of the novelty of computer delivery without utilizing its intrinsic properties."[39] To her filmed plays we might add the televised plays of the 1950s, which took advantage of television's novel delivery system without exploring its intrinsic properties. But television and the process of television viewing have evolved significantly since television's so-called Golden Age. *ER*, with its shattered proscenium arch, illustrates just how television might differ from the theatrical drama. Further, the VCR, DVR, DVD box sets of television shows, video iPod, and remote control have radically altered the viewer's power over the television. As Caldwell contends, "Increasingly, television has come to be associated more with something you can hold, push into an appliance, and physically move around with a controller."[40] In short, television has become increasingly interactive. Similarly, it is in interactive movement that we will find one of the truly revolutionary characteristics of the digital realm.

For Murray, interactivity and movement are inextricably interwoven into "four essential properties" of digital environments: "Digital environments are procedural, participatory, spatial and encyclopedic."[41] The first two properties, in her view, are what define interactivity. We may *participate* in a digital world by clicking buttons with our mouse, manipulating a joystick, or wearing a virtual reality helmet; and that world will respond with behaviors that are grounded in certain *procedures* or rules. Murray continues, "Procedural environments are appealing to us not just because they exhibit rule-generated behavior but because we can induce the behavior. They are responsive to our input."[42] Murray's insight helps us understand the unique function of space and, more importantly, the function of *movement* on the Web and in other digital environments. As she puts it,

> The new digital environments are characterized by their power to represent navigable space. Linear media such as books and films can portray space, either by verbal description or image, but only digital environments can present *space that we can move through* [emphasis added].[43]

Thus Murray identifies navigable space as one of the key pleasures of Web browsing or other activities in digital environments.

Returning to our specific examples of *ERTV* and *ERLive*, we can see how significant navigation is. Each homepage presents a navigation scheme, as can be seen in these details from *ERTV* and *ERLive* as they appeared in 1998 (Figures 4.26, 4.27, respectively). Although both seem to be just text, just lists of words, they actually have a spatial dimension. In HTML (Hypertext Markup Language) terminology, they are "image maps;" *ERTV*'s map is ori-

Figure 4.26 A horizontal navigation bar for *ERTV* is an image of text, an "image map" on which users may click to navigate to other pages.

ented horizontally, and *ERLive*'s vertically. They are not so much text as they are *images resembling text.* The area of the image that users click determines what they will see next. Or, in more spatial terms, we could say that various regions of the text image have become hotspots, the HTML code determining the action triggered by clicking those spots. Position your cursor over the image of the word "Video," press a mouse button, and this webpage will be replaced with another one. Thus, in webpages, text *is* space. Clicking on an image map or on a regular bit of text that has been programmed as a hypertext link allows users to "move" metaphorically to another location, another webpage. But this is not literal movement. The text/graphics of one page do not usually slide off the screen while another slides on—*à la* a video wipe. Rather, the space of one page is replaced by that of another—more like the displacement that happens when an editor makes an Eisensteinian montage of attractions or a television viewer changes channels with a remote control.

During the 2000s, the image map was "deprecated," to use a term commonly employed by computer programmers. It became obsolescent and was largely replaced by more powerful programming techniques for visual navigation—specifically, JavaScript, cascading style sheets (CSS), and Flash animation. The fundamental spatial principle of the image map persists (that is, click an area of

Figure 4.27 ERLive's navigation bar is also an image map that serves the same purpose, but is oriented vertically.

the screen and something happens), but these newer techniques also permit instantaneous visual changes based solely on the position of the cursor on the screen, which is not possible with a simple image map. On the official NBC homepage for *ER* during its final season, one can find another horizontal navigation bar (Figure 4.28, as observed on December 11, 2008), much like the *ER* image map in Figure 4.26. When one rolls over the 2008 navigation text with the mouse cursor, however, the text changes—indicating one's choices if one clicks that spot. Mouse "rollovers" are constructed using a programming language and are thus an illustration of the inducing of rule-based behavior. Examining the HTML source code of this *ER* page reveals which programming technique controls this drop-down list: a JavaScript named "nbcDropDown."[44] Initially nbcDropDown displays the word "Video" in the navigation bar, but when we mouse over that text, it changes from black to white, its background color shifts from white to green, and additional text is presented to us below it:

*WATCH FULL EPISODES
*TWO-MINUTE REPLAYS
*INTERVIEWS
*HIGHLIGHTS

This simple user action, one that we now perform without a second thought, was not possible in the days of image maps. Nonetheless, both the image map and JavaScript offer navigable space to us and both are governed by rules and procedures that are codified in their programming languages. The "pleasure" we get from initiating action through a visual navigation bar is not exactly *jouissance*, but it is fundamental to our online experience.

Displacement and hypertextual

Figure 4.28 During the 2008–9 season, the *ER* website dispensed with image maps and used JavaScript to create drop-down menus for its navigation bar.

"movement" are not the only forms of spatial activity on the Web. We can also identify movements in the Web environment that are quite literal. The simplest and most fundamental is the movement of the mouse-controlled cursor across the screen. Let's dissect this simple, but consequential, interaction. Users move a mouse on a flat surface and the on-screen cursor responds by moving in a corresponding direction.[45] For users who have grown up on computers with graphical user interfaces (GUI), it seems unimaginable that computers would ever function without the mouse; but, of course, the GUI is a relatively recent phenomenon. Up until the mid-1980s, most computer users were staring at text-filled screens and cursors were mainly controlled by the keyboard on strict x- and y-axes. Whether mouse- or key-controlled, the cursor is central to Web interactivity. It is the main embodiment on screen of what Murray calls "agency:" "the satisfying power to take meaningful action and see the results of our decisions and choices."[46] The placement of the cursor upon the webpage and the pressing of a mouse button results in the predominant user-controlled movements on webpages: vertical and, to a lesser extent, horizontal "scrolling." In Wolf's taxonomy of on- and off-screen movement in computer-based games, he notes the significance of scrolling movements. Scrolling video games—as with scrolling webpages—move fixed screen elements (text and graphics) up or down or side to side. Early video games from the late 1970s and 1980s tended to scroll on a single axis—whether horizontally or vertically. Wolf notes *Defender* (1982), *Stampede* (1981), and *Space Jockey* (1982) as examples of horizontal scrolling and *Skiing* (1980) and *Street Racer* (1978) as examples of vertical scrolling. Our initial sense of power over the webpage comes from this ability to scroll, to decide what shall be on screen and what shall be off. This scrolling is a very basic form of visual navigation. By manipulating the mouse, touchpad, or keyboard we can explore the navigable space of the page. This is quite unlike anything one can do at the cinema or while watching television, where the border between on-screen space and off-screen is always strictly determined by the director and the camera operators. On the Web, that border becomes malleable.

The metaphorically loaded terms "scrolling" and "webpage" help us to understand an important property of this movement. Just like the turning of a paper scroll or the movement of a paper page on a desk, the motion of web-pages is planimetric—as in Bordwell's discussion of film staging. The space is flat, with little sense of a third, z-axis poking out at the viewer or receding into the background. Planimetric Web movement is like the sliding of a typewritten page across a desk. It is true that webpages can develop a sense of depth, but it is still planimetric. In *On the History of Film Style*, Bordwell discusses planimetric staging in the silent film *Barbe Bleu* (1907). In one shot, there are two distinct planes of action (a woman in the foreground and several women, in a line, in the background), but, as Bordwell notes, "In such compositions each layer lies parallel to the picture plane and often to the background planes as well ... A sense of depth is conveyed primarily through comparative size and overlapping edges."[47] In the *ER* webpages there are dim, muted background images that the text appears to float above. Figure 4.29 illustrates this use of text, with the text and graphics hovering on top of a tiled image of operating surgeons wearing surgical masks, which is shown in detail in Figure 4.30. Thus, just as in *Barbe Bleu*, there are two planes, but they do not connect to one another—much like the animation created by Disney's multi-plane camera.

The earliest webpages—constructed solely of text and no images—only allowed vertical scrolling of the text. There was no horizontal movement because the width of the text would automatically adjust to the width of users' browsers and thus horizontal scrolling was unnecessary. Moreover, the page usually loaded at its top, which meant that the vertical movement was only in one direction—downward. The introduction of images and HTML "tables" to the Web, and the release of the first widely popular browser with a GUI (NCSA Mosaic, 1993) created the ability for horizontal scrolling, but only in one direction. Images/text could now extend beyond the right side of the

Figure 4.29 In *ERTV*'s main page, text and images appear to float above a background image, which...

Figure 4.30 ...is enlarged here.

browser and the user could scroll to the right (and the right only) to view them. When viewed on a standard sized monitor of the time (800 × 600 pixels), the two *ER* homepages only permit vertical scrolling because their graphics and text are narrower than the standard width.[48] Since the entire width of the image is immediately visible, there is no need for scrolling. However, both pages are longer than the standard height and thus they both permit and induce the user to move the page downward.

The shape of the browser "window," its aspect ratio, is yet another source of user agency that is quite distinct from television and film. As the film and television industries know from the battles over widescreen and letterboxing, and now over the 16:9 ratio of high definition television, aspect ratio can be a volatile subject, with both aesthetic, technological, and economic ramifications.[49] But, much like Steadicam movements, aspect ratio is not something most television or film viewers can influence.[50] Aside from choosing whether to view a letterbox or pan-and-scan version of a film that's been transferred to video, viewers of television texts have minimal control over aspect ratio. It's somewhat startling, then, to realize that Web users have full control over the size of their browser windows. Browser resizing is a form of animation, of movement, over which users hold full agency. They decide if they will view the Web at 640 × 480, 800 × 600, 1024 × 768 pixels or *anywhere in between.*[51] Users need not even respect the 4:3 and 16:9 ratios that determines the outer bounds of standard monitor screens. To a large extent, then, the designer's carefully conceived use of space must submit to the user's choice. In some respects, the evolution of scrolling has been marked by a battle for agency between users and designers—with the designers gradually asserting more and more control. New graphic design software and programming/scripting languages such as JavaScript, CSS, and Flash animation empower designers with the ability to determine the spatial layout of the screen and limit users' ability to change it, but users can still resize their browsers and choose to view only a portion of these fixed layouts.

Beyond Planimetric Movement: Going "Deep Inside the Hidden Areas"

> ERLIVE.com [takes] you straight to the set with our very own Virtual Reality Sets. Rush into the Admitting Area, take a break in the Hospital Lounge, and visit the hectic Trauma Center—all from the comfort of your very own computer screen! With your mouse and keyboard, you can go deep inside the hidden areas of the ER! Click here to begin your tour of the Virtual Reality Sets![52]

The history of visual media is littered with promises of full verisimilitude, of total television and cinema, of a simulacrum that is indistinguishable from reality. Ad copy for Cinerama, for instance, claimed, "you won't be gazing at a movie screen—you'll find yourself swept right *into* the picture, surrounded with sight and sound."[53] To prove their point they provided images of a man in a movie seat flying over water skiers in bikinis and a woman levitating in the middle of a concert hall. Similarly, *ERLive* promises to take us "deep inside the hidden areas of the ER." In short, it promises immersive movement along the *z*-axis (i.e., in depth). It should be no surprise that Cinerama and *ERLive* don't deliver on their promises, but I find their failures interesting and instructive—helping us to understand what virtual reality is not.

ERLive's "Virtual Tour" consists of three QuickTime VR "movies" (as they are called by Apple):[54] "Admitting Area," "Hospital Lounge," and "Trauma Center." They are blandly presented on the *ERLive* "QuickTime VR" page, in a style that recalls Murray's "multimedia scrapbook" (Figure 4.31). An image from the movie entices users to click on the word "Windows" or "Mac" to load the version appropriate to their platforms. By moving the mouse over the VR image, they may pan right or left and, to a much lesser extent, they may even tilt up or down (e.g., the QuickTime VR movie of the trauma room; note the objects that persist from one frame to the next in Figures 4.32–4.34). The only other permitted movement is a zoom, where a section of the image is enlarged or reduced (e.g., a zoom in on the doors and clock in Figure 4.34, enlarged in Figure 4.35). Thus, there is movement here and the inducement of human agency, but is it really virtual reality?

In her chapter on "Television Graphics and the Visual Body: Words on the Move," Morse describes the "weightless flight" of television spectators as they watch words and graphic design elements fly towards and "past" them.[55] "A development began in television graphics at the end of the 1960s," she notes, "when a vortex seemed to pull the viewer virtually 'inside' the [television] set and into a miniature cosmos occupied by an animated logo."[56] For Morse these moving, twisting, gyrating textual objects reveal a back side of the text. We are allowed to view "precisely what is forbidden in monocular perspective and, one might add, representation in the photograph and the classic fiction film."[57] The "hidden areas" of *ERLive*'s "Virtual Reality Sets" promise us a similar forbidden pleasure. They offer to show us the opposite side of the 180-degree line, the reverse angle that classical cinema represses. The irony of such a promise in *ER* is that its directors have already revealed all four walls of the program's sets—through the use of the Steadicam (Figures 4.10–4.16). In a sense, there is nothing new or forbidden to see.[58]

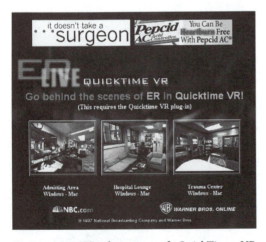

Figure 4.31 *ERLive*'s menu of QuickTime VR movies arranges its thumbnail images as if they were in a paper scrapbook.

There is more to the allure of VR than just the uncovering of

Figure 4.32 ERLive: a QuickTime VR of the trauma room grants the user control to look left…

*Figure 4.33 …*and right…

*Figure 4.34 …*around the set. The user may also zoom into the image…

*Figure 4.35 …*which results in an enlarged, but visually degraded, image, with chunky pixels.

normally forbidden space—although the ability to go into virtual worlds that would be too dangerous or physically impossible for real humans is quite significant. This ability explains why, for example, the U.S. military has invested so heavily in flight simulators, which permit pilots to experience dangerous situations "virtually" without placing themselves at risk. But what truly makes VR a virtual simulacrum of its referent is the illusion of z-axis movement under the control of the user. The sense of agency is, of course, paramount. Morse's flying logos are not true virtual realities because viewers have no control over them. Their "weightless flight" is piloted by the television apparatus. Consumers did not become their own pilots (and tank commanders and race-car drivers) until the arrival of video game arcades in the 1980s. According to Wolf, "The first commercial game to offer a first-person perspective of an interactive three-dimensional environment was the arcade game *BattleZone* (1980)."[59] *BattleZone*'s virtual world is constructed of stick-figure tanks and mountains; but despite its crudity it generates a strong sense of immersion—of *being* in that world—because of the user's ability to move on the z-axis (Figure 4.36).[60] The 1998 remake of *BattleZone* for the personal computer (Figure 4.37) and popular "first-person shooter" games of the 1990s and early 2000s—such as *Doom* (1993; Figure 4.38), *Half-Life* (1998; Figure 4.39), and the *Call of Duty* series (2003–8; Figure 4.40, from *Call of Duty 4: Modern Warfare* [2007])—have progressively improved the verisi-

Figure 4.36 The early arcade game, *BattleZone*, allows the user to move a tank *into* a primitive landscape, along the *z*-axis.

Figure 4.37 Updated versions of *BattleZone*, to be played on the home computer, improve the photo-realism of the original's landscape.

Figure 4.38 *Doom* was among the early first-person shooter games, which provide navigable space to the user.

militude of these virtual realms, but the principle of navigable space remains the same. As the user navigates these computer-generated realms, a first-person narrative evolves and it evolves in real time: "I am moving, commanding, my tank through this world. A tank shoots at me. I shoot back. A missile attacks me and I'm killed." Murray specifies some of the "pleasures specific to intentional navigation: orienting ourselves by landmarks, mapping a space mentally to match our experience, and admiring the juxtapositions and changes in the perspective that derive from moving through an intricate environment."[61]

Morse calls these sorts of environments "fictions of presence" in that the space and time of the simulacrum is the same as that of the user/viewer/interactor.[62] Echoing Barthes' photo effect and the application of it to television by Heath and Skirrow and Ellis, she maintains that print and film "media *represent* a world that is past and elsewhere; television and the computer *present* virtually shared worlds, unfolding temporally in some virtual relation to our own, if not always actually simultaneously."[63] This emphasis on the time of virtual reality is also stressed by Lev Manovich. In *The Language of New Media*, he charts the genealogy of the screen from the "classical screen" of Renaissance painting to the "dynamic screen" of the cinema and television.[64] For him the defining characteristic of the computer screen is its ability to interact with the user in real time. For this reason, he refers to it as the "real-time screen."[65]

Thus we arrive at what Morse, Murray, Manovich, and others propose as the generally accepted axioms of virtual reality:

Figure 4.39 The increasing verisimilitude of video games can be observed in 1998's *Half-Life* and...

Figure 4.40 ...2007's *Call of Duty 4: Modern Warfare.*

1. navigable space;
2. movement along the *z*-axis;
3. user control of that movement;
4. a virtual sense of shared space; and
5. a match of the time of the signification with the time of the user.

To understand how and why *ER*'s VR fails to meet these criteria it is useful to understand a little about how QuickTime VR movies are created. QuickTime VRs are constructed from still photos of a space. The camera is rotated on a tripod and one image is taken every 30 degrees (more or less). The photos are loaded into a QuickTime VR program and similar points on the adjoining images are matched. Based on these matching points, the photos are then stitched together. This creates one long continuous photograph—a panorama that can be viewed flat (in an aspect ratio even wider than Cinerama) or looped together into a 360-degree image, as has been done on *ERLive*. A QuickTime VR "movie" is, thus, no movie at all. Essentially, it is a cylindrical still image that places the spectator in the center of the cylinder. It is as if one were inside a zoetrope looking out (Figure 4.41). The QuickTime movies, failure as virtual reality has several implications.

First, because these unmoving "movies" are just still photographs they present a digitized photo effect. They have a very strong sense of "this is was," of "presence-absence," in Ellis's words. "These *were* the sets of the program *ER*," they seem to signify, not "these *are* the sets, and you *are* moving inside them." The immediacy that comes with immersion into a virtual reality is absent. Second, there is no true *z*-axis movement. The zooms in QuickTime VR do not actually change the angle of view, the perspective, of the spectator. Rather, they simply enlarge the image itself—appearing to bring it closer to you

Figure 4.41 The nineteenth-century zoetrope arranged still images around the inside of a cylinder, much like a QuickTime VR movie.

(or, of course, shrinking it or moving it further away; Figures 4.34–4.35). As Zettl argues, "When zooming in on an event, the event seems to come toward you.... During a dolly-in, you will seem to be moving with the camera toward the event."[66] In the case of the digital medium, this enlargement blows up the pixels, quickly leading to blocky distortion and the breakdown of the illusion of reality (Figure 4.35). It's impossible to maintain an illusion of reality when the constituent elements of the image are made so obvious. True, these zooms are under the control of the user and thus provide some sense of agency, but they fall well short of virtual reality because they lack the "juxtapositions and changes in the perspective that derive from moving through an intricate environment."[67] Without the change in perspective, there is no sense of user mobility.

Further, there are no moving objects or characters within these sets. This stands in stark contrast to the hectic visual style of the program—where cameras and actors are constantly careening toward one another. Drs Benton, Greene, Weaver, and the rest are but ghostly presences in these virtual spaces. In *Battle-Zone, Doom* and many other video games, tanks, missiles, and combatants rush along the z-axis toward users—interacting with them in ways that threaten their virtual lives. A true VR realm based upon *ER* would take a page from ELIZA, one of the first artificial intelligences on the Web. Developed by Joseph Weizenbaum in 1966, ELIZA's users typed questions to "her" and she would respond with therapeutic replies. Blending ELIZA with *Doom*, one can imagine an *ER* VR in which—with a palpable sense of *real time*—the user *chooses* (agency) to be a doctor or a patient and *moves through* (z-axis) hallways and into the trauma room where virtual lives could be saved or lost. In the place of *Doom*'s monsters, speeding at us with weapons firing, we could find Dr Eliza on a psych consult—extending a sympathetic hand along the z-axis.

Divergence in Converging Times: the 1990s

In *ER*, we see the effects of techno-industrial convergence and competition upon contemporary television in the 1990s. It has been obvious since the advent of cable television that the old broadcast models won't last forever. This prospect became increasingly evident at the end of the twentieth century. From 1997 to 1999, the average annual hours per person spent watching U.S. broadcast television dropped 9.3 percent while online and video-game time increased 126.6 percent.[68] *ER*'s response to the threats of competitors and converging technology combined the schema of an older, more prestigious medium (the cinema) with the technologies of newer media (the Web and VR movies) whose prestige factor inevitably generated curiosity, debate, and increased viewership. This pastiche succeeded more in its skillful application of cinematic style than in its pale attempts at virtual reality, but its overall success cannot be disputed, as *ER*'s high Nielsen ratings attest.

Ratings success aside, *ER*'s attempts at distinguishing itself from the rest of television illustrate the stylistic function of product differentiation. In a time of convergence, *ER* strained to diverge from the pack, to establish a unique (for television) visual style, and to incorporate elements of new media. In so doing, it provides an interesting test case for the signifying function of style. Unusual production practices like the live show, unconventional set design, and camera movement, and digital media such as Web pages and VR movies were all elements in its battle for uniqueness. *ER*'s disturbances of conventional television style allow us to examine anew the significance of television style and to gauge its strategies for making meaning.

Divergence in Converging Times: the 2000s' First Decade

A decade's worth of media convergence has occurred since this chapter was initially conceived. During that time, the broadcast networks have acquiesced to the necessity of new distribution systems—providing miniature versions of their products through iTunes and websites such as Hulu and Joost. Even venerable *ER* is offering hours of online video that, in sheer bulk, dwarfs the material provided on *ERLive* in the 1990s. Yet after the attempt analyzed here, *ER* never again launched a new effort representing the show in a "virtual reality" setting, perhaps recognizing that online virtual worlds and games such as *Second Life* and *World of Warcraft* (2004–) would humble anything its producers could devise.[69] A major technological factor enabling new online video offerings has been the phenomenal increase in the bandwidth available to home users. When *ER* debuted in 1994, home access to the Internet was limited to dial-up connections via telephone modems.[70] Today's cable and DSL modems are capable of receiving data over 200 times faster than those dial-up modems.[71] With higher speeds has come the ability to download video over the Internet or to view it instantaneously. Initially, such videos were frustratingly small, but "high-definition" video is becoming more and more common, a clear sign of things to come.

If we examine the navigation and spatial style with which these new offerings are presented, however, we find quite modest changes since 1997, when the *ERLive* website was launched. Despite the mid-2000s proselytizing for a new, supposedly revolutionary, "Web 2.0," many design principles have not changed, especially for television programs' companion websites.[72] Hulu, for instance, carries *ER* and many other NBC programs and is among the most popular websites providing online video. Yet its homepage relies on a format that improves very little on Murray's multimedia scrapbook (Figure 4.42). Sophisticated JavaScript and Flash animation are used to slide images across the frame's top, which would have been difficult in 1997, but the rest of the page consists of a pedestrian horizontal navigation bar and a simple grid of thumbnails—no more revolutionary than paper photographs attached to a scrapbook's page. Users' navigation of the page involves only a modest increase in their sense of agency, or control, over its visual space. Hulu's pop-up information about a specific video (Figure 4.43), for example, does afford the user more agency over the site's space as it only appears when the user elicits it through a mouse-over. However, video sites in general take great pains to *curtail* user agency. NBC and Warner Brothers are deathly afraid that users will appropriate their intellectual property and distribute

Figure 4.42 NBC's Hulu.com still relies on a scrap-book-style layout of thumbnail images.

it illegally. Consequently, a cat-and-mouse game has evolved in which producers endeavor to lock down their online video while users (and hackers) yearn to free those images. Hulu's video player software uses various controls to block the downloading of its video, but computer-savvy users can get around them and download the video to their own hard drives.

ER's producers have encouraged some forms of restricted Internet distribution by users. Hulu's system allows users to embed an *ER* video in their own websites, as well as to "share" the video through email, instant messaging, and social-network pages like Facebook and MySpace. The producers' obvious goal is to turn their product into a "viral video," a video that users, not the producers themselves, spread through the Internet like a virus.[73] Conflicting with that goal, however, is the desire to retain control over intellectual property, which is why Hulu and similar sites do not allow the sharing of the video itself. Rather, they promote the sharing of a *link* to the video on their site. Users cannot distribute actual video clips, they can only operate as shills for Hulu, encouraging their friends to visit that site.

And yet, recognizing viewers' desire to gain agency over television's intellectual properties, producers and advertisers have experimented with the online manipulation of their work by users—with mixed results. Warners' site for its television network, The WB, implores users to "Create TV:" "Remix shows, start a channel and make The WB yours."[74] An online non-linear video editor allows users to "own" The WB's content and alter its stylistic schema—reediting select video clips from WB programs and combining them with new captions, graphics, and music (Figure 4.44). The resulting remix cannot be downloaded, but can be, again, shared as a link via email, in which the recipient is invited to "Remix, mash and create your own [video]!" Viewers of WB programs are thus hailed and exhorted to engage with the programs, but the potential for video piracy and vandalism is minimized. Chevrolet was not so fortunate in its 2006 experiment with user agency. It provided online

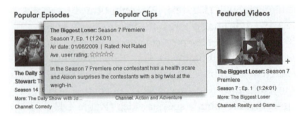

Figure 4.43 A detail from Hulu.com contains a pop-up box elicited by user action—rolling the mouse over a thumbnail image. A drop shadow suggests that it's floating over the background.

video of its Tahoe SUV and invited users to recombine shots and add text and music as they wished— resulting in over 30,000 do-it-yourself car commercials that were automatically posted online. The experiment backfired, however, when environmentalists used these stylistic elements to political effect. The newly edited "commercials" attacked the SUV for guzzling gas.[75] As Chevrolet

Figure 4.44 Warner Brothers grants users limited freedom to create video mash-ups online.

found out, user agency and its implementation have become increasingly complicated as television culture and online culture have blended.

The issue of agency and spatial control extends to the aspect ratio and size of online video players. A Web browser, as I note above, is a source of user agency in terms of the shape of the browser window. Users can make it narrow or wide, a small rectangle or one that fills the entire screen. Online video players like Hulu's cede some of that power to the viewer, much more than does a conventional television set. Whereas the aspect ratio is fixed at 16:9 when watching *ER* on Hulu, the size of the image is not. Viewers can make that 16:9 frame 160 pixels wide or 1,600 pixels wide, if they choose. In fact, one need not watch the video embedded within Hulu's webpage at all: users can choose to fill their computer screens with the image, or to pop the player out of the page into a new window. That window may then be resized as the user wishes, and positioned anywhere on his or her screen. This degree of user agency would be impossible in the conventional livingroom viewing situation, and was not supported in *ER*'s online video in 1997. At that time, users were forced to view videos at one small size.

The development of immersible virtual realities in the 2000s—particularly within the realm of video games—might lead one to expect a less planimetric organization of space in contemporary graphical user interfaces, and there have been experimental, three-dimensional GUIs that labor to bring visual depth, a *z*-axis, to the user experience. Some elements of them have even found their way into mainstream operating systems. For example, the Aero GUI theme included with Windows Vista has a feature known as Windows Flip 3D which presents windows as if they were flat pieces of paper floating in space (Figure 4.45). And Cooliris, a Web browser add-on, transforms multimedia scrapbooks into moveable walls of images that glide past users, at their control, and on modified *z*-axes (Figure 4.46).[76] When an image is selected, a window floats up toward the user and a video starts playing. Despite these developments in GUI design, the interfaces of the websites that provide *ER*'s video, Hulu included, still have only a modicum of three-dimensionality.

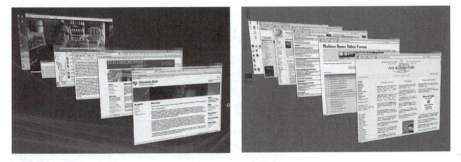

Figure 4.45 Windows Vista's Flip 3D feature floats your documents into virtual space.

Hulu's pop-up frames, for instance, do very little spatial "popping" toward the user. Small drop shadows outlining them do suggest a minuscule bit of depth, but pop-ups themselves still appear to be flat pieces of paper sliding over flat virtual desktops. Thus, in terms of the organization of navigable space, the lack of a movement on the z-axis, and the user's limited sense of agency, *ER*'s Web presence in 2009 is surprisingly similar to its 1997 efforts.

I have argued above that movement along the z-axis is but one common axiom of virtual reality. Another is the time of the signification matching the time of the user—Manovich's real-time screen and Morse's temporal simultaneity. Has this changed in terms of *ER*'s online presence in 2009? Hulu's representation of *ER* video—as with any of the video scrapbook sites—emphasizes the *lack* of temporal simultaneity. It heightens Barthes' photo effect of *this is was*. It is an artifact from a past time that can be manipulated by the viewer. When watching a video online one can pause it, rewind it, skip ahead or backwards. The illusion of it occurring at the same time that you're watching it, of Ellis' immediate presence, is extremely faint. The more agency that a user can hold over the moving image, the less "live" it seems. Were *ER* episodes to be streamed live, with little viewer control over the stream, then temporal simultaneity would return. Such streams are extremely common online, making *ER*'s lack of simultaneity more obvious by contrast. A service such as Ustream.TV, for example, encourages the live streaming of video by non-professionals—including "Personal milestones such as holiday gatherings, weddings, grade school events, parties, even births."[77] Ustream.TV's live events take advantage of their temporal simultaneity and provide a sidebar or overlay where viewers post comments

Figure 4.46 Cooliris attempts to transcend the multimedia scrapbook by portraying thumbnails on a moveable wall. Click one and it floats "up" toward the viewer.

as the stream is presented. The interactivity is instantaneous. There is no photo effect.

When Ellis wrote about the differences between television and cinema in 1982, years before Tim Berners-Lee developed the protocols on which the Internet was built, he contended, "Gazing is the constitutive activity of cinema. Broadcast TV demands a rather different kind of looking: that of the glance."[78] Online video on a real-time screen demands the gaze, but must satisfy itself with the glance. When *ER* or any other television program appears on someone's computer screen it is often just one window among many. And it may well be the smallest window on the screen. Until recently, highly compressed videos from sources such as YouTube degraded rapidly if they were enlarged beyond a quarter-screen. Such a video presence earns only a *glance* from users while they devote their *gazes* to the instant-message session for which they are actively typing messages or the massively multi-player online role-playing game (MMORPG) in which they are moving through virtual spaces, on z-axes, battling evil elves with magic potions. While it is true that the resolution, and potential on-screen size, of video delivered online is rapidly increasing and that this video can now fill a conventional digital television set in a viewer's living room, these developments will not eliminate the increasing number of distractions drawing us away from the video screen. Just how television will respond to these competing screens is still to be determined.

YouTube and MMORPGs, along with the social network Facebook, the user-created encyclopedia Wikipedia, and other collaborative online efforts, share a defining Web 2.0 characteristic that broadcast-era television utterly lacked: their content is created by masses of individuals contributing small bits to them and sharing a networked experience. Online marketers refer to these texts as "user-generated content" (UGC) and one study found 44.4 percent of all U.S. Internet users, 88.8 million users, produce some form of UGC.[79] Thus, *nearly half of these Internet users are also producers*. Characteristically of UGC sites, the "you" in YouTube's name is meant to refer to the viewers/users themselves. Its website proclaims, "YouTube is empowering them to become the broadcasters of tomorrow."[80] UGC emerges from Pierre Lévy's "collective intelligence," which he defines as "a form of *universally distributed intelligence*, constantly enhanced, coordinated in real time, and resulting in the effective mobilization of skills."[81] In YouTube's case, the networked collective submits videos and it also rates them, comments upon them, and distributes them to their friends, causing them to "go viral." YouTube's phenomenal success—it remains the most popular online video source by a very wide margin—was built not just on collective intelligence, but also on thousands of copyright violations by its users.[82] YouTube's video upload page emphatically states, "Do not upload any TV shows, music videos, music concerts, or commercials without permission unless they consist entirely of content you created yourself."[83] But users blithely ignore this warning and upload all manner of copyrighted material. The legal implications of this and YouTube's ability to invoke passages in the Digital Millennium Copyright Act to shield itself from crippling lawsuits are of less interest to a student of television style than the impact of YouTube on television stylistic schemas. YouTube culture rewards fragmentation, remix, and pastiche, which serve as mainstays of its stylistic schema. As Lévy notes, "Image and text are being increasingly subjected to sampling and rearrangement. In cyberculture every image is potentially the raw material of another image."[84] YouTube users are blocked from uploading entire television episodes as videos must be under ten minutes; so all television-originating video is necessarily fragmented. And those fragments are commonly re-edited or have a new soundtrack or graphics laid over them or a user lip syncs his or her own music video. This radical pastiche is what The WB's video remix (discussed above) both aspires to and can never fully become. It results from users taking full agency over the television text and Warner's concerns over intellectual property would never allow that. Of course, such unauthorized use of intellectual property is frequently removed by the YouTube administration because of its violation of copyright, but once a video is released online, it is difficult to reign it back in again. Thus, on YouTube we can see what happens to television stylistic schemas when they are appropriated by the online community. It is more difficult to gauge the impact of online appropriation and pastiche on the stylistic schema of a scripted program such as ER. Will its producers fight back with episodes that are YouTube-proof in some manner? Or will they develop material that is more easily appropriated by YouTube viewers?

Consider, by way of conclusion, one example of a potential viewer of ER online: Chris Pirillo (Figure 4.47). Pirillo is not a typical viewer because he himself used to appear on "regular" television. He was a frequent contributor to The Screen Savers, a technology-oriented program on the cable network, TechTV.[85] After leaving cable television, Pirillo began his own live video stream. Twenty-four hours a day, seven days a week, he offers a portrait of himself as homo internetus.[86] He gazes intently at one window on one computer screen, but he is surrounded by two other screens at which he might glance. He could easily have ER running in a window on one of those screens, but how much attention would he pay to it? And consider the users that are watching Pirillo watch his screens. According to the graphic at the bottom of Figure 4.47, 630 "viewers" are currently tuned in, a tiny audience compared to TechTV's, but still it means hundreds of users have Pirillo's image somewhere on their computer desktop. And three viewers—identified as cipher_nemo, LJGoose, and Granit—are sufficiently engaged with the broadcast that they have posted comments: e.g., "Hi Brigitte and asasin;". Although their comments are not sparkling examples of collective intelligence, they do illustrate the real-time collaboration of the group. And, besides, Lévy allows that "collective stupidity" is as common online as collective intelligence.[87] In Pirillo's gaze, Figure 4.47 illustrates television's sought-after viewer, fully engaged with the moving image and available for the pitching of products. In the comments of cipher_nemo et al., Figure 4.47 presents the interactivity and collective intelligence that broadcast television of the network era could only approximate and never truly achieve.

The future of media convergence, like the future of the moving image itself, depends upon media companies' ability to compete with the real-time screen's user agency, navigable space, temporal simultaneity, and virtual sense of shared space. However, as of January 20, 2009, the "superiority" of the real-time screen as the moving-image's medium of choice is far from certain. On that date, Barack Obama was inaugurated as presid-

Figure 4.47 Chris Pirillo, *homo internetus*, streams his time in front of the computer onto the Internet. Six hundred and thirty viewers were "tuned in" at this moment, with three of them offering comments.

ent of the United States. Numerous online services provided real-time streaming of the event, challenging conventional television's coverage. CNN.com allied itself with Facebook and created an interface in which Facebook members could share their thoughts with their Facebook "friends" and with "everyone watching" (Figure 4.48). CNN.com attracted a record number of concurrent live video streams: 1.3 million users. It was a major technological feat and yet it was also a failure. The quality of the CNN.com stream—as with the other online services' streams—was poor, with the image freezing and the audio stuttering, making it difficult to watch for any extended period.[88] Conventional broadcast television at the same time was able to handle nearly ten times as many viewers without any deterioration in its signal.[89] In fact, while CNN.com offered a small, 569-by-320 pixels video image, broadcast television presented the event in high-definition

clarity, with commensurate audio. On this day, it was broadcast television that offered a superior screen experience and it provided it to a significantly greater number of people. To return to Pool's dictum: there is "no immutable law of growing convergence." On inauguration day, convergence grew (1.3 million concurrent streams!) and shrank (stuttering, distorted

Figure 4.48 Barack Obama's inauguration was both a high point and a low point for online video on social networks such as Facebook. Millions connected online, but the video quality was poor.

streams paling in comparison to HD television!). So shall it be for the next few years, at the very least. The only thing that is certain is that television's stylistic schemas will either adjust to the fluctuating characteristics of the contemporary media environment, or they will wither and die.

Notes

1. Henry Jenkins, *Convergence Culture: Where Old and New Media Collide* (New York: New York University Press, 2006), 10.
2. The essay on which this chapter is based was written in 1999 and 2000, initially presented to the Society for Cinema Studies on March 11, 2000, and published in the winter 2001 issue of *Screen*. As I write these words in January 2009, ten years have passed since I first considered the topic.
3. Ithiel de Sola Pool, *Technologies of Freedom* (Cambridge: Belknap Press, 1983), 54. Jenkins dubs him the prophet of convergence and quotes Pool, *Convergence Culture*, 11.
4. As one new-media marketing website queried, "Is all of [online video] monetizable?" "Online Video Growth Continues," eMarketer.com, January 15, 2009, www.emarketer.com/Article.aspx?id=1006868 (accessed January 16, 2009). And the mission of Pixsy, a media search platform, is "to dramatically enhance traffic and monetization for website owners." "Pixsy Corporation," Pixsy, 2007, www.pixsy-corp.com (accessed January 22, 2009).
5. Jenkins, *Convergence Culture*, 12.
6. "Press Releases," *ERLive*, January 5, 1998, www.ERLive.com/press.html. "Warner Bros. Online" as a distinct entity no longer exists. It has splintered into divisions within the Warner Bros. Home Entertainment Group: Warner Bros. Digital Distribution, Warner Bros. Advanced Digital Services, and Warner Bros. Interactive Entertainment. The WB's website proclaims, "WARNER BROS. ADVANCED DIGITAL SERVICES provides full-service, cutting-edge interactive solutions for Warner Bros. Entertainment subsidiaries. WBADS also oversees all aspects of warnerbros.com, which serves as the entry point into, and aggregator of all things Warner Bros," www.warnerbros.com/main/#/page=company-info/divisions/home_entertainment/divisions_advancedmediaservices.
7. "Online Events," *ERLive.com*, January 5, 1998, www.ERLive.com/events.html.
8. Ken Neville, "Minor Wounds, Killer Ratings for Live 'ER'", *E! online*, February 28, 2000, www.eonline.com/News/Items/0,1,1833,00.html.
9. Jack Spellman, "Re: Captions on live ER episode," e-mail to the author, March 3, 2000.
10. Ellis himself assays television in the new millennium in *Seeing Things: Television in the Age of Uncertainty* (New York: I.B. Tauris, 2000).
11. Charles Derry, "Television Soap Opera: Incest, Bigamy, and Fatal Disease," *Journal of the University Film and Video Association* 35, no. 1 (1983): 4–16.
12. Although *Chicago Hope* was not on the air nearly as long as *ER*, it did manage a respectable six-year run. During their first seasons the two programs were broadcast against one another on Thursday nights, with *Chicago Hope* moving off the Thursday schedule after losing the ratings battle to *ER*.
13. Ken Kwapis, telephone interview, February 24, 2000.
14. David Bordwell, *On the History of Film Style* (Cambridge: Harvard University Press, 1997), 168.
15. Ibid., 306.
16. Herb Zettl, *Sight Sound Motion: Applied Media Aesthetics*, 3rd edn (Belmont: Wadsworth, 1999), 141–63.
17. Kwapis, telephone interview.

18. Zettl, *Sight Sound Motion*, 41.

19. Dziga Vertov, *Kino-Eye: The Writings of Dziga Vertov*, ed. Annette Michelson, trans. Kevin O'Brien (Berkeley: University of California Press, 1984), 17.

20. This has continued into the 2000s, as can be seen in long-running programs such as the *Law & Order* franchise and newer efforts such as the critically revered *Mad Men* (2007–). However, as the decade is coming to a close, more and more single-camera programs are shifting from film to high-definition video. Examples include *Battlestar Galactica* (2004–9), *Weeds* (2005–) and *Dexter* (2006–).

21. Personal correspondence with Ken Kwapis. It may be noted that the scene as it was edited cut this movement into two shots. Nonetheless, Kwapis' plan for movement illustrates the house style of *ER*.

22. *ER*'s reliance upon the Steadicam was confirmed by Kwapis. *Sports Night* and *The West Wing* were both directed/produced by Thomas Schlamme, who's known to favor Steadicam movements and was responsible for the direction of *ER*'s live "Ambush" episode.

23. "Ambush," *Shot Logger*, December 9, 2008, www.tcf.ua.edu/slgallery/shotlogger/TitleListDetailPage.php?recordID=211 (accessed December 18, 2008).

24. Peter Wollen, "Godard and Counter Cinema: *Vent d'Est*", *Afterimage* 4 (autumn 1975): 6–17. Reprinted in *Readings and Writings: Semiotic Counter-Strategies* (London: Verso, 1982), 79–91.

25. For more on Fox "reality" programs, see Tarleton Gillespie, "Narrative Control and Visual Polysemy: Fox Surveillance Specials and the Limits of Legitimation," *Velvet Light Trap* 45 (2000): 36–49.

26. It goes without saying that handheld shots do not always signify this documentari-ness. Most commonly they're used to signify subjective camera, as may be seen in innumerable scenes of characters stalking one another. Further, the initial popularity of handheld shots—in the early 1960s under the influence of French New Wave directors—was also interpreted as emblematic of modern disorientation and angst.

27. Jean-Pierre Geuens, "Visuality and Power: The Work of the Steadicam," *Film Quarterly* 47, no. 2 (1993–4): 16.

28. André Bazin, *Jean Renoir*, trans. W. W. Halsey II and William H. Simon (New York: Simon and Schuster, 1973), 46.

29. For examples from *As the World Turns*, see Jeremy G. Butler, "Notes on the Soap Opera Apparatus: Televisual Style and *As the World Turns*," *Cinema Journal* 25, no. 3 (1986): 59.

30. John Ellis, *Visible Fictions: Cinema Television Video* (New York: Routledge, 1992), 106.

31. Ibid., 108.

32. Roland Barthes, "Rhetoric of the Image," in *Image Music Text*, ed. and trans. Stephen Heath (New York: Hill and Wang, 1977), 44.

33. Stephen Heath and Gillian Skirrow, "Television, a World in Action," *Screen* 18, no. 2 (1977): 61.

34. "Press Releases."

35. Heath and Skirrow, "Television," 7–59.

36. Viewers in the Mountain Time Zone saw a tape of the Eastern/Central broadcast. The U.S. DVD release uses the East Coast version for most of the episode, but shifts to the West Coast version for the final ten minutes.

37. For additional differences between the two, see Ken Neville, "Minor Wounds, Killer Ratings for Live 'ER.'"

38. Mark J.P. Wolf, "Inventing Space: Toward a Taxonomy of On- and Off-Screen Space in Video Games," *Film Quarterly* 51, no. 1 (1997): 11–23.

39. Janet H. Murray, *Hamlet on the Holodeck: The Future of Narrative in Cyberspace* (Cambridge: MIT Press, 1997), 67.

40. John Thornton Caldwell, *Televisuality: Style, Crisis, and Authority in American Television* (New Brunswick: Rutgers University Press, 1995), 264.
41. Murray, *Hamlet on the Holodeck*, 71.
42. Ibid., 74.
43. Ibid., 79.
44. The beginning of the navigation code starts with and HTML comment, "<!– begin nav ->", after which the JavaScript is invoked with this line of code: <script type="text/javascript" charset="utf-8">nbcDropDown('ul#er_nav');nbcHideMe[0] = 'er_nav';</script>.
45. Mechanical mice contain a ball mechanism which rubs x- and y-axis rollers inside the mouse and the cursor responds by moving along those axes. In the 2000s, such mice were mostly replaced by devices using optical sensors to track the mouse's movement.
46. Ibid., 126.
47. Bordwell, *On the History of Film Style*, 168.
48. Using a fixed-width table, *ERTV*'s main page is set to a width of 500 pixels while *ERLive*'s width is 600 pixels.
49. John Belton, *Widescreen Cinema* (Cambridge: Harvard University Press, 1992).
50. Widescreen televisions have changed this marginally. Many of them allow you to zoom into the image or change your display to/from letterboxing and windowboxing. Some, however, force the viewer to accept whatever aspect ratio is their default.
51. 640×480, 800×600, and 1024×768 were the most common monitor settings in the 1990s, but 1280×1024 and larger/wider displays are widespread in the late 2000s.
52. "It's a WRAP!!!" *ERLive*, January 5, 1998, www.ERLive.com/wrap.html.
53. Quoted in Belton, *Widescreen Cinema*, 98.
54. *QuickTime VR Authoring*, June 12, 2000, www.apple.com/quicktime/qtvr.
55. Margaret Morse, *Virtualities: Television, Media Art, and Cyberculture* (Bloomington: Indiana University Press, 1998), 91.
56. Ibid., 71.
57. Ibid., 87.
58. *ER*'s "sinuous z-axis moves" have been commented on by Morse, *Virtualities*, 224.
59. Wolf, "Inventing Space," 20.
60. *Battlezone*'s wireframe graphics were displayed on a black-and-white CRT monitor, with green and red overlays providing some limited color.
61. Murray, *Hamlet on the Holodeck*, 129.
62. Morse, *Virtualities*, 21.
63. Ibid., 20. It will be interesting to see how the digital video recorder (DVR) affects viewers' sense of time and interactivity. Boddy provides an early assessment of the possible impact of devices such as TiVo: William Boddy, "Television in Transit," *Screen* 41, no. 1 (2000): 67–72.
64. Lev Manovich, *The Language of New Media* (Cambridge: The MIT Press, 2001), 95–6. Also available online: Lev Manovich, "An Archeology of a Computer Screen," Lev Manovich, www.manovich.net/TEXT/digital_nature.html (accessed December 18, 2008).
65. Manovich, *The Language of New Media*, 99.
66. Zettl, *Sight Sound Motion*, 255.
67. Murray, *Hamlet on the Holodeck*, 129. Quoted above.
68. "Mass Distraction: Media Consumption in Dollars and Hours", *Wired*, May 2000, 105.
69. In *Second Life* one creates a visual identity, an avatar, that can travel through a virtual world that is simultaneously connected, via the Internet, with thousands of other users. It's less a game than an environment. *World of Warcraft*, a massively multiplayer online role-playing game (MMORPG), also supports visual avatars and online interaction, but also includes combat with other users.

70. In 1994, the fastest online consumer access was via a modem transmitting data at 28.8 Kbps (kilobits per second).

71. The speed of consumer-grade Internet access is highly variable—depending on both technological and economic factors. Nonetheless, it is common for consumers currently accessing the Internet via cable modems to achieve download speeds of 6,000 Kbps.

72. One of the first to identify Web 2.0 was Tim Reilly who contends that principal among the new online "rules" is, "Build applications that harness network effects to get better the more people use them." Tim O'Reilly, "Web 2.0 Compact Definition: Trying Again," Oreilly.com, December 10, 2006, radar.oreilly.com/archives/2006/12/web-20-compact.html (accessed January 8, 2009).

73. One notable example is the "Dick in a Box" excerpt from NBC's *Saturday Night Live* (December 16, 2006). Its posting to YouTube allowed it to go viral. And among 2008's most viral videos was Weezer's music video, *Pork and Beans*, which itself features individuals from homemade viral videos—including Gary Brolsma (aka the Numa Numa Guy), Tay Zonday (famous for his rendition of "Chocolate Rain"), and Chris Crocker (who proclaimed, "Leave Britney [Spears] alone!").

74. "Create TV," TheWB.com, www.thewb.com/wblender (accessed January 16, 2009).

75. Frank Rose, "Commercial Break," *Wired* 14, no. 12 (December 2006), www.wired.com/wired/archive/14.12/tahoe.html (accessed January 20, 2009).

76. "Cooliris," Cooliris, January 29, 2009, www.cooliris.com (accessed January 29, 2009).

77. Sites such as Ustream.tv facilitate live, interactive "broadcasts" by persons outside the world of big media. According to its website,

> [It] enables anyone with a camera and an Internet connection to quickly and easily broadcast to a global audience of unlimited size. In less than two minutes, anyone can become a broadcaster by creating their own channel on Ustream or by broadcasting through their own site, empowering them to engage with their audience and further build their brand.
>
> ("About Us," Ustream.TV, www.ustream.tv/about [accessed January 16, 2009])

78. Ellis, *Visible Fictions*, 50. Some 18 years later, Ellis maintains that "the aesthetics of television" still demand a "relatively low level of audience attention." Ellis, *Seeing Things*, 100.

79. Paul Verna, "User-Generated Content: More Popular than Profitable," eMarketer, January 2009, www.emarketer.com/Reports/All/Emarketer_2000549.aspx (accessed January 29, 2009).

80. "Company History," YouTube, January 20, 2009, www.youtube.com/t/about (accessed January 20, 2009).

81. Pierre Lévy, *Collective Intelligence: Mankind's Emerging World in Cyberspace*, trans. Robert Bononno (Cambridge: Perseus, 1997), 13.

82. In a report from August 2008, the Nielsen Company found that YouTube "broadcast" 4,762,883,000 video streams that month and that its nearest competitor (Fox Interactive Media) could muster only 278,375,000. "Top Online Streaming Video Sites: August 2008," Nielsen Wire (September 24, 2008), blog.nielsen.com/nielsenwire/online_mobile/top-online-brands-august-2008 (accessed January 30, 2009).

83. "Video File Upload," YouTube, January 20, 2009, www.youtube.com/my_videos_upload (accessed January 20, 2009).

84. Pierre Lévy, *Cyberculture*, trans. Robert Bononno (Minneapolis: University of Minnesota Press, 2001), 151.

85. Originally known as ZDTV and later as G4.

86. Chris Pirillo, "Live Streaming Internet Broadcast," January 13, 2009, chris.pirillo.com/live (accessed January 13, 2009).

87. Lévy, *Cyberculture*, 11.

88. Erick Schonfeld, "The Day Live Web Video Streaming Failed Us," TechCrunch, January 21, 2009, www.techcrunch.com/2009/01/21/the-day-live-web-video-streaming-failed-us (accessed January 22, 2009).
89. According to a television industry newsletter,

> during 11a to 1230p, NBC averaged almost 11.5 million total viewers and a 4.0 A25–54 rating; ABC averaged 11.0 million total viewers and a 3.5 A25–54 rating; CNN drew in 7.3 million total viewers and a 2.4 demo rating; and CBS had nearly 7.2 million total viewers and a 2.3 demo rating.
>
> ("Cynopsis," Cynopsis Media, January 22, 2009, www.cynopsis.com/content/view/4133/53 [accessed January 22, 2009])

5.

Televisuality and the Resurrection of the Sitcom in the 2000s

In my consideration of commercials above, I had occasion to allude to Bertolt Brecht in that unlikely context. I must invoke him once again—perhaps unadvisedly—in my explication of style in yet another lowly television context: the genre of the situation comedy. The sitcom is one of television's founding genres—having existed on radio before making the transition to television, much like the soap opera. And, like the soap opera as well, it is a genre said to be in decline.[1] Within the past ten years, however, it has radically reinvented itself and that reinvention has largely occurred within the realm of style. Therefore, I feel it is not wholly inappropriate to compare the contemporary situation comedy with Brecht's revolutionary work in the 1920s and 1930s. And, if I may paraphrase his notes to the opera, *Rise and Fall of the City of Mahagonny* (1930), I contend that the modern sitcom is the televisual sitcom.[2]

Many say the sitcom is already dead—killed off by reality television and the YouTubian attention span of network television's few remaining viewers.[3] The genre's ratings have been disastrously low for several years, and the writers strike during the 2007–8 season pushed them lower still. In the two seasons before the strike, the Nielsen ratings' top-20 programs included just one lonely sitcom—the critically reviled *Two and a Half Men* (2003–). Looking back over the genre's various peaks in the ratings, we can see that in 1978–9 all of the top ten programs were sitcoms and, exactly one decade later (1988–9), 16 out of the top 25 were sitcoms—the highest sitcom saturation in the history of U.S. television.[4] The current low ratings only tell part of the story. Within the television industry, there is a pessimism about the genre. Larry Gelbart, who developed the long-running sitcom, *M*A*S*H* (1972–83), expressed it succinctly, "It is just over."[5]

Perhaps the most reliable indication that a genre is becoming moribund is the frequency with which it is ridiculed, whether gently or not. Some of the more notable parodies since the 1990s include Weezer's cannibalization of *Happy Days* for the Spike Jonze-directed music video, *Buddy Holly* (1994, available on TVStyleBook.com) and a 2009 titles sequence of *The Simpsons* in which the family appears as if they were in several iconic sitcoms, presenting a virtual history of the genre in just a few seconds.[6] A shot based on *The Honeymooners* (1955–6)[7] is rendered in black-and-white and casts Homer as Ralph Kramden, Marge as Alice Kramden and Bart as Ed Norton (Figure 5.1). The sitcom, *Scrubs*

Figure 5.1 In black-and-white, *The Simpsons* parodies *The Honeymooners*, with Homer and Marge as Ralph and Alice Kramden, and Bart as Ed Norton.

(2001–), engaged in genre parody in a manner that is especially significant for the study of television style. In the episode, "My Life in Four Cameras" (February 15, 2005), young doctor, J.D. (Zach Braff), suffers through a difficult day in Sacred Heart Hospital. When, in voiceover, he muses, "There are moments when we all wish life was more like a sitcom," he is instantly transported into one (Figures 5.2–5.3). The camera zooms back to reveal video cameras on pedestals, shooting J.D. on a hospital set, with a visible lighting grid (Figure 5.4). The voiceover continues, "J.D.'s sitcom fantasy will be back after these messages." And a fade to black takes us into a commercial break. Once the episode resumes, *Scrubs'* diegetic world becomes the sitcom fantasy world—with a laugh track, "bad" sitcom jokes and the announcement, "J.D.'s sitcom fantasy is filmed in front of a live studio audience."[8] This episode of *Scrubs* is a particularly telling parody because it goes beyond the more obvious targets: the sitcom's self-congratulatory laugh track, its conventions of plot and dialogue, and its presumed complicity in sexist, racist, and classist ideology (e.g., in *Leave It to Beaver* [1957–63] and *Father Knows Best* [1954–60]). As indicated by the episode's title, "My Life in Four Cameras," *Scrubs* here addresses and deconstructs the sitcom's standard mode of production: the multiple-camera set-up.[9] And it's only able to do so because *Scrubs'* standard mode of production is not multiple-camera. Rather, it relies on single-camera production.[10]

The multiple-camera mode that was obtained in 1978 and 1988 when the sitcom was a dominant television force is currently being challenged by a new crop of narrative comedies that aggressively implement the single-camera shooting style. *Scrubs* is one such comedy. During the 2006–7 season, NBC strategically grouped four of these on Thursday nights when *My Name Is Earl* (2005–), *The Office* (2005–), *Scrubs*, and *30 Rock* (2006–) huddled together—striving to regain the prestige, if not the unattainable ratings, of NBC's blockbuster, "must-see" television night of years past. *Scrubs'* parody of the sitcom's mode of production crystallizes the genre's hyperconsciousness of the craft practices of four-camera production and a perceived need to transcend that mode of production to evolve the genre. As *Scrubs* producer Bill Lawrence explains,

> What we're trying to do in the middle of it [the multiple-camera parody], even though we're doing sitcommy stories and sitcommy things, is ultimately have a great experience for the fans. Which means we're still writing funny jokes. So I hope people will like it on two levels—hopefully they'll watch it and laugh because we took time to write really funny stuff, and on some level be enjoying the fact that we're tweaking the format a little bit.[11]

If *Scrubs* can derive humor from "tweaking the format," from the defamiliarization of the number of cameras used to shoot a program, then we need to explore the significance and functions of production modes to the sitcom genre and, more globally, to television style.

Single-camera comedies are experimenting with television style on a complex variety of levels. Moreover, as is often the case in comedy, these experiments can be quite extreme. It is useful, therefore, to invoke once again Caldwell's concept of televisuality, which I have traced through *Miami Vice* (Chapter 2) and television commercials (Chapter 3). To review: he proposes "to describe an important historical moment in television's presentational manner, one defined by excessive stylization and visual exhibitionism."[12] At the time that he was writing, the early 1990s, the sitcom was anything but excessively stylized or visually exhibitionistic. On his way toward defining televisuality, he accurately describes the then-prevalent sitcom mode as exemplifying the "zero-degree studio style," the opposite of the televisual—discussed above in terms of attenuated continuity in the soap opera (Chapter 1) and *Dallas* (Chapter 2).[13] He writes about so-called "quality" sitcoms:

> The reemergence of serious drama and writing as center stage in television brought with it a renewed and dominant preoccupation with zero-degree studio style in television. Television art, in effect, had been redefined as theater. Cinematic and videographic influences took a back seat as television entered an *ascetic* period during the first half of the 1970s.[14]

Figure 5.2 A *Scrubs* episode's transition from single-camera to multiple-camera production is signaled by a shift in lighting from low-key, almost film-noir style lighting to…

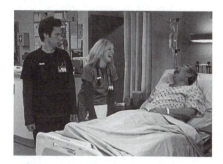

Figure 5.3 …bright high-key lighting.

Figure 5.4 A wide shot of the *Scrubs* studio set up for multiple-camera production, which it normally did not use.

"Quality" sitcoms—such as those produced by Norman Lear and MTM Enterprises—placed a premium on "liveness, character acting, and sensitive writing" over "television's stylistic capabilities."[15] *Scrubs* and its ilk reject this ascetic approach to sitcom production and revel in television's stylistic capabilities, raising the possibility that they qualify as televisual programs.

In analyzing the single-camera comedy, I wish to account for the sitcom's visual and sound style in terms of its manipulation of the audience's experience and its ability to create meaning and humor on its own. To do so, I first revisit the multiple-camera proscenium schema introduced in Chapter 1 and ruminate on the sitcom's particular implementation of it. Second, I describe the breaching of that schema by the televisual sitcom. Finally, I offer some thoughts on the significance and functioning of this new television style. In so doing, I hope to follow Bordwell's suggestion:

> in order to explain continuity and change within film styles, we ought first to examine the circumstances that impinge most proximately on filmmaking—the mode of film production, the technology employed, the traditions, and the craft routines favored by individual agents.[16]

The Multiple-Camera Proscenium Schema

The conventions of the multiple-camera sitcom evolved early in the post-World War II history of American television. Making the transition from radio to television, early sitcoms such as *Mama* (1949–57) and *The Goldbergs* (1949–56) were broadcast live, from a proscenium-style theater with an audience.[17] Within this presentational mode, the proscenium and its curtain need not be effaced or concealed—as it would be in later sitcoms. George Burns, for example, addresses the audience from in front of the curtain and teases the operators of the large television cameras (Figure 5.5)—on *The George Burns and Gracie Allen Program* (1950–8). In their mode of production and their overarching aesthetic, these programs owe more to American vaudeville and British music hall traditions than they do to narrative radio programs shot in a studio. Radio programs could construct diegetic worlds set indoors, outdoors, or, indeed, on the surface of the moon—limited only by the resources of their sound effects departments and their listeners' imaginations.

Figure 5.5 The George Burns and Gracie Allen Show: George Burns teases a camera operator after having spoken directly to the studio audience from in front of a proscenium curtain.

Figure 5.6 A vaudeville performance. Vaudeville shaped the style of early live television performances.

Early live television looked more like a vaudeville stage (Figure 5.6) with modest, shallow sets, broad lighting and what Bordwell, after art historian Heinrich Wölfflin, calls "planimetric" staging—"spread[ing] the performers out like clothes on a line, along a single plane"[18] rather than having them move in depth, up and down stage, as it were.

This mode of production favored a tradition of comic performance that relied upon an audience for its timing and to sustain its energy. In *Television Sitcom*, Brett Mills extensively considers the implications of this performance tradition and its antecedents. I don't wish to pursue this line of inquiry here as it focuses on performance style rather than style of sound and image, but it is evident that this performance tradition motivated the most significant development in the sitcom's mode of production and its use of a recording technology in the 1950s: the introduction of *film* recording to multiple-camera shooting in 1951. The story is frequently told of Lucille Ball and Desi Arnaz's investment of their own money in *I Love Lucy* so that their sponsor, Philip Morris cigarettes, and their network, CBS, would agree to record their live performances on film—and not on the visually inferior kinescope that could be recorded from a live broadcast. In return, Ball and Arnaz would control the syndication rights to the program, which turned out to be substantial enough that they could form Desilu Studios with the profits. In addition to the shift from live to live-on-film broadcasting, Ball and Arnaz were largely responsible for the sitcom shifting from a true proscenium-style theater to a television studio where the audience sat on bleachers, rising up from the stage floor instead of conventional theater seating—as can be seen in a photo of Arnaz addressing the studio audience (Figure 5.7). The arrangement of a line of sets in front of bleachers has persisted in programs shot with audiences (Figure 5.8)—resulting in a studio layout markedly different from live-on-tape narrative productions, such as soap operas (see discussion of *As the World Turns* in Chapter 1, Figure 1.34). In contrast to the *I Love Lucy* layout, another early sitcom, *The Honeymooners*, recorded Jackie Gleason and Art Carney with three Electronicams, on the curtain-framed proscenium stage of the Adelphi Theater in New York City.[19] Despite *The Honeymooners'* old-fashioned use of a theatrical stage, its recording technology was more advanced than that of *I Love Lucy*.

Essentially, the "DuMont Electronicam TV-film system" was a video-assist system that permitted the live transmission of a program at the same time that film was being recorded.[20] In the same year (1956), Jerry Lewis devised a closely related system for use in motion picture production.[21] The end product of both DuMont's and Lewis' systems were motion-picture films—films that, as with *I Love Lucy*, were clearly superior to a kinescope.

Thus, by the mid-1950s, the sitcom's aesthetic traditions (from vaudeville and

Figure 5.7 Desi Arnaz speaks to the studio audience of *I Love Lucy*.

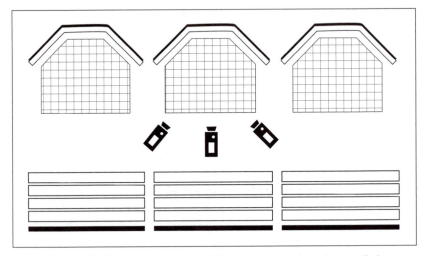

Figure 5.8 In multiple-camera sitcoms with live studio audiences, three-walled sets are arrayed in front of the audience. Video cameras are positioned between the audience and the sets.

radio) had been assimilated and its mode of production (multiple-camera) and fundamental technology (film or live broadcast) had been established.[22] Moreover, this stylistic foundation has changed little in the past 50 years. This consistency—the persistent "standardized craft practices"[23] (Bordwell)—of the multiple-camera sitcom may be identified through close textual analyses. To that end, I have dissected scenes from an early sitcom episode (from October 1, 1955: *The Honeymooners*) and a recent, popular sitcom (from January 8, 2007: *The New Adventures of the Old Christine*). (See Tables 5.1 and 5.2; video clips are included on TVStyleBook.com.) Despite superficial differences—black and white versus color, editing pace—the two scenes share numerous characteristics.

Before proceeding, it is important to clarify that schemas are rooted in modes of production, but they are not wholly determined by those modes. Schemas refer to stylistic conventions *as they appear in the texts*. Through convention, the schemas become linked to on-the-set craft practices and contemporary technology, but they may also become detached from those practices and that technology. For instance, laugh tracks originated in and are semiotically linked to the on-the-set practice of having an audience close to microphones on the stage and would thus appear to be one of Peirce's indexical signs—that is, an indexical signifier of the presence of an audience. However, the laughter on a laugh track is indexical in appearance only as it may well have been fabricated by a sound technician with no audience present. Indeed, it is common practice in contemporary sitcom production to splice together different takes of a scene. In such a situation, the audio from one take may be inserted on top of the image from another. Further, the distinctions between multiple-camera and single-camera that I make are also referring to elements of videography, *mise-en-scène* and editing *as they appear*

Table 5.1 The Honeymooners scene découpage

Shot Number, Scale, and Length	Figure	Sound
1 long shot 19 secs. (*Figures 5.9–5.16*)	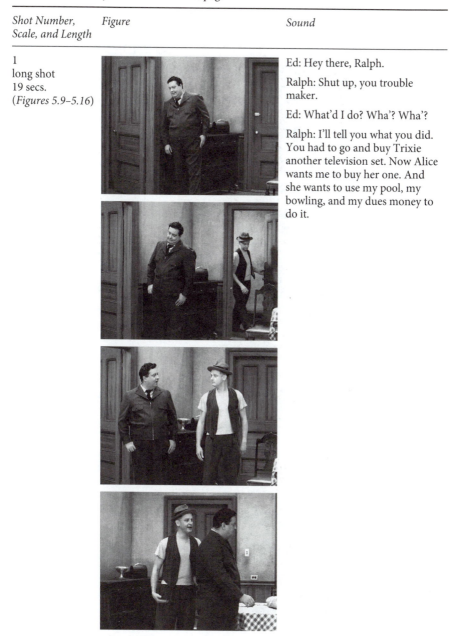	Ed: Hey there, Ralph. Ralph: Shut up, you trouble maker. Ed: What'd I do? Wha'? Wha'? Ralph: I'll tell you what you did. You had to go and buy Trixie another television set. Now Alice wants me to buy her one. And she wants to use my pool, my bowling, and my dues money to do it.

continued

Table 5.1 continued

Shot Number, Scale, and Length	Figure	Sound

Shot Number, Scale, and Length	Figure	Sound
2 medium long shot 24 secs. (*Figure 5.17*)		Ed: How come Alice found out about such a thing as television, Ralph? I thought you kept her in the dark about things like that. Well, if you're going to buy a television set then I guess what I came down to see you about is out. I was down pricing those television sets and they're pretty steep, pretty expensive. I can't afford one right now. I figured maybe I'd borrow a little money from you.
3 medium long shot 6 secs. (*Figure 5.18*)		Ralph: Why should you do that? Why don't you go down and get it like you got everything else— on time?
4 medium long shot 21 secs. (*Figure 5.19*)		Ed: I can't. They won't give me any more credit down there at the store. I got eighteen accounts going already. No, nineteen. I bought a water softener last week. Well, I guess just for the next two, three months I got to go without television. Boy, I'm going to miss it, too. I couldn't come at a worse time. Do you realize that tomorrow afternoon Captain Video takes off for Pluto?

continued

Table 5.1 continued

Shot Number, Scale, and Length	Figure	Sound
5 medium long shot 26 (*Figures 5.20–5.22*)		Ralph: Hey, wait a minute. Wait a minute, I got the solution to the whole thing. Look, you haven't got enough money to buy a set. I haven't got enough money to buy a set. But if we put our money together, we got enough dough to get a great set. It solves the whole problem. You can see Captain Video. I can go bowling. And Alice can sit around here watching television all day if she wants.
6 medium long shot 32 secs. (*Figure 5.23*)		Ed: I gotta go along with you, Ralph. The whole route, all the way, except for one thing. How come automatically the television set lands down here instead of up there? Ralph: I've seen some babies in my day, but you are the champ. Alright, we'll flip a coin to see where the television set goes. Give me a coin. Alright. Heads I win, tails you lose. Right? Tails, you lose.

Shot Number, Scale, and Length	Figure	Sound
7 medium long shot 14 secs. (*Figure 5.24*)		Ralph: Now… Ed: Wait a minute, wait a minute. Ralph: What's wrong? Ed: I hope I don't insult you, Ralph, but would you mind giving me back my coin? Ralph: Oh, yes, yes.
8 medium long shot 9 secs. (*Figure 5.25*)		Ralph: Right about here, it ought to go, pal.

on the screen and may, or may not, be the result of one or four cameras on the set at the time of shooting. One could conceivably use a single camera on set to replicate multiple-camera style and, more commonly, more than one camera is employed on the set these days—even for theatrical films—to create programs that still maintain a "single-camera" look. As director Tom Cherones explains, it has become common practice in so-called single-camera shoots to set up two cameras on the same angle—one for a wide shot and one for a close-up.[24] The dramatic program, *24*, for instance presents a single-camera schema, but, as its cinematographer, Rodney Charters, reveals:

> We always shoot with two cameras. A-camera … is always handheld and B-camera … is always on a dolly. The two are usually 90 degrees apart, which makes it difficult to light too specifically. Frequently we'll also have a C-camera floating around. We go through whole scenes from beginning to end and then do the scene again with the two cameras in different positions.[25]

Thus, craft practices and technology certainly shape stylistic schema, but they also can be detached from them conceptually. In the final analysis, the schema identifies stylistic practices as they are manifest in the television text.

During my discussion of the multiple-camera proscenium schema in soap opera, I summarized its components in Table 1.3—dividing them into *mise-en-scène*, videography, editing, and sound. Since the focus of this chapter

Table 5.2 The New Adventures of Old Christine scene découpage

Shot Number, Scale, and Length	Figure	Sound
1 long shot 6 secs. (*Figures 5.26–5.28*)	  	Music starts and stops before dialogue. Christine: Hey, guys. Matthew: Hey. Christine: Ritchie, weren't you supposed to have a playdate with the girls.
2 medium shot 1 sec. (*Figure 5.29*)		Ritchie: I did.
3 medium shot 2 secs. (*Figure 5.30*)		Christine: Well, what happened?
4 medium shot 1 sec. (*Figure 5.31*)		Matthew: Do you want to tell them what happened?

Shot Number, Scale, and Length	Figure	Sound
5 medium shot 1 sec. (*Figure 5.32*)	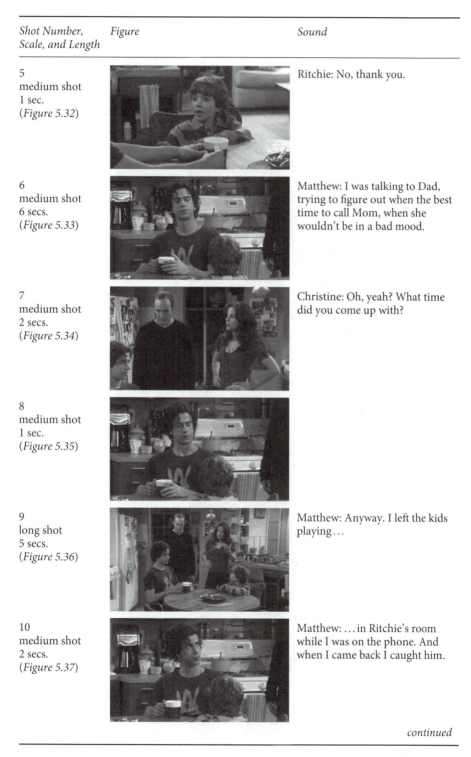	Ritchie: No, thank you.
6 medium shot 6 secs. (*Figure 5.33*)		Matthew: I was talking to Dad, trying to figure out when the best time to call Mom, when she wouldn't be in a bad mood.
7 medium shot 2 secs. (*Figure 5.34*)		Christine: Oh, yeah? What time did you come up with?
8 medium shot 1 sec. (*Figure 5.35*)		
9 long shot 5 secs. (*Figure 5.36*)		Matthew: Anyway. I left the kids playing…
10 medium shot 2 secs. (*Figure 5.37*)		Matthew: …in Ritchie's room while I was on the phone. And when I came back I caught him.

continued

Table 5.2 continued

Shot Number, Scale, and Length	Figure	Sound
11 medium shot 1 sec. (*Figure 5.38*)		
12 medium shot 2 secs. (*Figure 5.39*)		Richard: What were you doing?
13 medium shot 2 secs. (*Figure 5.40*)		Ritchie: I was just playing house with my friends.
14 medium shot 1 sec. (*Figure 5.41*)		
15 medium shot 1 sec. (*Figure 5.42*)		Matthew: And…?
16 medium shot 2 secs. (*Figure 5.43*)		Ritchie: And I was the husband. So I kissed them.

Shot Number, Scale, and Length	Figure	Sound
17 medium shot 8 secs. (*Figure 5.44*)		Christine: Ritchie! Richard: All three of them?
18 long shot 10 secs. (*Figure 5.45*)		Christine: [pauses for laughter] Ritchie, those girls are your friends. And you don't kiss your friends. You don't.
19 medium shot 3 secs. (*Figure 5.46*)		Christine: No matter how much you want to. You don't.
20 medium shot 1 sec. (*Figure 5.47*)		
21 medium shot 2 secs. (*Figure 5.48*)		Christine: Alright, listen…
22 long shot 9 secs. (*Figures 5.49–5.51*)		Christine: …go upstairs and get going on your homework and I'll be right there. Richard: Don't feel bad. It's just nature.

continued

Table 5.2 continued

Shot Number, Scale, and Length	Figure	Sound

23
medium shot
5 secs.
(*Figure 5.52*)

Christine: No, I don't accept that. Listen, Matthew, you have friends that are girls, right?

24
medium shot
less than 1 sec.
(*Figure 5.53*)

Matthew: Sure.

25
medium shot
1 sec.
(*Figure 5.54*)

Richard: That you haven't slept with?

26
medium shot
7 secs.
(*Figure 5.55*)

Matthew: Oh, no. One! Oh, no. No.

Shot Number, Scale, and Length	Figure	Sound
27 long shot 8 secs. (*Figure 5.56*)		[Children's screams are heard from off-stage] Christine: What, the girls are still here? You didn't send them home?
28 medium shot 5 secs. (*Figure 5.57*)		Matthew: I didn't know what to do. They're bossy. They called me super dork. So I just grabbed Ritchie and ran.
29 long shot 11 secs. (*Figures 5.58–5.63*)	   	Christine: Ritchie! Ritchie! Richard: Man, all three. [Music starts at end of dialogue, continues briefly into the next scene.]

continued

Table 5.2 continued

Shot Number, Scale, and Length	Figure	Sound

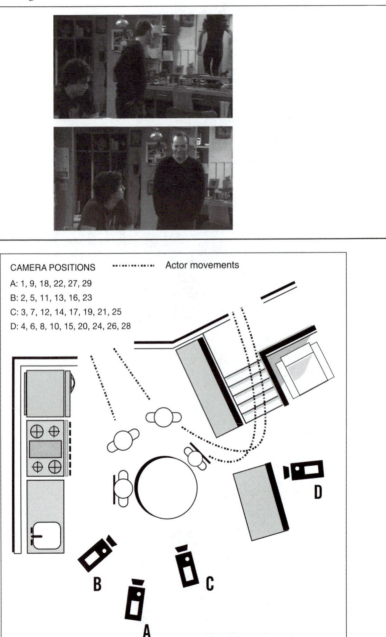

Figure 5.64 The set design of *The New Adventures of Old Christine* emphasizes side-to-side blocking, but permits some use of depth.

is how schema change and not how they persist, I will not discuss each item in that table, but I do need to highlight the predominant elements that mark the sitcom as adhering to this schema. Further, the sitcom does implement this schema in ways that diverge from the soap opera, as one would expect with a genre that is comedic rather than dramatic; but, as we shall see, most of those divergences are overshadowed by the convergences.

The *mise-en-scène* of the sitcom shares the soap opera's limitation to recurring interior and in-studio exterior sets—with high-key lighting and no ceilings.[26] Both *The Honeymooners* and *The New Adventures of Old Christine* (commonly abbreviated as *Old Christine*) spend the lion's share of their diegetic time in a living room/dining room/kitchen. Much like the soap opera, these sets mirror the emphasis on home and workplace situations in the sitcom and encourage a preponderance of dialogue rather than action. Sitcoms do incorporate physical humor and Jackie Gleason, Art Carney, and Julia Louis-Dreyfus are all capable of humorous physical performances, but no one would ever mistake a sitcom for a Buster Keaton comedy. The humor relies more heavily on comic tropes, double-entendres, word play, catch-phrases (e.g., Ralph's "Bang! Zoom! Straight to the moon, Alice!" and "Baby, you're the greatest") and the description of situations by characters. The set design of these interiors has become increasingly elaborate over the decades— as is clearly seen by contrasting the homes of the Kramdens and Christine— but the locations themselves have changed very little. It is true that recent sitcoms travel outside the studio more than their predecessors, but even *Seinfeld*, the definitive 1990s multiple-camera sitcom, built elaborate sets instead of shooting on location. For example, an Emmy-winning episode that transpires entirely in a parking garage was filmed in the *Seinfeld* sound stage— requiring its wholesale renovation:

> Jerry's apartment and the studio audience seating was removed. Every shot used showed the entire set so it constantly required shooting from different angles. Mirrors all around the perimeters of the stage gave the illusion of further depth and with just a dozen cars, the illusion of being in a giant parking garage was complete.[27]

The economies of sitcom production are such that even a massive set is more cost efficient than shooting on location.

As we have seen in soap opera, the sitcom tends to stage its actors on the *x*-axis—moving them laterally across the relatively shallow set. The planimetric staging of *The Honeymooners* is quite obvious, with Ralph and Ed pacing about within the truncated depth of the room (Table 5.1, Figures 5.9–5.16; see TVStyleBook.com for a video clip)—a function of the fact that this episode was shot on a stage with a true proscenium.[28] *Old Christine* is shot on a sound stage, with more potential for in-depth staging, but the bulk of this typical scene occurs around the kitchen table with the actors grouped on one side of it (Table 5.2, Figures 5.36, 5.65; see TVStyleBook.com for a video clip). Although sitcoms and soap operas alike seldom stage significant action in depth,

Figure 5.65 Orson Welles blocks the *Citizen Kane* suicide scene in depth, with a glass and a bottle of sleeping medicine looming large in the foreground.

we can see in both of these scenes that characters can enter/exit from "upstage" (i.e., the back of the set). Christine and Richard (Clark Gregg) enter the scene from a rear door (Figure 5.27) and Christine exits into the back, too (Figures 5.58–5.63, 5.65). Even the spartan set design of *The Honeymooners* facilitates Ed's entrance from the rear of the set (Figure 5.10). However, the "aggressive foregrounds" and "aperture framing" (foreground objects obstructing our view) that Bordwell finds in deep-space staging of 1940s films by directors such as Orson Welles and William Wyler are notably missing from the sitcom.[29] It is difficult to imagine a composition such as that in Figure 5.65, from *Citizen Kane* in *The Honeymooners* or *Old Christine*. Both the physical dimensions of their sets and the time required to light and block such a shot prohibit it.

As discussed above, the DuMont Electronicam employed by *The Honeymooners* was an advanced method for bridging the gap between video (or live television) and film. Similarly, *Old Christine* is on the current forefront of video technology that interfaces with film—shot on high-definition video cameras (Sony F950 CineAltas) that have been "designed primarily to function as an alternative to 35mm film production … [and] to emulate the look of film."[30] In fact, the Sony F950 was at the leading edge of the evolution of film to high-definition video, as it was used by HD advocate, George Lucas, to shoot *Star Wars Episode III: Revenge of the Sith* (2005).[31] *Old Christine's* images are thus as high-resolution as theatrical-film images shown on television. The choice of HD recording also means a widescreen aspect ratio of 1.78:1, expanding television's old 1.33:1 ratio, but falling short of theatrical film's most common ratios of 1.85:1 and 2.40:1.[32] *Old Christine's* HD format causes a disjunction between the photo effect (from Barthes) associated with the cinema and the liveness cues provided by multiple-camera production (see the discussion of liveness in soap opera, Chapter 1). Its high-definition visual resolution and widescreen aspect ratio signal to the viewer the this-is-was of the cinema, but this photo effect is overwhelmed by signifiers of liveness, of "immediate presence," as Ellis would say.[33] However, developments in high-definition video seriously challenge Ellis's argument, which is predicated on video being a degraded, lower-resolution image than the cinema:

> The regime of cinematography presents an image which can claim a far higher fidelity and level of complication than any current video system, broadcast or not. The cinematic image is therefore in some sense the perfection of photography: superior in its ranges of nuance of color or black-and-white to video; firmly within the paradoxical regime of presence-yet-absence that can be called the "photo effect."[34]

What happens when the cinema can no longer make such claims to higher fidelity? And could Barthes find the photo effect in photography now that it has itself become an electronic medium—founded on the same digital technology as high-definition video?

Old Christine and soap operas that have converted to high-definition production present a paradox: the resolution and aspect ratio of the image link them to the cinema, but virtually all other elements of their videography connect them to broadcast presentations that we know to be live. First among these is approximate, imprecise framing—as cameras struggle to follow the action. Shot three from the analyzed scene—with Matthew's head popping into the frame's lower left corner and Richie's (Trevor Gagnon) hair appearing at the bottom of the frame (Figure 5.30)—does not fit into the single-camera schema of compositional precision. Similarly, the end of shot 22 includes Richie's shadow on the right side of the frame as he leaves the room (Figure 5.49–5.51) and shot 28's framing captures a small bit of Christine's gesture with her thumb, also on the right of the frame (Figure 5.57). Single-camera craft practices would avoid such distractions, minor though they may be. Consider this: if these *Old Christine* shots were part of a film directed by a meticulous visual stylist such as Alfred Hitchcock, would he "previsualize" a storyboard with images framed thus?

The videographic elements of camera position and shot scale in *The Honeymooners* and *Old Christine* also mark them as multiple-camera productions. In each, the camera stays back, outside the proscenium—literal, in *The Honeymooners*; virtual, in *Old Christine*. The closest framing of Ralph and Ed is a very loosely composed medium close-up, almost a medium shot, as Ralph crosses in front of Ed (Figure 5.21). A notorious improvisor, Jackie Gleason kept his camera operators guessing about his location and line readings. To accommodate that performance style, his directors gave him plenty of space to work within the frame. Even contemporary performers like Julia Louis-Dreyfus and her co-star, Hamish Linklater, who have a less flamboyant performance style than Gleason's, are shot in medium shot and medium close-up, with only the occasional close-up—as can be seen in shots 23 and 24 (Figures 5.52–5.53). The widescreen frame makes the loose framing even more evident, with more space on the sides of the performers than in a 1.33:1 shot of the same scale. Compare, for example, the medium close-up of Christine in Figure 5.52 with the medium close-up of *As the World Turns*' Brad in Figure 1.3. In both shots, we see actors framed from the waist up, but Brad occupies more of the width of the frame than Christine does.

In addition to the relatively distant framing, the proscenium "boundary" in multiple-camera sitcoms also makes it difficult for cameras to be moved into the set, to come close to the axis of action or achieve subjective shots placed in the actor positions. This is quite obvious in any *Honeymooners* scene, but it is slightly less clear in *Old Christine*. Since *Old Christine* is shot on a sound stage without a true proscenium, cameras can be moved *slightly* into the set, as in the shots from behind Richie's head (shots four, six, eight, etc.; camera position D in Figure 5.64), which appear to have been shot by a camera near the counter visible in shot 29 (Figure 5.61). Note, however, that the reverse shot of Richie from near Matthew's point-of-view cannot achieve a conventional over-the-shoulder shot as would be done in continuity editing. Instead of a "true" POV shot, we see Matthew's arms from a camera position near the front of the table (Figure 5.32, camera position B in Figure 5.64). The camera operator is unable to enter the set far enough to actually shoot over Linklater's shoulder. Thus, the multiple-camera proscenium schema is determined by the logistical restrictions endemic to the mode of production, which itself has been determined by the economics of sitcom production. This mode of production, with its limited application of classical shooting conventions, constructed an attenuated classical continuity system.

To this juncture, I have discussed the convergence between multiple-camera sitcoms and multiple-camera soap operas. However, the presence of a studio audience on multiple-camera sitcom sets and the mode of production necessitated by the audience cause the sitcom to diverge from the soap opera. The most notable difference is clearly the laugh track, which might more accurately be called an "audience track" as it presents more than laughter. The audience track contains applause, gasps, sighs, even whistles. Linking the genre to other television shows with live audiences (game shows, talk shows, sports programs, etc.), the sitcom's audience track is another marker of immediate presence as it encourages viewers to experience the program as if they were members of that audience that witnessed the program live. Further, the audience track interpellates viewers—hailing them to join the experience that the live audience is having. Even though viewers know this experience occurred weeks or months before they see it on television, its presentational mode is one of contemporaneity: this comedy is going on *now*, *live*, as you can tell by the audience's response that you are hearing *in the present*.[35]

One last distinction between multiple-camera genres is rooted in the sitcom's editing process. As we have seen, soap operas are largely shot live-on-tape, with the shots mostly switched while the scenes are performed. The intensive schedule of grinding out daily programs prevents much reshooting. Although sitcoms are also shot in a single day—usually in one evening with a live audience—there are commonly multiple takes of each scene, which are edited together in post-production. (*The Honeymooners* and early sitcoms are more like soap operas in this regard.) The editing process is slightly more leisurely, because sitcoms are on weekly, not daily, schedules and produce perhaps one-quarter as many shows annually as soap operas do. As I noted above, live-on-tape editing preserves a temporal continuum that single-camera editing must construct out of fragments. The editing of multiple takes in sitcoms bends, but does not break, live-on-tape's temporal continuity. Essentially, sitcom editors have variations of complete scenes that they reassemble into final continuous temporal structures. However, the multiple-*take* editing schema, as we might call it, does allow editors to cut to a more rapid pace and to vary the original material. Our *Old Christine* scene, for example, has an average shot length (ASL) of 3.66 seconds—significantly shorter than the 4.84 seconds ASL of the contemporaneous *As the World Turns* sample discussed above.[36] Further, nine out of the *Old Christine* scene's 29 shots—almost one-third—were only one second long and the median shot length was just *two* seconds. A pace like that would be extremely difficult to maintain in a live-to-tape recording. Sitcom editors may shorten shots or, minimally, expand them—shaping time to fit the rhythm of the comedy. One additional small signifier of multiple-take editing is the continuity error that inevitably sneaks in. For example, at the end of shot 15 in our *Old Christine* scene, Matthew is holding his coffee cup with two hands, but at the start of the following shot, only one hand is on the cup (Figures 5.42–5.43). Continuity errors, unless particularly egregious, are concealed through continuity editing's conventions. The cut from shot 15 to shot 16 is from a camera angle over 30 degrees different than the previous shot—giving the viewers new visual information to digest and hiding the continuity error. If shot 15 had been cut to a shot from a similar angle, a jump cut would have resulted. In any event, the point is that such an error never occurs in live or live-on-tape recordings as they are transmissions/records of a single performance.

We've now seen how the sitcom employs the multiple-camera proscenium schema that it shares with the soap opera. Our next task is to assay how the contemporary sitcom has challenged this schema in single-camera programs. Although I risk getting ahead of myself, I have counterposed the characteristics of the multiple-camera proscenium schema with the single-camera televisual schema in Table 5.3. This table arrays schematic elements in ways that hark back to previously discussed schematic tables—characterizing the anti-traditional visual style of film noir (Table 2.1, from Janey Place and Lowell Peterson)[37] and counter-television videography in the commercial (Table 3.1). Table 5.3 was also inspired by Peter Wollen's explication of the "deadly sins" of classical cinema versus "cardinal virtues" of counter cinema, which itself is rooted in Brecht's table of "Dramatic Theatre" versus "Epic Theatre."[38] In each instance, two schemas are in opposition to one another—which accurately represents the sometimes contentious ways that schemas evolve. Often a stylistic schema exists as a retort to a previous, aging schema, or as an unfriendly modification of one. As we shall see with the single-camera televisual schema below, there can often be resistance toward changing schemas.

The Single-Camera Televisual Schema

In the current attention to single-camera sitcoms, it is often forgotten that the single-camera mode of production has been with us since the very beginning of the genre. NBC's *The Life of Riley*—the pilot for which was telecast April 13, 1948—was a single-camera film production.[39] In fact, in just the second year that the Academy of Television Arts & Sciences awarded Emmys, *The Life of Riley* won in the category with the unwieldy title of "Best Film Made for & Viewed on Television in 1949–1950." The Academy and the television industry themselves distinguished clearly among technologies and modes of production—emphasizing them over today's genre-based categories (e.g., "outstanding comedy series").[40] Other major awards in 1950, for example,

Table 5.3 Multiple-camera and single-camera schemas

Multiple-camera Proscenium Schema	Single-camera Televisual Schema
Cinematography	
Imprecise framing	Precise framing
Reliance on medium shots	Close-ups and *extreme* close-ups
Post-independent	*Post*-dependent (VFX)
No subjective shots	Subjective shots
Zoom	Track/dolly/Steadicam
Cameras outside fourth wall/proscenium	Cameras inside fourth wall/proscenium
x-axis movement	*x*- and *z*-axis movement
Eye level (or slightly higher)	Low/high angle
Large depth-of-field (due to MS's, camera- object distance, and lighting)	Choice of shallow focus (camera close to object) or deep focus (w/composition in depth)
Balanced composition	Imbalanced composition
"Normal" speed	Variable speed action (slo-mo, fast action)
Text/graphics only in credits	Text/graphics during narrative
Mise-en-scène	
Interiors and *studio* exteriors	Interiors *and* exteriors
High-key lighting	Low-key, more modeled, chiaroscuro
Proscenium set design (three-wall sets)	Three-dimensional set design (four-wall sets)
x-axis blocking, some diagonals	*x*- and occasional *z*-axis blocking
Unobstructed views	Aperture framing
Editing	
Fixed axis of action	Moveable axis of action
Gaps; missing action	Total control of action
Few POV cuts	POV cuts
Reaction shots	POV or subjective shots
No montage	Montage
Theatrical-scene time	Cinematic time
Theatrical-scene space	Cinematic space
Linear editing	Spatio-temporal discontinuity
Laugh-based rhythm (slower)	Narrative-based rhythm (faster)
	Non-diegetic visual jokes/puns
	Intellectual montage
Sound	
Laugh track	No laugh track
Studio audience response (gasps, etc.)	No audience sounds
Limited non-diegetic music	Copyrighted music, with lyrics
Functional, supports narrative	Self-reflexive, intertextual and/or symbolic
No non-diegetic dialogue	Tendency toward voice-overs
Catchphrases	
Miscellaneous	
Appearance of liveness/presence	Photo effect/present absence
Stand-up comic based	Actor based
Performer-oriented	Medium-oriented
Controlled by performance	Controlled by director
Gag oriented	Narrative oriented
	Animated

went to "best kinescope show" and "best live show."[41] In the 2000s, the Academy still emphasizes mode of production in categories oriented around visual and sound style, which are often divided into "multi-camera series" and "single-camera series" regardless of their genres. Art direction, cinematography, and sound and picture editing are all segregated into "multi-camera" and "single-camera" categories.[42]

Single-camera programs such as *The Life of Riley*, *Petticoat Junction* (1963–70), and *The Andy Griffith Show* (1960–8) exemplify what David Barker calls "1960s telefilm values."[43] They do not contain the stylistic exuberance required for Caldwell's televisuality. Despite their single-camera mode of production, they still qualify as zero-degree television, similar to the attenuated continuity I discussed in *Dallas*.[44] Or, to put it another way, these programs employ a zero-degree schema despite their single-camera mode of production. Thus, we can see again that the single-camera mode of production and the televisual stylistic schema are not necessarily linked. The overarching distinction that I feel is worth making, however, is not between single-camera and multiple-camera modes of production, but between a schema organized to capture live performance and one organized to allow the medium itself to perform. In the televisual schema, style is aggressive, roughened, and opaque, not smooth and transparent. It carries meaning. It makes jokes. It might call attention to itself. It can even make familiar things seem strange, creating art as technique—as if Russian formalist Viktor Shklovsky had been exhumed and asked to direct situation comedies.[45] Kristin Thompson in *Breaking the Glass Armor: Neoformalist Film Analysis*, borrows the term "parametric" from Noël Burch to refer to "those films that allow the play of stylistic devices a significant degree of independence from narrative functioning and motivation."[46] I've already discussed how parametric form may be used in commercials to hail viewers. In the televisual sitcom, we see much the same thing. Clearly, the "My Life in Four Cameras" episode of *Scrubs* is one in which style has come unhinged from narrative and put in service of humor creation. Moreover, it sharply illustrates the more salient differences between the multiple-camera proscenium schema and the single-camera televisual schema by containing both within a single episode. To illuminate these differences I will drill down to the first scene of the episode, which typifies single-camera shooting and is representative of how most *Scrubs* episodes appear in terms of *mise-en-scène*, cinematography, editing, and sound. I will refer out from this scene to other scenes/shots in the episode—in particular, the scenes produced in multiple-camera mode.

First, in terms of *mise-en-scène*, *Scrubs'* mode of production gives it the freedom to shoot outdoors (Figure 5.66) or indoors, but the nature of this hospital-based program is such that its stories lend themselves to interior settings: J.D.'s apartments, Sacred Heart Hospital's patient rooms, cafeteria, and so on. *Scrubs* contains many of the same themes and narrative preoccupations as the soap opera (death, life, disease, romance, and so on), but, obviously, presents from a comedic instead of a tragic perspective. It is not surprising, therefore, that *Scrubs'* set design resembles that of the soap opera. However,

Figure 5.66 Scrubs: exterior, high-angle shot.

Figure 5.67 Physical humor is facilitated by *Scrubs'* set design and location shooting, as in this shot of J.D. crowd surfing.

the single-camera mode of production has much greater flexibility when it comes to set constructions and does not rely on the same sort of standing sets as audience-oriented, multiple-camera sitcoms such as *The Honeymooners* and *Old Christine*. Consequently, *Scrubs* uses more sets—and of more varied design—than sitcoms that must constrain themselves to sets that can be effectively positioned in front of audience bleachers. In fact, many of the interior locations in the show are shot in a defunct hospital, the North Hollywood Medical Center, which was renovated to accommodate *Scrubs* and other television shows and films (e.g., *The One* [2001]). Obviously, a show that relies on an in-studio audience does not have options such as this. *Scrubs'* flexibility in set design and location shooting facilitate physical humor—as when J.D. surfs the crowd outside the hospital (Figure 5.67). *Scrubs* still relies heavily on verbal humor, but its varied set design can also host varied forms of humor.

The blocking of this episode's first scene illustrates another televisual aspect of *mise-en-scène*. In this scene, J.D., his girl-friend, Kylie (Chrystee Pharris), Turk (Donald Faison), and Carla (Judy Reyes) compete to see which couple is more romantically compatible (see Table 5.4). In shots one and three of the analyzed scene, director Adam Bernstein has positioned the actors in depth: J.D. in the foreground, Kylie in the middle ground, and Carla in the background (Figure 5.70). The planimetric, *x*-axis blocking that we have seen in the extreme in *The Honeymooners* and gently modified in *Old Christine* is thus dispensed with in these two shots, which are instead designed along the *z*-axis. Although perhaps falling short of Wellesian aggressive foregrounds from the 1940s (as in Figure 5.65), these shots do present significant narrative information in foreground and background. In shots one and three, J.D. paces in the foreground, Kylie sits on the couch in the middle ground and Carla opens beer cans in the back. The deep-space staging is not merely used to get characters in and out of a scene, as we saw previously in *The Honeymooners* and *Old Christine*. In addition, since the sets do not have to be designed for viewing by an in-studio audience, they may be configured in depth—as in a scene from the end of this episode where J.D. walks down a deep-space hallway, towards the camera (Figure 5.91). Sets such as this are designed solely for the view of a single camera—clearly exemplifying what Bordwell calls pyramidal space:

Table 5.4 Scrubs scene *découpage*

Shot Number, Scale, and Length	Figure	Sound
1 long shot 7 secs. (*Figures 5.68–5.71*)		J.D.'s Narration: Things were amazing with Kylie. But before I could get more emotionally invested… J.D.'s Narration: …I needed answers to some questions that were very important to me.

continued

Table 5.4 continued

Shot Number, Scale, and Length	Figure	Sound
2 medium long shot 5 secs. (*Figures 5.72–5.73*)	 	J.D.: Name three spin-offs of the sitcom *Happy Days*.
3 long shot 3 secs. (*Figure 5.74*)		Kylie: *Mork & Mindy, Laverne & Shirley,* and *Joanie Loves Chachi.*
4 medium shot 3 secs. (*Figure 5.75*)		Turk: You marry her. You marry her now! You marry her! J.D.: Okay…

Shot Number, Scale, and Length	Figure	Sound
5 medium long shot 3 secs. (*Figure 5.76*)		J.D.: … okay, we passed section one: "Sitcoms about or involving Asian-American diner owners."
6 long shot 1 sec. (*Figure 5.77*)		J.D.: Now on to section two: …
7 medium long shot 3 secs. (*Figure 5.78*)		J.D.: … "Fat, tubby TV husbands and the crazy-hot women that would never actually be married to them."
8 medium long shot 3 secs. (*Figures 5.79–5.80*)		Carla: Hey, we're missing *Sanford and Son*!

continued

Table 5.4 continued

Shot Number, Scale, and Length	Figure	Sound

9 medium shot 3 secs. (*Figure 5.81*)		Turk: What? Carla: Yes! J.D.'s Narration: Turk was…
10 medium long shot 6 secs. (*Figures 5.82–5.83*)	 	J.D.'s Narration: …freaked out because Carla never joins us on *Sanford and Son* night. Or *Cheers* night. I think it was because she was…

Shot Number, Scale, and Length	Figure	Sound
11 medium shot 1 sec. (*Figure 5.84*)		J.D.'s Narration: ...feeling a little romantically competitive...
12 medium shot 2 secs. (*Figure 5.85*)		J.D.'s Narration: ...with Kylie and me. [*Sanford and Son* theme music begins.]
13 medium long shot 4 secs. (*Figure 5.86*)		Turk: Woman! Woman! I am not a lollipop!
14 medium shot 2 secs. (*Figure 5.87*)		

continued

Table 5.4 continued

Shot Number, Scale, and Length	Figure	Sound
15 medium shot 4 secs. (*Figure 5.88*)	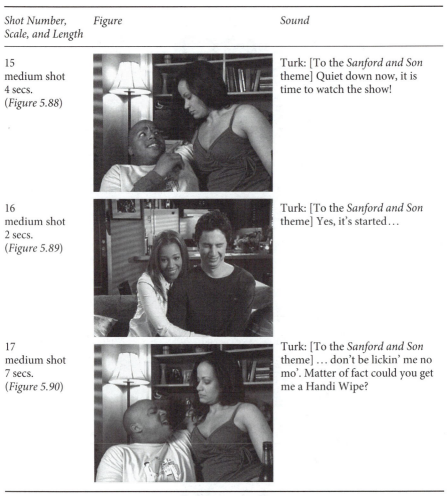	Turk: [To the *Sanford and Son* theme] Quiet down now, it is time to watch the show!
16 medium shot 2 secs. (*Figure 5.89*)		Turk: [To the *Sanford and Son* theme] Yes, it's started...
17 medium shot 7 secs. (*Figure 5.90*)		Turk: [To the *Sanford and Son* theme] ... don't be lickin' me no mo'. Matter of fact could you get me a Handi Wipe?

On the proscenium stage the playing space is broad and comparatively shallow, so directors tend to spread actors across the horizontal expanse for the benefit of many sightlines in the auditorium. But in cinema only one sightline matters—that of the camera. Thanks to projective optics, the playing space of cinema constitutes a horizontally tipped pyramid, with light rays gathering at the lens. This yields a very narrow but rather deep area of visibility.[47]

In Figure 5.91 we can imagine the point of Bordwell's horizontal pyramid to be the single camera lens—the mirror image of the vanishing point within the frame. (The lines painted on the walls lead back toward the vanishing point, as if diagramed by Leon Battista Alberti.[48]) His argument about multiple sightlines in the theater may be adapted to help understand multiple-camera set design. In

this context, however, it is the sightlines of four cameras that must be accommodated instead of hundreds of theatergoers. The wide and shallow set design in
multiple-camera productions does support the sightlines of in-studio audiences,
but their views are incidental to the final product. In practice, audience members
often have badly obstructed views of the sets—whether due to obstructive
camera dollies and production personnel or viewers sitting in the bleachers off to
the side of the set that is currently being used. During most of an evening's
sitcom recording, audience members must rely on in-studio monitors to follow
the action. Thus, the hundreds of sightlines of the in-studio audience do not
influence set design and blocking, but the four sightlines of the cameras certainly
do. Single-camera sitcoms, in contrast, may design sets and block action that
present the view to just one sightline.

Figure 5.91, J.D. in the hallway, exemplifies an aspect of lighting found in the
single-camera schema and not in multiple-camera: visible lights in the ceiling.[49]
We don't see lights in the ceilings of multiple-camera programs because, simply
enough, we don't see ceilings in those programs. Lighting grids are hung in the
place of ceilings because this is the quickest—and thus cheapest—way to broadly
light a standing set in front of an in-studio audience—as may be seen in the shot
when J.D. recognizes that he's in a sitcom fantasy and the cameras and set are
revealed (Figure 5.3, the only shot of the fantasy that is non-diegetic like this).
Multiple-camera mode of production makes a logistical choice based on the economics of television production. One of the most striking visual ways that "My
Life in Four Cameras" signifies the shift from single-camera to multiple-camera
is through the lighting. The shots just before the transition have a dark, film-noir
look, with light cut by Venetian blinds (Figure 5.1). (This shot is also composed
in depth, with a patient in the foreground, J.D. and Elliot [Sarah Chalke] in the
middle ground, and an X-ray in the background.) After J.D. slips into his fantasy,
the lighting instantly becomes broad, bright, and hyperbolically high-key (Figure
5.2). Unlike in the multiple-camera sitcom and the soap opera, where this lighting is the norm and thus semiotically insignificant, the high-key lighting here has
meaning. It signifies "multiple-camera sitcom-ness" and contributes to the
parodic humor of the episode. Here we can begin to see how style becomes parametric, has been roughened and is being
used to generate humor.

In this *Scrubs* episode, the dissimilarity
between the two forms of sitcom is also
defined by contrasting cinematography
with videography. The single-camera
portion is a cinematographic production. It
was shot on film—as is standard practice
on *Scrubs*—using the Super 16 mm format
and Aaton XTR Prod cameras. The multiple-camera portion is a videographic production, recorded with the studio video
cameras pictured in Figure 5.3.[50] The difference is a subtle one and, as remarked upon

Figure 5.91 Pyramidal space in *Scrubs*: J.D.
walks toward the camera in a hallway,
emphasizing its visual depth.

previously, the film-video distinction is coming to matter less and less as high-definition cameras such as *Old Christine*'s Sony F950 replace film cameras. Super 16 is still a common format for single-camera programs because, as Kodak maintains, "although 35 mm is still the imaging standard, Super 16 offers a cost-effective method for producing TV programming."[51] For most of its history, the single-camera comedy has also been the single-*film*-camera comedy, but this was only because video cameras provided such a comparatively degraded, low-resolution image. Single-camera shows *could* have been created with single-*video*-camera technology in the 1980s and 1990s, but their producers made the *aesthetic* choice to shoot on film, despite the *economic* disincentive of it being more expensive. In this case, the aesthetic choice was a matter of product differentiation, of producing television that looked significantly different from material shot with video cameras for multiple-camera sitcoms such as *The Cosby Show* (1984–92) or game shows, talk shows and newscasts.[52] Today, single-camera sitcoms can no longer claim a videographic superiority over multiple-camera sitcoms now that high-definition cameras are becoming the standard craft practice.

Other videographic elements beside resolution are significant and signifying aspects of the single-camera schema—rendering the *mise-en-scène* in ways that are uncommon or impossible in multiple-camera production. Despite its high-definition image, *Old Christine* still frames its actors imprecisely. In contrast, *Scrubs* director Bernstein holds tight control over framing. The previously discussed deep-space blocking of shots one, three and six in the analyzed scene is enhanced by framing that keeps all three characters visible. And shot four manages to keep Turk's moving finger just inside the camera frame (Figure 5.75). This shot also illustrates how the single-camera varies camera height in a way that's extremely difficult for multiple-camera shooting. In the latter, as seen in Figure 5.3, cameras on dollies are usually set at eye level or just a little above. Shot four is a low-angle shot of Turk, as are several of the shots of J.D. in this scene. Low angles are particularly "dangerous" for multiple-camera shoots because they risk revealing the missing ceilings. High angles, such as the one of J.D. crowd surfing (see Figure 5.67), are just as uncommon in multiple-camera productions.

Closely related to choices of camera height are shot scale and camera position. *Scrubs* contains a wide range of shot scales—from tight close-ups (Figure 5.92) to extreme long shots (Figure 5.66). In "My Life in Four Cameras," that variety of framing disappears when we shift into the sitcom fantasy. In its place is a reliance upon medium close-ups, medium shots, and long shots (Figures 5.93, 5.94, and 5.95 respectively)—all virtually from the same camera height. Even more significant is the ability of single-camera productions to break the proscenium and move the cameras into the set. If we look closely at the shots in the episode's first scene, it becomes evident that the camera has been positioned inside the proscenium and that, indeed, we see all four walls of that living room set. For shot one, the camera dollies from behind the television, moving out of blackness and then positioning itself behind J.D., showing us most of the room (Figure 5.68). Barely visible on the left of the frame are Turk's legs, where he's sitting in a chair to the left of the television. If this were a standard multiple-camera shoot, the audience would be positioned behind the camera, but the first cut shows us the wall behind J.D., where the audience would have been. The camera in shot two is positioned behind Kylie's right shoulder and, in shot four, we return to a camera position even farther to Kylie's right, looking up at Turk (Figure 5.75). The camera is now deep within the set and it remains there for the shots of Carla kissing Turk. First, in shot eight, Carla exists frame left (Kylie's right, Figure 5.80). Then she enters Turk's shot from frame right (Turk's left, Figure 5.81), further establishing that Turk is on the left side of the set, based on our original orientation. The remaining camera positions are from the front of the set (a medium shot of Kylie and J.D. sitting on the couch) and from Kylie's right. Later scenes in the episode show us even more of J.D.'s apartment, revealing that the four-wall set design and the positioning of the cameras within it obliterate the virtual proscenium of programs like *The Honeymooners* and *Old Christine*. Most likely, this was accomplished by first building all four walls of the set, but making some of the walls "wild"—industry parlance for flexible walls that may be removed quickly. Thus, grips may "wild out" a wall from a four-walled set in order to make room for cameras and crew.

Figure 5.92 Scrubs: a tight close-up of Carla.

Figure 5.93 Multiple-camera programs prefer looser framing than that seen in single-camera programs. The multiple-camera *Scrubs* episode depends on medium close-ups...

*Figure 5.94 ...*two shots and...

*Figure 5.95 ...*long shots.

The ability to move cameras beyond the proscenium opens up the possibility of true point-of-view shots. As we saw in *Old Christine*, the POV shots in multiple-camera editing are often displaced from where they would normally be in continuity editing, resulting in an attenuated continuity system. *Scrubs* illustrates more conventional POV framing in shot two, where we clearly see Kylie's head as she watches J.D. (Figure 5.72).

This discussion of camera position brings us to the editing of single-camera productions. Single-camera editing, rooted in the continuity system, exists on the opposite end of the editing continuum from the switched-live editing of *The Honeymooners* and soap operas. In *Scrubs*, scenes are more constructed from fragments than captured whole. Building scenes from fragments is a much more controlled process than capturing a live event. As we've seen in soap operas and *Old Christine*, significant action is sometimes missed in multiple-camera editing—although less so in sitcoms, due to their multiple takes, than in soap operas. *Scrubs* follows the craft practices of continuity editing in its construction of scenes, with each shot conveying maximum narrative information. As we saw in the analysis of a commercial from *As the World Turns*, individual shots serve precise diegetic functions. In the first scene of "My Life in Four Cameras," Turk breaks into a song that fits words to the theme music to the sitcom, *Sanford and Son* (1972–7). John Michel, who won an Emmy for the editing of this episode, cuts from Turk in shot 15 to Kylie and J.D. nodding their heads to the music (Figure 5.89). He then cuts back to Turk at the exact moment that they, in unison, turn their heads toward him. Their looks cue the cut in a precise manner that is difficult to manage in multiple-camera editing.

Single-camera editing is also more rigorous because it does not have to pause for laughter to die down, which is a skill that actors must develop as well. Lawrence comments that the *Scrubs* actors had to modify their line delivery for the live-audience portion of "My Life in Four Cameras:"

> When we first cast this [episode], I told everyone that it was a show built on pace. So even if you have a joke in the middle of a speech, John McGinley [Dr. Cox], I want you to—people are gonna process that joke— but I want you to get through that speech the way people talk, and haul ass. And now John has a monologue in the [multiple-camera segment of the] sitcom with like four laughs in it, and he's going to have to, overnight, learn the skill of getting a laugh, holding, then continuing on with the speech as if that's the way somebody talks.[53]

Thus, the audience's presence tends to slow the pace of a program—recognizing, of course, that much of the audience track is fabricated by the sound editor and that laughs may be as long, or as short, as is desired. The lack of an audience track in single-camera productions offers the opportunity for them to be edited more quickly, but that is not borne out by the average shot lengths of segments of "My Life in Four Cameras." The single-camera portion of the episode has an ASL of 4.14 seconds. The multiple-camera portion's ASL is considerably shorter—3.64 seconds. In both segments, the median shot length is three. Preliminary Shot Logger data show the ASLs of some 1980s–1990s sitcoms range from 3.8 seconds (*Friends*, January 21, 1999) to 5.5 seconds (*The Cosby Show*, December 13, 1984), but at this point the sample is too small to generalize.

Despite the inconclusive ASL data, this episode does illustrate in individual scenes how single-camera editing can be much quicker than multiple-camera editing and, further, can be used for humorous effect. For example, when J.D. and Elliot interview patients about their possible E. coli symptoms (vomiting and diarrhea), a quick montage of six shots is presented in four seconds—close-ups of individuals looking at the lens, or just off-camera, and exclaiming, "No" (Figure 5.96). The humor arises from the quick juxtaposition of the patients and is done in fashion that would be difficult for a multiple-camera program and impossible in a live-on-tape show.[54] To create these shots, the camera was moved inside the proscenium and six actors were shot, probably one after the other. Since this could not be done live-on-tape, a multiple-camera production would have to pick up these shots after the main scenes were shot—not impossible, but not cost effective. Thus, although a multiple-camera program *could* create a montage like this, its craft practices and logistics work against it.

Figure 5.96 Scrubs: A quick series of close-ups with actors looking directly at the camera, which would be difficult to achieve in a multiple-camera show.

Scrubs is known for generating humor through visual effects (VFX) added in post-production, but it is less "postdependent," as Caldwell puts it, than several other single-camera sitcoms that rely on post-production work.[55] In fact, a comedy-drama crossover program, *Ally McBeal* (1997–2002), is almost single-handedly responsible for bringing *digital* visual effects to television narrative comedy.[56] From the start of its run, *Ally McBeal* featured digital animation and VFX to illustrate the title character's fantasies. The single most famous example of digital animation on the show is the so-called "dancing baby," a baby in a diaper that dances to Blue Swede's recording, "Hooked on a Feeling" (see Figure 5.97). Ally repeatedly imagines the baby as

Figure 5.97 The "dancing baby" fantasy scenes in *Ally McBeal* helped bring digital animation to television.

she struggles with her feelings toward motherhood. The baby figure was digitally rendered through the animation program, 3D Studio Max, incorporating the Character Studio plug-in, and was intended solely to be a product demonstration.[57] However, versions of it began circulating around the Internet in 1996—an early example of a viral video—and producer David Kelley decided to incorporate it into *Ally McBeal*. Thus, the dancing baby has an extratextual presence that other animations do not. Most of the animations on *Ally McBeal*, and, moreover, the digital visual effects on single-camera sitcoms, qualify as televisual elements, but the dancing baby extends further into an intertextual, postmodern realm.

Taken together, the videographic and editing aspects of the televisual single-camera sitcom approach Bordwell's intensified continuity.[58] I first presented this concept in the context of commercials (Chapters 1 and 3) and then in *Miami Vice* (Chapter 2). Intensified-continuity techniques that Bordwell specifies include accelerated editing, extremely long and extremely short focal lengths, very tight close-ups in dialogue scenes and hyperactive camera movement, as well as handheld camera and certain visual effects (manipulated color schemes, slow motion, and so on). Crucial to Bordwell's argument is that these techniques are not counter to Hollywood classicism, but, rather, are a heightened implementation of its conventions. Similarly, *Scrubs* and other televisual programs employ intensified continuity without jettisoning all classical storytelling principles. It would be overstating their radicalness to suggest that they do. What is intriguing to examine is how intensified continuity can be employed for humorous effect. Moreover, the cliches of intensified continuity may even become the targets of televisual humor—as is handheld camera in mockumentaries such as *The Office* and *Reno 911!* (2003–).

To this point, my examination of televisual sitcoms has centered on visual style (as does Bordwell's consideration of intensified continuity), but we cannot ignore the importance of sound to televisual form. The audio mix of single-camera sitcoms can be highly stylized, especially if we view the norm of narrative-television audio as the spartan, recorded-on-the-set audio of the soap opera and the multiple-camera sitcom. The boom mic above the actors that typifies this form of recording is visible in Figure 5.3. Its audio pick-up pattern creates a sound perspective that is the audio equivalent of a medium shot—not picking up every nuance of actors' voices, as happens in close-miking techniques (used, for example, by radio announcers), and recording much of the ambient sound of the room. In feature-length film production, the on-set audio is heavily processed and even wholly replaced through looping, but soap operas and sitcoms don't have enough time between an episode's recording and its broadcast to engage in much modification. Both multiple-camera and single-camera productions share this approach to dialogue recording, but there are still ways that single-camera productions stylize audio.

First, and most noticeably, single-camera televisual sitcoms dispense with a laugh track. The laugh track had been such a staple of the sitcom—both multiple-camera and single-camera—that its absence became significant. Stemming from its roots in radio, television is a medium that relies heavily on sound to hail viewers and maintain their interest in the visuals. In 1972, when the producers of *M*A*S*H* (1972–83), a single-camera sitcom, wished to dispense with a laugh track they had to do battle with a network and eventually settled upon a compromise where the laugh track would be silenced during the operating-room scenes, but not the rest of the program. It wasn't until the late 1980s that single-camera comedy programs such as the short-lived *Frank's Place* (1987–8) and *The Days and Nights of Molly Dodd* (1987–91) could exist without laugh tracks. Removing laugh tracks meant that the programs would have to rely more heavily upon the visuals to capture the viewer's attention. It also freed programs to create more intricately layered sound mixes.

Second, voiceovers are exceedingly common in single-camera productions, but almost unheard of in multiple-camera shows. J.D.'s voiceover commentary in *Scrubs* continues a single-camera audio tradition that may be traced back as far as 1988 and *The Wonder Years* and is rooted in Dobie Gillis' asides to the camera in *The Many Loves of Dobie Gillis* (1959–63). Most commonly, these are diegetic narrators—characters offering their thoughts on events as they happen or, as in *The Wonder Years*, from a perspective much later. When these voiceovers fold back over themselves and become self-reflexive they enter into the televisual realm. *Arrested Development* (2003–6) made significant use of this self-reflexivity with its third-person narrator—voiced by one of the show's producers, Ron Howard, who often makes allusions to himself as an actor/producer/director and to *Arrested Development* as a television program (including barely veiled comments on its cancellation by Fox). In one episode, the lead character, Michael Bluth (Jason Bateman) comments, "You know, your average American male is in a perpetual state of adolescence, you know, arrested development." And the narrator offers this rejoinder, "Hey. That's the name of the show." In another episode, Howard alludes to his previous appearance on *The Andy Griffith Show*. Andy Griffith, the actor, has been hired by the Bluth family to assist them in a legal matter:

> LINDSAY (PORTIA DE ROSSI): Bad news. Andy Griffith turned us down. He didn't like his trailer. [The camera pans over to reveal the log cabin truck.] He thought we were making fun of him.
> NARRATOR: They were not making fun of Andy Griffith. This cannot be stressed enough.[59]

The self-mocking word play breaks the virtual fourth wall and acknowledges the viewer as a viewer and television as television—a frequent component of televisuality.

The music of single-camera sitcoms serves a different function from that of the soap opera and most multiple-camera sitcoms. It can, of course, operate as a diegetic support, as it does in the soap opera, but there are times in the single-camera sitcom when music's signifying function shifts and it comes to comment on the narrative. *Scrubs* is dotted with music allusions to other texts. In "My Life in Four Cameras" the first scene includes the theme song for the multiple-camera sitcom, *Sanford and Son*. Initially, it's just the theme, with no lyrics, but then Turk sings his own version, starting with: "Quiet down now, it is time to watch the show." And, at the end of the episode, J.D.'s narration sums up the preceding events, talking about how "real-life" issues are not resolved as easily as in a sitcom. There is some irony here, of course, because *he* is a sitcom character. Under his voice, a version of the *Cheers* theme song plays—not that show's original music, but a slightly melancholic version sung by Colin Hay.[60] We then see J.D. sit in front of the television to watch a sitcom, presumably *Cheers*. We don't hear actual dialogue or music from *Cheers*, but a laugh track softly plays. These two theme songs—neither of which is heard in its original version—exist in different relationships to *Scrubs'* narrative. The *Sanford and Son* theme is hijacked by the text, absorbed as a piece of bricolage into *Scrubs'* narrative. In televisual fashion, Turk's dialogue has been processed through the antecedent text of *Sanford and Son*. The second instance of a theme song is less televisual. Although it is clearly intertextual—referring to *Cheers*, its camaraderie and easily resolved sitcom crises—it is also just a piece of music that offers an implicit commentary on the diegesis. A popular love song could comment on a scene in a soap opera in just the same fashion and would hardly be televisual.

Televisuality's History and Significance to Television Comedy

Where does the televisual strain begin in narrative television comedy? Space does not permit a full historical overview here (see Table 5.5 for a list, in chronological order, of the most significant single-camera programs). Suffice to say that there are glimmers of televisuality as early as *The Many Loves of Dobie Gillis* (1959–63) and that trace elements of it may be located in *The Addams Family* (1962–6), *M*A*S*H* (1972–83), *Buffalo Bill* (1983–4), *Frank's Place* (1987–8), and *Doogie Howser, M.D.* (1989–93). However, the first fully formed televisual sitcom is *Parker Lewis Can't Lose* (1990–3), which makes delirious use of the single-camera mode of production. Since that show's debut in 1990, we have seen perhaps two dozen programs in the United States that could conceivably be said to utilize the single-camera televisual schema—including *Dream On* (1990–6), *The Larry Sanders Show* (1992–8), *Ally McBeal, Curb Your Enthusiasm* (2000–), *Malcolm in the Middle* (2000–6), *Arrested Development* (2003–6), *The Office* (U.S., 2005–), *My Name Is Earl* (2005–), and *30 Rock* (2006–). This list could be expanded further if we include animated series, especially *The Simpsons* (1989–), as significant sitcom rule-breakers.

There have been enough single-camera sitcoms now that a reaction against them has developed in the press. A *Variety* review of *Old Christine* typifies the backlash, dismissing televisual videography as "gimmickry" and praising *Old Christine* for not indulging in it:

> What's really refreshing amid this year's uneven crop of laughers, though, is how conventional *Christine* turns out to be while still being flat-out funny. It's a reminder, perhaps, that producers and nets have become

Table 5.5 Significant single-camera U.S. sitcoms (*animated shows)

Title	Start Year	End Year	Proscenium/ Not (P or N)	Laugh Track (Y or N)
Topper	1953	1955	N	Y
Father Knows Best	1954	1960	N	Y
Leave It to Beaver	1957	1963	N	Y
Many Loves of Dobie Gillis, The	1959	1963	N	Y
Andy Griffith Show, The	1960	1968	N	Y
Flintstones, The	1960	1966	N	Y
Mister Ed	1961	1966	N	Y
Addams Family, The	1962	1966	N	Y
Beverly Hillbillies, The	1962	1971	N	Y
My Favorite Martian	1963	1966	N	Y
Petticoat Junction	1963	1970	N	Y
Gilligan's Island	1964	1967	N	Y
Munsters, The	1964	1966	N	Y
Bewitched	1964	1972	N	Y
F-Troop	1965	1967	N	Y
Get Smart	1965	1970	N	Y
I Dream of Jeannie	1965	1970	N	Y
Hogan's Heroes	1965	1971	N	Y
Monkees, The	1966	1968	N	N
Flying Nun, The	1967	1970	N	Y
Bill Cosby Show, The	1969	1971	N	N
Partridge Family	1970	1974	N	Y
M*A*S*H	1972	1983	N	Y/N
Happy Days	1974	1984	N/P	Y
Square Pegs	1982	1983	N	Y
Frank's Place	1987	1988	N	N
Days and Nights of Molly Dodd, The	1987	1991	N	N
Wonder Years, The	1988	1993	N	N
Annie McGuire	1988	1988	N	N
Doogie Howser, M.D.	1989	1993	N	N
Simpsons, The*	1989		N	N
Parker Lewis Can't Lose	1990	1993	N	N
Dream On	1990	1996	N	Y
Herman's Head	1991	1994	Y	Y
Hi Honey, I'm Home!	1991	1992	P	Y
Larry Sanders Show, The	1992	1998	P/N	Y/N
Bakersfield P.D.	1993	1994	N	N
Tick, The	1994	1997	N	N
Arli$$	1996	2002	N	N
Sabrina, the Teenage Witch	1996	2003	N	Y
King of the Hill*	1997	2009	N	N
Secret Diary of Desmond Pfeiffer, The	1998	1998	P	Y
Family Guy*	1999	2002	N	N
Futurama*	1999	2003	N	N
Curb Your Enthusiasm	2000		N	N
Malcolm In The Middle	2000	2006	N	N
Bernie Mac Show, The	2001	2006	N	N
Scrubs	2001		N	N

continued

Table 5.5 continued

Title	Start Year	End Year	Proscenium/ Not (P or N)	Laugh Track (Y or N)
Grounded for Life	2001	2005	P/N	Y
Andy Richter Controls the Universe	2002	2003	N	N
Watching Ellie	2002	2003	N/P	N/Y
Arrested Development	2003	2006	N	N
Oliver Beene	2003	2004	N	N
Reno 911!	2003	2009	N	N
Everybody Hates Chris	2005		N	N
My Name Is Earl	2005	2009	N	N
Office (US), The	2005		N	N
*American Dad!**	2005		N	N
30 Rock	2006		N	N
Samantha Who?	2007	2009	N	N
Worst Week	2008	2009	N	N
Better Off Ted	2009		N	N
Modern Family	2009		N	N

overly preoccupied with single-camera gimmickry and improve when
wedding a star to the right material can still click.... Coupled with the net's
consistently endearing freshman *How I Met Your Mother* and Monday
anchor [*Two and a Half*] *Men*, CBS is proving that the traditional sitcom—
itself seduced and abandoned—still has some life left in it, too.[61]

As I have previously discussed in the context of commercials, Pauline Kael
believes that such techniques are "impersonal—dexterous, sometimes clever,
but empty of art."[62] More reasonable interpretations of televisual sitcoms have
begun to arise. Brett Mills and Ethan Thompson have both addressed the significance of televisual sitcoms which are either mockumentaries (as in the U.K.
and U.S. versions of *The Office*) or adopt a documentary style without proclaiming the program to be a faux documentary (as in *Arrested Development*, in the
U.S., and *The Royle Family* [1998–], in the UK).[63] Both of them offer the term,
"comedy *vérité*" as a label for this inflection of the sitcom. And they both consider how comedy *vérité*, as Mills' argues, "indicates a use of television comedy
to interrogate the processes and representations of media forms, in a manner
similar to the aggressively involved characteristics of *cinéma vérité*."[64] He continues, "the sitcom has finally abandoned its music hall origins, and begun to
interact with aspects of television to create meaning. This is, then, sitcom *as* television."[65] Mills and Thompson are quite correct in arguing for the sitcom as a
genre that is now capable of breaking apart other media forms. I would take
their argument beyond the mockumentary branch of sitcoms to say that televisual sitcoms can target more than documentary forms. As we've seen in *Scrubs*,
they can deconstruct their own genre, as is quite common in comic genres in all
media. And, importantly, televisual sitcoms can interrogate many other television forms—soap operas, medical dramas, Westerns, talk shows.

Formal interrogation/deconstruction is thus one significant function of tele-visuality. A second function is product differentiation. In an increasingly clut-tered media landscape, the single-camera televisual sitcom stands out from others in the genre—especially those from the 1970s and 1980s when the sitcom dominated narrative television. In this regard, the televisual sitcom is no differ-ent than the televisual commercial. Its distinctive look and sound make it stand out. To *Variety*, this is in bad taste, but it's a standard aspect of genre evolution that new works must resemble the old, but bring something different to the form. The televisual sitcom must distinguish itself to survive. And the sitcom genre as a whole must change to survive. Moreover, the single-camera aesthetic adds prestige to sitcoms as it associates them with prime-time dramas and the-atrical releases—as is discussed above in *Miami Vice* and *ER*.

Also in common with the commercial is a third function of televisuality: the Althusserian hailing of the spectator. For decades, the sitcom relied upon the laugh track to hail viewers, asking them to join the virtual audience in their enjoyment of the program. Even if one were not in the same room as the televi-sion set, the sound of a program's laughter—as with crowd response in a foot-ball game—draws you to it, entreating you not to miss out on the fun. Since most televisual sitcoms have no laugh tracks, they must rely on other devices to lure the viewer—much like experimental films rely on devices other than narra-tive hooks. Commonly, televisual sitcoms achieve this through "sheer semiotic density of visual signs," as Caldwell refers to this phenomenon in a different context.[66] These programs contain a layering of signifiers and a surfeit of allu-sions that entreat and challenge the viewer to decode them—as with the opening scene of *Scrubs* and its musical quotation from *Sanford and Son*. Thompson quotes one of the writers/producers of *Arrested Development*, Mitchell Hurwitz: "We're really making a show for the new technology here. We're making a show for TiVo, and we're making a show for DVD, and it really becomes part of our objective in making this thing."[67] In other words, Hurwitz constructs a spectator position that demands active, engaged viewers—viewers that might pause their DVRs or DVDs in order to review a segment of the text or ponder an allusion. Of course, pastiche is nothing new for comic texts—as *Tristram Shandy* (1765–9), *Monty Python's Flying Circus* (1969–74) and *Mystery Science Theater 3000* (1988–99) readily illustrate—but it is mostly absent from multiple-camera proscenium sitcoms. The proscenium sitcom, with its visual poverty, warrants little more than a distracted glance at the screen. In the televisual sitcom, as Caldwell contends regarding televisuality in general, are "images that spectacularize, dazzle, and elicit gazelike viewing."[68]

The absence of semiotic activity may also serve televisual functions. Silence in televisual sitcoms is, ironically, a device for hailing viewers. Television in the broadcast era was a noisy medium, a "lava lamp with sound," as one critic put it. And programs with chuckling, sighing, applauding studio audiences were among the loudest. In this context, a show with silences demands your attention—as does someone whispering softly in a crowded room. Televisual programs like *The Larry Sanders Show*, *The Office* and *Curb Your Enthusiasm* are marked by an audacious use of silence, frequently *awkward* silences (see clip on TVStyleBook.com). This use of silence is confirmed by Ken Kwapis, who has directed and/or produced a significant number of episodes for *The Larry Sanders Show* and *The Office*:

> People don't even think about the fact that *The Office* features no music at all other than the opening theme, which is something it shares with *Larry Sanders* and pretty much no other show. It's all part of our mandate to work without a net and use awkward silences to distinguish the humor.[69]

The silences of these programs might be their most antitraditional characteristic, because the imperative to call out to the viewer is one of broadcast-era television's main tenets.

One final function of the single-camera televisual sitcom that is often overlooked in any discussion of television, is pure aesthetic pleasure. The programs contain a visual dexterity that, as I wrote in a review of Caldwell's book, "invite the viewer to revel in the pleasure of the image, in the delirium of stylistic excess."[70]

The Televisual Continuum

In this chapter I've stressed the differences between the televisual, single-camera sitcom and multiple-camera productions in order to highlight the former's televisual characteristics. However, it is more accurate to view televisuality in terms of a continuum—from the stylistically utilitarian to the stylistically exhibitionistic. On one end of the spectrum is a play that is recorded from a single vantage point with no editing—the camera positioned at the "best seat in the house." The silent cinema's *Film d'Art* was mostly shot in this fashion, as are innumerable school plays today. In this instance, the camera and microphone add little, or nothing, to the live event. On the other end of the spectrum is a wholly abstract animation or wholly processed image, one that could not exist without the medium itself. As Caldwell argues, "images become artifactual objects and pictures, not replications of the real."[71] They therefore depend upon the "picture effect" instead of the "reality effect."[72] Norman McLaren's *Begone Dull Care* would be one such example (Figure 5.98). In narrative television, the closest to this extreme is the animated program, particularly in segments that contain visuals impossible to generate with a camera and real actors. Better examples, however, are displayed in non-narrative television: the visually abstract commercial or the credit sequence built through visual effects. An example of the former is Apple's ad campaign for the

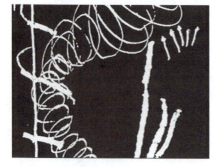

Figure 5.98 Abstract animation in *Begone Dull Care.*

iPod and iTunes, which relies heavily on abstract imagery (Figure 5.99, from a commercial featuring "Shut Up and Let Me Go," by The Ting Tings).

Figure 5.99 An Apple iPod commercial relies on abstract imagery.

With this continuum in mind, we can still mark some distinct schema that have had significant use in film and television. I identify these schema largely based on the actual mode of production used to create them, but I must emphasize again that modes can be dislodged from their schema—as when a fiction film poses as a documentary. Table 5.6 provides an overview of six stages in this continuum. The overarching division of these stages is based on whether the performance is recorded or constructed. By this I mean, is it a record of a pre-existing performance or does the television text construct the narrative through sound/image fragments? The distinction is, I admit, a bit fuzzy and relies on a presumed event in a presumed "real world"—laying the notion open to the same criticisms that are made of Peirce's iconic sign—but I contend that, in its most extreme forms, the distinction is evident in the texts themselves. A comparison of a video of a school play with *The Simpsons* confirms this. Table 5.6 illuminates how elements of those extremes are contained in a spectrum of television programs. Televisuality might not exist in a "pure" form, but its implementation within the sitcom illustrates how it can have an impact on genre evolution and shifts in television style.

Has the Sitcom Died?

Having considered the significant and signifying changes that the single-camera televisual sitcom has wrought, can we agree with Mills that the televisual sitcom, *The Office*, in its British incarnation, "vividly signals an irrevocable sea change for sitcom and highlights the point at which the traditional sitcom form died in Britain and Australia"?[73] Does the U.S. version and its televisual brethren accomplish the same thing?

If there's one thing that Janet Staiger's book on *Blockbuster TV: Must-See Sitcoms in the Network Era* teaches us, it is that the sitcom was remarkably resilient *while the broadcast industry* was remarkably resilient. If the network era is truly over, then the sitcom is likely over, too. But the broadcast networks and the genres that thrived during it, in my view, are not finished. Rather, they are in the midst of a genre-altering evolution. Death is an essential aspect of this evolutionary process, of natural selection. I suspect that the multiple-camera proscenium schema will indeed die off, but that some mutated version of the single-camera televisual sitcom will survive. As with any mutation, the new, hybrid species will be more hearty than its ancestors.

Table 5.6 A televisual continuum

Performance	Space	Proscenium	Image	Sound	Editing	Examples	Comments
recorded	theatrical	literal	one camera, fixed in place	post-independent	none	Film D'Art, school-play recordings, the first TV shows	The purest form of the multiple-camera proscenium schema
recorded	theatrical	literal	multiple cameras, moveable	post-independent	attenuated continuity	The Honeymooners, The George Burns and Gracie Allen Show	
recorded	sound stage	virtual	multiple cameras, moveable	post-independent	attenuated continuity	I Love Lucy, The New Adventures of Old Christine, As the World Turns	These examples do occasionally shoot on-location, but their principal mode of production is in-studio.
constructed	sound stage, or on location	virtual	single camera	post-dependent	attenuated continuity	The Andy Griffith Show, Petticoat Junction, Dallas	Telefilm values.
constructed	sound stage, or on location	none	single camera, post-dependent	post-dependent	intensified continuity	Parker Lewis Can't Lose, Scrubs, Miami Vice	The purest form of the single-camera televisual schema. Style as a source of humor or carnivalesque pleasure.
constructed	none	none	post-dependent	post-dependent	intensified continuity or discontinuity	The Simpsons, commercials and credit sequences	

Notes

1. In 2000, *Advertising Age* bemoaned the "sorry state" of the sitcom. Ed Martin, "Sitcom Slip No Laughing Matter for Nets," *Advertising Age* 71, no. 21 (May 15, 2000): 28.
2. See Bertolt Brecht, "The Modern Theatre is the Epic Theatre: Notes to the Opera *Aufstieg und Fall der Stadt Mahagonny*," in *Brecht on Theatre: The Development of an Aesthetic*, ed. and trans. John Willett (London: Methuen, 1964), 33–42.
3. To select one example among many: Steve Lopez, "Death Of The Sitcom: It's not the First Time Sitcoms have Fallen on Hard Times. But with More Networks and Fewer Wits and Sages, this is Anything but the Golden Age of Comedy. Is there still Hope, or are we Squeezing the Last Laughs out of TV's Ailing Genre?," *Entertainment Weekly* 481 (April 16, 1999): 26+(1), Academic OneFile, Gale (accessed June 18, 2008).
4. Stephen Winzenburg, *TV's Greatest Sitcoms* (Baltimore: Publish America, 2004), 243–6.
5. Quoted in Lopez, "Death of the Sitcom."
6. The sequence of sitcoms in "How the Test Was Won" (March 1, 2009) is chronological: *The Honeymooners*, *The Dick van Dyke Show* (1961–6), *The Brady Bunch* (1969–74), and *Cheers* (1982–93). In the latter, the program engages in even more intertextuality. Sideshow Bob appears in that segment and he is voiced by Kelsey Grammer, who was part of the actual *Cheers* cast.
7. *The Honeymooners* has a very complicated broadcast history as it initially appeared as a segment within Jackie Gleason's variety programs, debuting in 1951 on *Cavalcade of Stars*. The only standalone *Honeymooners* episodes were broadcast 1955–6.
8. This was not a fabrication. The episode actually was shot before a studio audience.
9. All of *Scrubs'* episode titles begin with "my," emphasizing the show as J.D.'s story.
10. Another single-camera sitcom to use the multiple-camera mode of production for fantasy sequences is *My Name Is Earl* (2005–9). During the 2007–8 season, the main character is in a coma, during which he fantasizes about his life as if it were a sitcom—including a shot of the stage showing the lighting grid.
11. Rick Porter, "*Scrubs*, Filmed Before a Live Studio Audience," *Zap2It*, February 14, 2005, tv.zap2it.com/tveditorial/tve_main/1,1002,271|93580|1|,00.html (accessed June 27, 2008).
12. John Thornton Caldwell, *Televisuality: Style, Crisis, and Authority in American Television* (New Brunswick: Rutgers University Press, 1995), 352.
13. Ibid., 56.
14. Ibid., 56.
15. Ibid., 57.
16. Ibid., 40.
17. With their emphasis on families and interpersonal stories, these comedies were also significant antecedents for the soap opera.
18. David Bordwell, *On the History of Film Style* (Cambridge: Harvard University Press, 1997), 168.
19. For an illustration, see Chuck Pharis, "The DuMont ELECTRONICAM," October 12, 2003, www.pharis-video.com/p4589.htm (accessed March 1, 2007)—featuring backstage photographs of the *Honeymooners* episode, "Mind Your Own Business," which aired May 26, 1956.
20. The Electronicam film recordings were made for the 1955–6 season, when 39 episodes were created as standalone programs and not as part of Gleason variety show.
21. Michael Frediani, "On the Set with Video Assist," *Operating Cameraman* (fall/winter 1995/6) www.soc.org/opcam/07_fw9596/mg07_vidassist.html (accessed March 2, 2007). First put into production by Lewis on *The Bellboy*.

22. The sitcom genre itself was not so well established at that time. It is perhaps surprising to note that *I Love Lucy* was one of only three or four sitcoms to break into the Nielsen top-20 during any one television season in the 1950s and, moreover, it was sometimes the only sitcom in the top ten. The dominant years of the genre were yet to come.

23. Bordwell, *On the History of Film Style*, 4.

24. Personal interview with Tom Cherones, March 6, 2007.

25. "The Clock Starts Ticking on Season 6," *Videography*, January 2007, 22.

26. Specifics of the lighting scheme for *Old Christine* are detailed in Elina Shatkin, "New Cinematography Tools for *The New Adventures of Old Christine*," *Videography*, May 2006, 23–4.

27. "The Parking Garage," *Sony Pictures*, 2008, www.sonypictures.com/tv/shows/seinfeld/episode_guide/?sl=episode&ep=306 (accessed June 20, 2008).

28. For the implications of theatrical versus cinematic staging see David Bordwell, "Feuillade, or Storytelling," in *Figures Traced in Light: On Cinematic Staging* (Berkeley: University of California Press, 2005), 43–82; and Ben Brewster and Lea Jacobs, *Theatre to Cinema: Stage Pictorialism and the Early Feature Film* (Oxford: Oxford University Press, 1997).

29. For more on "aggressive foregrounds," see Bordwell, *Figures Traced in Light*, 111–12. For more on "aperture framing," see Bordwell, *On the History of Film Style*, 180.

30. "HDCAM FAQs—HDW-F900," Sony.com, 2005, bssc.sel.sony.com/Professional/production/productsite/cinealta/900faq.html?m=0&p=2&sp=19&sm=0&s=&cpos = (accessed June 20, 2008).

31. For more on Lucas' digital advocacy, see Paula Parisi, "By George," *The Hollywood Reporter*, February 18, 2004, www.hollywoodreporter.com/hr/search/article_display.jsp?vnu_content_id=2094216 (accessed June 20, 2008).

32. A summary of common aspect ratios is provided by David Bordwell and Kristin Thompson, *Film Art: An Introduction*, 8th edn (New York: McGraw-Hill, 2008), 183–7.

33. John Ellis, *Visible Fictions* (Boston: Routledge & Kegan Paul, 1992), 106.

34. Ibid., 38.

35. Much like the soap opera, sitcoms were once performed live and in recent years the genre also has produced ratings stunts where programs were broadcast live. See the "Drew Live" episode of *The Drew Carey Show*, broadcast live on November 10, 1999; and the entire 1992–3 season of *Roc*.

36. Of course, no surprising results come from comparing current, speedy sitcoms with those from television's beginnings. Still, for the record, "TV or Not TV" (1955), the analyzed *The Honeymooners* episode, has an ASL of 17.7 seconds and *I Love Lucy* episodes from 1951 and 1952 have ASLs from nine to 11 seconds. See ShotLogger.org for more details.

37. Janey Place and Lowell Peterson, "Some Visual Motifs of Film Noir," in *The Film Noir Reader*, eds. Alain Silver and James Ursini (New York: Limelight, 1996), 64–75.

38. Peter Wollen, "Godard and Counter Cinema: Vent D'est," in *Readings and Writings: Semiotic Counter-Strategies* (London: Verso, 1982), 79; and Bertolt Brecht, "The Modern Theatre is the Epic Theatre," in *Brecht on Theatre*, 37.

39. Its regular season did not begin until October 4, 1949.

40. "Advanced Primetime Awards Search," Academy of Television Arts & Sciences, www.emmys.org/awards/awardsearch.php (accessed March 2, 2007). The Academy's database permits the listing of individual year's awards through its "year range" option.

41. Interestingly, another sitcom, *The Goldbergs*, was nominated that year, but did not compete with *The Life of Riley* as it was in a different category (best kinescope show), for which it lost.

42. Examples include "Outstanding Art Direction for a Multi-camera Series" and "Outstanding Art Direction for a Single-camera Series."

43. David Barker, "Television Production Techniques as Communication", in *Television: The Critical View*, 6th edn, ed. Horace Newcomb (New York: Oxford University Press, 2000), 169–82. Originally in *Critical Studies in Mass Communication* (September 1985): 234–46.

44. Caldwell, *Televisuality*, 55.

45. Viktor Shklovsky, "Art as Technique," in *Russian Formalist Criticism: Four Essays*, ed. and trans. Lee T. Lemon and Marion J. Reis (Lincoln: University of Nebraska Press, 1965).

46. Kristin Thompson, *Breaking the Glass Armor: Neoformalist Analysis* (Princeton: Princeton University Press, 1981), 247.

47. Bordwell, *Figures Traced in Light*, 62.

48. For more on Alberti, see Anne Friedberg, *The Virtual Window: From Alberti to Microsoft* (Cambridge: The MIT Press, 2006).

49. An earlier shot in the episode further emphasizes *Scrubs'* use of ceilings. In it, the camera starts with a shot of the ceiling and then tilts down to reveal J.D. and Elliot interviewing patients about E. coli. These shots were likely captured in *Scrubs'* real-world hospital location.

50. *The Larry Sanders Show* (1992–8) similarly counterposed film and video—at a time when the difference was more substantial.

51. "Motion Picture Super 16 Film," *Kodak*, www.kodak.com/global/en/service/faqs/faq2109.shtml (accessed June 25, 2008).

52. Caldwell discusses how technical devices can serve to "stylistically individuate" shows. Caldwell, *Televisuality*, 89.

53. Rick Porter, "For One Week Only, It's *Scrubs*, the Sitcom," *Zap2It*, January 20, 2005, tv.zap2it.com/tveditorial/tve_main/1,1002,271|93072|1|,00.html (accessed June 27, 2008).

54. In a humorous montage from the "My Quarantine" episode (February 8, 2005), J.D. is asked how many clothes he tried on before picking an outfit. He says "Not many," but we then see 15 outfits in as many shots, squeezed into about three seconds.

55. Caldwell, *Televisuality*, 157.

56. For more, see Greg M. Smith, "Getting into Ally's Head: Special Effects, Imagination, and the Voice of Doubt," in *Beautiful TV: The Art and Argument of Ally McBeal* (Austin: University of Texas Press, 2007), 47–69.

57. Further details are available on the website of one of its animators: Ron K. Lussier, "Dancing Baby FAQ," *BurningPixel*, www.burningpixel.com/Baby/BabyFAQ.htm (accessed June 26, 2008). A QuickTime clip of the original animation is available here.

58. David Bordwell, "Intensified Continuity," *Film Quarterly* 55, no. 3 (April 1, 2002): 16–28, www.proquest.com (accessed June 27, 2008).

59. See "Memorable quotes for *Arrested Development*," *The Internet Movie Database*, www.imdb.com/title/tt0367279/quotes (accessed June 26, 2008).

60. Due to copyright clearance issues, this version is not heard on the DVD release.

61. Brian Lowry, "*The New Adventures of Old Christine*," *Variety Review Database*, March 2006, proquest.umi.com/pqdlink?did=1008533411 (accessed March 2, 2007).

62. Pauline Kael, "Trash, Art and the Movies," in *Going Steady* (New York: Bantam, 1970), 116. Available online at www.paulrossen.com/paulinekael/trashartandthe-movies.html (accessed June 17, 2008).

63. Brett Mills, "Comedy Vérité: Contemporary Sitcom Form," *Screen* 45, no. 1 (spring 2004): 63–78; Ethan Thompson, "Comedy Vérité? The Observational Documentary Meets the Televisual Sitcom," *Velvet Light Trap* 60 (fall 2007): 63–72.

64. Mills, "Comedy Vérité," 75.

65. Ibid., 78.
66. Caldwell, *Televisuality*, 138.
67. Thompson, "Comedy Vérité?" 71.
68. Caldwell, *Televisuality*, 158.
69. Ray Richmond, "ON THE LAUGH TRACK," *Hollywood Reporter*, June 4, 2007, S3–S4, S8, S12, S14–S15, www.proquest.com (accessed July 23, 2008).
70. Jeremy G. Butler, "Assaulting Orthodoxies in Screen Studies: Journalismo, Scopophobia, and Semiologos," *Semiotica* 116, nos. 2/4 (1997): 277.
71. Caldwell, *Televisuality*, 241.
72. Ibid., 152.
73. Brett Mills, *Television Sitcom* (London: BFI, 2005), 62.

Index